Campaign and Party Finance
in North America
and Western Europe

Campaign and Party Finance in North America and Western Europe

EDITED BY

Arthur B. Gunlicks

toExcel
San Jose New York Lincoln Shanghai

Campaign and Party Finance in North America and Western Europe

This edition published by toExcel Press,
an imprint of iUniverse.com, Inc.

For information address:
iUniverse.com, Inc.
620 North 48th Street
Suite 201
Lincoln, NE 68504-3467
www.iuniverse.com

ISBN: 0-595-00124-6

Contents

**PART FOUR
POLITICAL FINANCE ON THE RESEARCH
AGENDA IN COMPARATIVE POLITICS**

Preface

At least since Watergate and other scandals associated with the presidential election of 1972, there has been no dearth of books and articles on campaign financing in the United States. Still, one could argue that political money has not been a major focus of public attention during the past decade or more. Given recent revelations of scandals in the states and in Congress regarding influence peddling, e.g., "the Keating Five," and outright bribery (involving, for example, state legislators in South Carolina), it is not surprising that public financing of campaigns at the national, state and local levels has reemerged as an important public policy issue. What is perhaps surprising is that for twenty years there was no single volume containing information about foreign campaign and party financing practices that might serve as ideas for consideration in the United States until the publication of the book edited by Herbert Alexander, *Comparative Political Finance*, published by Cambridge University Press in 1989. As valuable as this book was and is, the chapter on the United States was limited to presidential elections, and some of the other chapters were too brief or general to provide much, if any, detailed information about practices abroad. There was also no chapter on France, which had just enacted important reforms providing public funds for campaigns and parties.

Like Herbert Alexander and others who have worked in the area of campaign and party finance, I believe that information about policies and practices regarding public financing abroad can help Americans develop their own ideas about reform possibilities. It is my hope that this book's somewhat narrower focus on North America and several Western European countries, countries about which many Americans are reasonably well informed, will encourage more readers to pay some attention to alternatives to American practices and to think about changes that would be both desirable and feasible. In reading about "comparative political finance," it is also important to realize that this term takes on different meanings in North America, especially in the United States, and in Europe. In North America it really means campaign and candidate finance. In Europe it is more likely to mean party finance. This is a reflection both of the stronger political parties in Europe and the candidate orientation of American politics. These differences must not be ignored when one ponders the possibilities of transferring ideas from one country to another.

A number of people deserve some thanks from me for assisting with the preparation of this volume. Miss Oscarlyn Brown was magnificent in applying her computer skills to this project and getting all of the manuscripts to conform to the publisher's standards and wishes. Mrs. Pat Thiel remained cheerful as always in spite of numerous provocations, including typing the translation of more than one manuscript in my handwriting. Ms. Amy Eisenberg and Ms. Jennifer Knerr of Westview Press were encouraging and helpful from the start. I received support from the Faculty Research Committee of the University of Richmond and Dean David Leary for miscellaneous expenses, for which I am grateful. And, again, my wife had to grin and bear it while I spent every weekend for several months working on "final details."

Arthur B. Gunlicks
Richmond, Virginia

PART ONE

Political Finance
in Comparative Perspective

1

Introduction

Arthur B. Gunlicks

As the 1992 elections approached, it was clear that many Americans were not only concerned and even apprehensive about the economy and the general state of the nation; they were also angry and frustrated about politics and politicians. Evidence was easy to find. Polls noted that seven of ten Americans thought the country was off track, an equal proportion thought that the government was controlled by special interests, and only three in ten had confidence that government would do the right thing all or most of the time.[1] There was widespread talk of term limitations for members of Congress and the state legislatures, and limitations were actually imposed on state legislators in California, Colorado, and Oklahoma. The arguments for such limitations were fueled in part by a series of financial ethics scandals in the late 1980s that led to the resignations of the Speaker of the House of Representatives, the Democratic Whip in the House, and a congressman from New York; a senator was disciplined for soliciting and accepting more money in speaking and other fees than was permitted. There were several sex scandals as well, but they did not appear to involve money.[2]

In March 1992 a check-writing scandal involving many members of the House of Representatives became a major news item, and it contributed much to the loss of primary election contests by several members of Congress. The growing role and potentially devastating influence of PACs (political action committees) and special interests were again revealed for all to see and hear for several months in 1991 during the dramatic hearings in the U.S. Senate on the "Keating Five." These were five senators accused of helping Lincoln Savings and Loan President, Charles H. Keating, Jr., avoid or delay regulatory oversight while his company was losing hundreds of millions of dollars in bad loans. Keating had contributed large sums of money to the senators and to the Democratic and Republican Parties, and he indicated in a news conference that he certainly expected his donations to have had some effect in his favor. Other,

3

sometimes bizarre, scandals involving state legislators and governors in various political financing schemes have been revealed in more than one-half of the states in recent years. When Americans were asked in a poll conducted in the fall of 1991 whether politicians generally were "financially corrupt" or "honest," it was no surprise that only 34 percent answered, "honest."[3]

The role of money in American politics was more apparent than ever before in the elections of 1988. More than $2.7 billion was spent for elections and referenda at all levels: $500 million for the presidential elections, and $458 million for congressional elections, including in both cases primary elections. In addition, the Democratic and Republican national parties spent over $328 million.[4] This was more than double the $1.2 billion spent in 1980 and nine times the expenditures of 1968 (not adjusted for inflation). In constant dollars, the increase in presidential spending alone from 1968 to 1988 was 268 percent.[5] Total congressional campaign expenditures in 1987-88 were $457 million. The average House winner spent about $400,000, the average Senate winner almost $4 million (which means he had to raise on average about $13,000 every week for six years). Most incumbents were able to raise large amounts of money, most challengers were not.[6] Herbert Alexander has noted that

> [f]ollowing the 1988 congressional elections, House incumbents held 25 percent more cash in reserve than their challengers had spent in the entire campaign. And the reelection rate in the House topped 98 percent for the second election cycle in a row. Few would argue that these two sets of statistics were unrelated.[7]

In the meantime, Congress has wrestled with a number of competing proposals for campaign finance reform. In the House of Representatives the Democrats have insisted on caps on PAC donations, some public subsidies, and campaign expenditure limits. These proposals have been rejected by the Republicans, including President Bush, who oppose both spending limits and public financing. The House and Senate passed a campaign finance bill in 1991, and differences between the two measures were ironed out in a conference committee meeting in early April 1992[8]; however, it was clear that the President would not sign the bill.

While American frustration with political money is anything but new,[9] there does seem to be a powerful desire today to "do something." One purpose of this volume is to make the reader aware of a wide variety of alternatives to the American system of political financing that can be found in various Western democracies. While it may not be feasible or even wise to borrow wholesale from the Canadian or Western European examples cited, there is surely no reason to believe that the experience of others is of no relevance at all to potential reform efforts in the United States.

Public Finance in Democratic Systems

According to Herbert Alexander, 21 countries had some form of public political financing in the mid-1980s,[10] which is more than half of the total number of countries that would have qualified as liberal democracies at that time. Since then the French have enacted public financing legislation, and a number of countries in Eastern Europe that have emerged from the collapse of Communism have already or will probably introduce some form of public party and campaign finance.

Why have so many democracies introduced public campaign and party financing in recent decades? The reasons are numerous and generally well known. The costs of party activities, both for routine organizational purposes and election campaigns, have risen everywhere, and in many countries the increases have been dramatic. Traditional sources of income, such as party dues, revenues from party meetings, profits from party newspapers, and generally small or modest contributions from the candidates themselves and their families and friends have become inadequate. Parties and candidates have turned increasingly to wealthy individuals and powerful interest groups for contributions. Political money from the private sector, however, can be based on a wide variety of motivations, ranging from the desire to participate as a good citizen in the political process to gaining access to decision makers, influencing the direction of public policy in specific cases, or even engaging in bribery. Citizens interested in running for office may lack the necessary funds for a campaign, and the parties and groups with which they identify may not be able to provide adequate financial assistance. Parties that do not appeal to powerful private interests may be unable to attract candidates in certain districts or regions due to lack of funding. Candidates and office holders who have few resources of their own or from their party may become dependent on private contributions, with obvious negative consequences for the political process. The issue of public finance, then, is concerned with questions of fairness, equal opportunity, competition, corruption, and with public assessments of the political process. It is, ultimately, a question of great importance to the political culture of a democratic society.

Some reformers have argued that tightening the regulation of parties and candidates, such as improved disclosure and reporting procedures, would "clean up" problems of political finance. Karl-Heinz Nassmacher suggests that the "puritan" streak in American political culture perhaps encourages such efforts, especially if they do not cost the taxpayers any money. Others have argued that public financing is the key to solving many of the problems raised by private money, whether by matching funds from private donors or by substituting public money for such funds. Still others have suggested, however, that government might become a new source of dependency, relieving the parties and office holders from their accountability to their voters and supporters.[11] We will see below, for example, in the chapter by Hans Herbert von Arnim and Peter Lösche, that this is a genuine concern in Germany, where public subsidies are among the most generous in the world.

The chapters that follow by Paul Herrnson and Ruth Jones on public campaign finance at the American national and state levels, respectively, show clearly that public subsidies in the United States, with the exception of the presidential campaign, are very limited when compared with most of the other countries in this volume. This can be demonstrated by numerous examples. Only the campaign expenses of the candidates running for President in the primary and general elections are covered in large part by public funds. There is no public funding for congressional candidates. The only public subsidy received by the political parties from the federal government is for the national presidential nomination convention every four years. The United States is the only country in which there is no free television and radio time made available to political parties; instead, parties and, especially, candidates at all levels may purchase as much time as they can afford. In the other countries the purchase of television and radio time by individual candidates is forbidden, and only in a few countries may the *parties* purchase a limited amount of time. There is no free poster space in the United States. Thanks to the Supreme Court, legal limits may not be placed on the personal expenditures of candidates or on so-called "independent expenditures" by groups not an official part of the campaign of individual candidates, on the grounds that such limits would be restrictions on free speech.[12] This has not prevented the Canadians and British, who presumably are also in favor of free speech, from limiting the amounts of money that individual candidates may spend in their own behalf, or, in the case of the British, from banning expenditures not authorized by the candidates or parties. In the 1970s the United States introduced the innovative and now inadequate $1 tax "check-off," but for presidential elections only. In the 1980s only 20-30 percent of the taxpayers participated in this scheme, with the rate of participation dropping over the decade. As Ruth Jones notes, almost two-thirds of the American states have considered or enacted some form of public subsidy, generally financed by tax "check-off" or "add-on" schemes.[13] In the latter case participation has been no higher than 2 percent. Not surprisingly, the amounts of money provided in the states are generally modest and limited to certain offices. In the two dozen states that have public financing, only eight provide some money for the political parties in contrast to candidates. The very limited federal tax deductions and credits for political contributions were eliminated by the tax reform legislation of 1986, whereas other countries--especially Germany, where tax credits and deductions are exceptionally generous--encourage citizen participation through their tax policies. It is sometimes argued that the American PACs encourage citizen participation by offering citizens the opportunity to promote specific interests (though without any tax benefits); however, as Paul Herrnson notes in his chapter on campaign financing in federal elections, the

PACs have weakened American parties and raised serious questions about the fragmenting and even atomizing effects of "special interests" in the political process. As a number of contributing authors note in their chapters, politics in the United States is *candidate oriented*, rather than *party oriented*, as in most other democracies, and this fundamental difference is reflected in public financing efforts as well as in the legal regulations that affect candidates, parties, and elections.

Political Systems, Party Systems and Political Finance

The contributors to this volume demonstrate in their respective chapters that there are numerous differences as well as similarities in the public financing measures of North American and European democracies. What is particularly striking, however, are the differences between the United States and the other countries. As Karl-Heinz Nassmacher notes, little theory has been developed in comparative politics to help us understand why these differences and similarities exist.

A number of potential explanations offer themselves. Ruth Jones, for example, notes that American federalism has encouraged the proliferation of elective offices, which are regulated by state law, and the effect has been to strengthen state parties at the expense of the national parties. This could help explain both candidate orientation and the relatively weak national efforts to enact general reforms or broader schemes of public finance. But federalism per se cannot explain the widespread opposition to public financing in the United States, because Canada, Germany, and, to a lesser extent, Austria, are also federal systems, and all three countries--especially the latter two--have more comprehensive and generous public financing schemes than the United States.

A factor that might explain the candidate orientation in the United States, and thus the weakness of the parties and their inability to bring about serious reform in their favor, is the single member district, plurality electoral system. While there can be no doubt that this system encourages a focus on the individual candidate, often at the expense of the party, this effect seems to be far more acute in the United States than in Canada and Great Britain, which also have single ballot, single member plurality systems. Yet the parties in these two countries, expecially in Great Britain, are far more important in the political process than their American counterparts. And while the British, like the Americans, have failed to introduce public financing for legislative candidates, they have placed restrictions on spending and banned the purchase of television time for candidates as well as parties.

A third factor that we might consider is the effect of the American presidential system versus the parliamentary systems of the other countries. It certainly seems plausible that this general system difference might be crucial in explaining the focus on candidates in the United States in contrast to the role played by parties in the other countries. After all, the majority party or the majority coalition of parties must have a high level of discipline and cohesion to sustain the government (cabinet), whereas the separation of powers in the United States permits the President and Congress to go in different directions with no danger of a negative vote of confidence by the Congress or a dissolution of the legislature by the President. On the other hand, the British have a parliamentary system with strong parties, and yet they have done little in the area of party and campaign financing beyond indirect measures such as providing free television and radio time during elections and placing limitations on the personal expenditures of individual candidates. One might note also that the French Fifth Republic, which is a semi-presidential or semi-parliamentary system, in which the political parties were generally weaker than elsewhere in Europe, now has a comprehensive system of public finance.

This may leave us with a fourth factor as the most important of all: political culture. Attitudes generally hostile to taxes and big government, or even to government at all, were tapped and further encouraged by the Reagan Administration during the 1980s, and public campaign and party financing certainly smacks of more government. Even without a recession, the support by Americans for public financing schemes is very limited, as can be seen in the 1-to-2 percent rate of taxpayer participation in state tax "add-on" programs. The public outcry against increasing the salaries of members of Congress, which can be seen also as a means of providing more financial independence and security for elected officials, is further evidence of public hostility toward politicians. It may be that voters in all democracies are skeptical of public subsidies for parties and candidates, but there appears to have been a more successful effort by political leaders in the other countries to persuade enough voters that public funding in principle is a means of bringing about a number of desirable benefits, such as lessening the influence of wealthy individuals and special interests and providing for fairer, more open and equal elections.

Political Finance in Comparison

As noted in the preface, political finance is a concept that can have different connotations. In North America, it generally refers to campaign finance for individual candidates, whereas it suggests party finance for both elections and routine organizational costs in Europe. The term might also incorporate the regulation of donations of money or contributions in kind to parties and candidates by individuals, groups and various special interests. While the chapters contained in this volume provide some information about the regulations affecting the financing of campaigns and parties, the focus is on direct and indirect public financing schemes.

Paul Herrnson reports that in the 1988 federal elections, about $1.5 billion was spent by candidates for federal offices in the United States, most of which came from private individuals and PACs. Relatively little money came from the individual candidates themselves, from the federal government or from the parties. In contrast to the other countries described in this volume, the parties are treated by federal law in many respects like interest groups. Though the amounts may differ, the parties are limited like PACs and individual contributors in the sums they may contribute to the campaigns of their candidates; indeed, they may not contribute to the campaigns of presidential candidates who have elected to receive public funds. This has not prevented large donors from giving larger contributions of "soft money" to state parties that do not fall under federal regulations, thus permitting the states to use this money for the presidential campaigns in their states or for other purposes. The focus on individual candidates in American elections is a theme that runs throughout the chapter, so that one could speak of *candidate* rather than *campaign* financing. This means, among other things, that politics in the United States has much to do with name recognition, and to gain such recognition the candidate, especially as the challenger, needs to spend a lot of money on expensive television commercials. The fact that individual candidates are not allowed to purchase television and radio time in the other, largely party-dominated, countries demonstrates clearly one of the most striking differences between the American and other party systems.

Ruth Jones notes the role of federalism and the electoral system on the political parties and their candidates in the American states. She points to the states as regulators of parties, candidates, and elections, and to the general lack of coordination among the states. Various limited public funding schemes for the candidates of certain offices exist in two dozen states and several cities. Many states have enacted public financing laws, including laws providing for tax "check-offs" as well as tax "add-ons." Rising costs of state services, combined with reductions in tax revenues and federal grants-in-aid, have combined to put the states under great financial stress, which makes state initiatives in the area of public campaign finance unlikely for the time being. On the other hand, recent scandals and the public concern for fair and open elections may bring enough pressure to bear on governors and state legislatures for them to take some action, at least in the form of more regulations.

William Stanbury's chapter on Canada is based in part on his participation in the hearings of the Royal Commission on Electoral Reform and Party Financing. The Commission's massive, four-volume report was released in the late fall of 1991,[14] and it is a goldmine of information about elections and political finance in Canada. It also contains many useful comparisons with other countries, especially but not only the United States. The Commission makes a large number of recommendations for various reforms in Canada, many of which are taken up by Stanbury. In spite of the focus on candidates, which

Nassmacher argues is typical of North America, there are, unlike the United States, spending limits and ceilings on election expenses (46,900 Canadian dollars in 1988!) and partial reimbursements to candidates who receive at least 15 percent of the vote in national elections. Parties also receive some reimbursement of expenses. Only parties may purchase time for political advertisements on television and radio, and free time is made available between 29 to 2 days before the election. All donations of $100 or more in cash or in kind must be disclosed in annual reports. Tax credits are allowed for donations up to $500, and no limits on contributions are imposed on individuals, business or union contributions; however, there are few large contributions by individuals and groups.

Ron Johnston and Charles Pattie describe several "eras" of party finance in British history. The "aristocratic" and "plutocratic" eras were replaced in large part at the end of the last and during the first half of this century by national regulations; however, these have not kept pace with developments over the past decades. British law applies above all to local campaigns, while in fact campaigns have become increasingly national. Trade union donations are more strictly regulated than corporate contributions. Union funds are collected from all but the few members who opt out, and these donations are crucial for the Labour Party. Spending limits are imposed on candidates running for the House of Commons, and only spending authorized by the candidate is permitted. Television and radio advertising is free for the parties, and no additional time may be purchased. British law does not require reporting of sources of income or expenditures outside of the official five-week election period, which means that the parties are relatively free to divulge as much information as they wish. British laws have changed little over the past decades, and there is little chance that there will be any reforms of political finance by the end of this century.

France was a kind of "black hole" in comparative party finance until 1988, when sweeping reforms were passed. Thomas Drysch points out that until then parties were generally ignored by French law, except that they were prohibited from accepting donations and party dues were limited in amount. This meant that the French parties and candidates engaged in a good deal of illegal fund raising, and there was little information available to assess the nature and scope of such activities. Nevertheless, there was before 1988 a modest reimbursement of presidential and parliamentary candidates with more than 5 percent of the vote and free television time for the parties. Since 1988 there is direct public funding of the parties as well as indirect funding via public reimbursement of the election expenses of presidential and parliamenatary candidates; however, ceilings have been placed on election expenditures. Private donations are limited for both individuals and corporations. Further additions to and revisions of the law of 1988 were made in 1990.

Germany represents in many ways a direct contrast to the United States in the generosity of tax benefits for political contributions and large-scale public funding of campaign expenditures incurred by political parties. In addition, sizable amounts of public funds are given to party groups (caucuses) and party foundations. These measures reflect the focus on parties rather than candidates, and they conform to the image of the "party state" in Germany. While they were designed to free the parties from private influences and also to give them the resources they needed for their recognized activities, public subsidies have made the parties dependent on the state in ways that alarm Hans Herbert von Arnim. Von Arnim argues that since the parties control the parliament and pass laws on party finance that are in their self-interest, there are few effective controls, other than the Federal Constitutional Court, on their generosity with taxpayers' money. The parties are required to account for their income and expenditures, but the reporting procedures are inadequate. Von Arnim notes the danger of party leaders' distancing themselves too far from the grassroots membership by becoming so dependent on public financing.

Peter Lösche raises several questions about "political money," and he suggests that problems regarding political finance are similar in democratic systems, especially the rising costs of party and campaign activities. He argues, however, that the main problem is not corruption but rather the *appearance* of corruption. Focusing on the United States and Germany, Lösche notes that there are significant differences in the political systems of the two countries. Dependency on public subsidies is a problem in Germany, whereas PAC and special interest contributions plague American politics. Still, it is the widespread perception, not the reality, of wrongdoing that is the core of the problem. Both countries need to introduce certain reforms. The United States should provide free media time for the political parties, which could decide how to allocate the time between party and candidates. Germany should change its public financing system to a system of matching funds for small donations and party dues. There needs to be better enforcement of reporting requirements in Germany, and the country would benefit from an institution like the American Federal Election Commission. Parties may be too strong in Germany, but they are too weak in the United States. PACs should be abolished, and parties should be given the responsibility of conducting and financing campaigns. American parties should be free to contribute generously to the campaigns of their candidates, and public funds should go to the parties rather than the candidates. In spite of numerous differences in their political systems, Germans and Americans can learn from each other.

The small democracies of Austria and Sweden have systems of public financing that are similar in important respects to German practices. Both have strong parties, and these are the recipients of public subsidies. Public finance is generous in both countries, but it seems to be better accepted by public opinion in Sweden. Public financing of parties in Sweden goes back to 1965, when, according to Gudrun Klee, "all members of parliament agreed that political parties fulfill an important function in maintaining democracy, and . . . therefore society has a responsibility to secure the existence of political parties." Public party financing at the national level in Austria goes back to 1975. Both countries distribute funds based on the number of seats won in the parliament. Political academies, roughly similar to the German party foundations, receive public funds in Austria, and the party press is subsidized in both countries. Free television and radio time is granted in both countries, and additional time may not be purchased. Dependency on public funds varies somewhat according to the type of party. Mass membership parties are less, cadre parties more, dependent on public funds in Austria. In Sweden parties in general appear to be dependent on public funds. Donations and dues are declining in importance in both countries. Large donations from the private sector are insignificant in Sweden today, while they are still important in Austria.

Karl-Heinz Nassmacher focuses on the crucial role of political parties in democratic systems, which raises the question of whether they therefore deserve public subsidies. He suggests that the public pays whether there is public financing or not. He notes the contrast between Germany, which provides lavish public subsidies, and Great Britain, which has no direct public funding. Canada, the U. S. and the Netherlands have taken a middle path.

Nassmacher points to the British reliance on private funding from unions for the Labour Party and from business for the Conservatives, with spending adjusted to the available funds. There are no tax incentives for donations. There are also no or few scandals regarding party finance. Germany has generous public funding, significant tax benefits, and scandals!

In discussing political finance as a subject of research in comparative politics, Nassmacher notes, for example, the problem of defining party units for purposes of analysis, the difficulty of discussing American primaries and PACs that do not exist elsewhere, and the problem of taking into account the costs of party leadership contests. He points to a lack of theory to help organize research. There is far more data available today than in the past, but data on all aspects of party activities are not available anywhere. We have to work with the data we have, which depend in part on the kinds of regulations found in the various countries studied. Obstacles such as deviating election cycles, varying inflation rates, and misleading foreign exchange rates also hinder progress in comparative research. Subsidies in kind and indirect public funding, such as free television time, can make comparison difficult, as can the fact that automatic registration in Europe makes U.S.-type voter registration drives unnecessary. Free television and radio time, free postal service, free billboard advertising space, as well as subsidies for youth groups and women's organizations related to parties are not untypical in Europe. Political foundations, used for educational and research purposes, are highly useful and flexible institutions in Germany and Austria.

Party and campaign costs are rising everywhere, but differences in expenditures do exist. The U.K., U.S., Canada, and the Netherlands have moderate expenditures, while Germany, Austria, Sweden and Italy have high expenditures. Nassmacher points out, however, that we do not know what the real costs are, due to inadequate reporting procedures, and we do not always know how to distinguish campaign expenditures from routine party expenditures.

Nassmacher suggests that there are three types of party and campaign financing: plutocratic, grassroots, and public funding. Grassroots funding is derived from membership dues and small voluntary donations, which are especially typical of left-of-center parties. Plutocratic funding from large private donors is more likely to characterized right-of-center bourgeois parties. The political levy of British trade unions is a special case. Other sources are connected with patronage politics, such as deductions from public salaries or "party taxes," kickbacks, and the like. The bulk of party funding comes from the public sector in Austria, Germany, Sweden and Italy. Public finance is less generous in Australia, Canada, the U.S. and the Netherlands. Britain and Japan provide subsidies in kind.

Public regulations of political finance vary widely. Full disclosure and reporting are not quite so strong in Europe as in North America. In the U.S., he suggests, motives for regulation may derive in part from "puritan expectations." Enforcement of laws regulating party finance by independent commisions such as the American FEC is weaker in Europe.

In his conclusion, Nassmacher points to political culture and the effect it has on defining political finance as candidate or party oriented. He also notes that of almost twenty countries with some form of public finance, five countries have not been studied in depth by any scholar. Data are becoming more available in more countries, and several new democracies should provide us with new subjects for comparative analysis. But we still have a way to go before we have the data and understanding we need for some adequate theories of comparative campaign and party financing.

Notes

1. Dan Balz and Richard Morin, "An Electorate Ready to Revolt," *The Washington Post National Weekly Edition*, November 11-17, 1991, pp. 6-7.

2. See the report on these and other scandals in *CQ Almanac* 45 (1989), pp. 36-48.

3. *New York Times*, Editorial, October 28, 1991.

4. Herbert E. Alexander and Monica Bauer, *Financing the 1988 Election* (Boulder: Westview Press, 1991), p. 3.

5. Ibid., pp. 3 and 13.

6. Ibid., p. 53.

7. Ibid., p. 109.

8. *New York Times*, November 26, 1991, p. A 17 and April 3, 1992, p. A18.

9. Margaret Latus Nugent and John R. Johannes, eds., *Money, Elections, and Democracy: Reforming Congressional Campaign Finance* (Boulder: Westview Press, 1990), pp. 1-5.

10. Herbert E. Alexander, ed., *Comparative Political Finance in the 1980s* (Cambridge: Cambridge University Press, 1989), p. 12.

11. Ibid., pp. 11, 16-17.

12. *Buckley v. Valeo* 424 U.S. 1 (1976).

13. See also Herbert Alexander, *Reform and Reality: The Financing of State and Local Campaigns* (New York: The Twentieth Century Fund, 1991), pp. 41-42.

14. Royal Commission on Electoral Reform and Party Financing, *Reforming Electoral Democracy*, 4 vols. (Ottawa: Minister of Supply and Services, 1991).

PART TWO

Political Finance
in North America

2

The High Finance of American Politics: Campaign Spending and Reform in Federal Elections

Paul S. Herrnson

In 1988 Americans spent roughly $1.5 billion to elect a President, 435 members of the U.S. House of Representatives, and 33 members of the U.S. Senate.[1] Most of this money was spent by individual candidates, who collected most of their funds from private citizens and political action committees. Political parties, the federal government, and the candidates themselves accounted for much smaller portions of the money spent in connection with federal campaigns.

Campaign finance in American federal elections is candidate-centered, pluralistic, and highly regulated. It reflects the unique features of the U.S. political system, including a constitutional framework that inhibits the formation of programmatic political parties, administrative and legislative structures that provide interest groups with significant access to high-level policymakers, and a population that is ambivalent about political parties and the role of money in politics. This chapter presents an examination of the major aspects of campaign finance in U.S. federal elections: the regulations that govern it, the actors that participate in it, and differences in the financing of presidential and congressional nominating contests and general elections. Recent developments as well as the prospect for reforming the present campaign finance law also are discussed.

The Road to Reform

For much of American history, campaign money flowed virtually

17

unchecked from businesses, trade associations, labor unions, political parties, and wealthy individuals to candidates for Congress, the Presidency, and other elective offices. Most of these groups gave money to candidates or parties with the hope of receiving a prestigious political appointment, lucrative government contract, or the opportunity to influence public policy. Campaign money also was routinely collected from other, less wealthy individuals who desired government jobs or other public benefits. It was not unusual for party bosses to extort money from those holding government positions; civil servants who failed to make a contribution often were threatened with dismissal. As late as the 1920s, candidates and parties directly purchased votes by distributing cash, alcohol, tobacco, or trinkets to voters. Prior to the passage of the 1974 amendments to the Federal Election Campaign Act, corruption was probably more the norm than the exception in the financing of American elections.

Many attempts have been made to regulate the flow of money in federal elections and to minimize the corrupting influence of money in politics.[2] Congress's first attempt took place in 1867, when it passed a naval appropriations bill that included provisions prohibiting naval officers and government employees from levying assessments on shipyard workers. Shortly thereafter, similar pieces of legislation, including the Civil Service Reform Act of 1883 (also known as the Pendleton Act), extended these provisions to prevent all federal employees from making or soliciting contributions in federal elections.

The Progressive Era brought with it a major impulse for campaign finance reform, resulting in the passage of the Tillman Act in 1907, the Publicity Act in 1909, and other measures designed to prevent corruption in federal elections. These regulations made it illegal for national banks and private corporations to make contributions to candidates for the Presidency or Congress. They also established expenditure limits and disclosure requirements for candidates for the House and Senate. Nevertheless, the lack of an adequate oversight agency to enforce the laws made it easy for unscrupulous politicians to break them.

During the period stretching from 1925 to 1947, Congress once again made a number of more-or-less futile attempts to clean up the financing of federal elections. The Corrupt Practices Act of 1925 was Congress's first attempt at comprehensive campaign finance legislation. It recodified many of the earlier reforms, adjusted spending limits for House and Senate candidates, and placed the onus for disclosing campaign receipts and expenditures on the candidates themselves.[3] Other measures passed during this period include the Public Utilities Holding Company Act (1935), the Clean Politics Act of 1939 (more commonly known as the Hatch Act), the Smith-Connally Act (1943), and the Labor Management Relations Act of 1947 (also known as the Taft-Hartley Act). Collectively, these measures prohibited public utilities and labor unions from giving contributions to parties or candidates; established limits for individual contributions to federal candidates; extended the spending limits for party and candidate committees to cover primary elections; and prevented individuals who worked for or did business with the U.S. government from contributing to federal campaigns.

The regulations had two overall weaknesses. First, they contained many loopholes. Candidates and parties, for example, could circumvent the overall spending limits by establishing a number of separate campaign committees, each of which could collect and spend the maximum amount allowed under law in a coordinated effort. Second, the regulations lacked an adequate enforcement agency. The Clerk of the House of Representatives, the Secretary of the Senate--the officials entrusted with administering the laws--had little authority, no staffs, and perhaps even less motivation to monitor the financial transactions of federal campaigns. Candidates could refuse to obey the disclosure provisions without fear of prosecution or potentially harmful publicity. Corporations, unions, and other big contributors went virtually unfettered in their contributing activities to federal candidates.

The dawn of the "new-style" politics during the 1950s drastically changed the nature of campaigning and introduced new pressures to reform the campaign finance system. The replacement of party-centered, labor-intensive campaigns that depended on volunteer party workers by candidate-centered campaigns that relied on mass media advertising, marketing techniques, and professional campaign consultants caused the costs of campaigning to skyrocket. Higher campaign costs placed greater pressure on politicians to raise money and heightened citizen concerns that wealthy contributors were gaining too much influence in the political process.

Several politicians responded to public opinion by proposing a number of reforms. President John F. Kennedy's Commission on Campaign Costs recommended using matching federal funds to finance presidential elections. Representatives Robert Ashmore and Charles Goodell and Senator Russell Long introduced bills to subsidize presidential election campaigns and to create a bipartisan commission to oversee the financing of federal elections. These proposals met with limited success in Congress, but they helped reinvigorate the dialogue on campaign finance and introduced at least a few ideas that would eventually become law.[4]

In 1971, reformers finally succeeded in changing some aspects of the laws governing the financing of federal elections. During that year, Congress enacted the Federal Election Campaign Act of 1971 (FECA). The FECA was the first comprehensive campaign finance legislation to be passed since the Corrupt Practices Act of 1925. It created ceilings on contributions by candidates to their own campaigns, set limits on the amounts that candidates could spend on mass media advertising, and tightened reporting requirements for federal candidates and political committees.[5] Companion legislation, contained in the Revenue Act of 1971, sought to encourage broader participation in elections by enabling individuals who made political contributions to claim a modest credit or deduction on their federal income tax returns.[6] The Revenue Act also created a tax checkoff that enabled individuals to designate $1 of their taxes to be placed in a special Presidential Election Campaign Fund that would be used to finance future presidential contests.

The Watergate Scandal renewed concern about corruption in American politics. The crimes committed by high ranking officials in the Nixon Administration and by Nixon's Committee to Reelect the President are too numerous to discuss fully here.[7] They include accepting illegal campaign contributions, giving ambassadorships and other high-level appointments to big contributors, granting price supports and other political favors to business executives in return for large campaign contributions, as well as the infamous break-in at Democratic Party headquarters in the Watergate Hotel. Watergate whipped up public sentiment for further campaign finance reform, energized the efforts of Common Cause and other reform groups, and called attention to all the glaring inadequacies in the regulations governing campaign finance.

In response to the public outcry, Congress revamped the law. The 1974 amendments to the FECA created new contribution and expenditure limits, introduced new disclosure and reporting requirements, and created the Federal Election Commission (FEC) to receive and analyze campaign finance reports, publicize campaign finance transactions, and enforce the law. In addition, the amendments introduced provisions for using the money collected in the federal income tax checkoff to fund presidential nominating campaigns, national conventions, and general elections.

Shortly after the 1974 amendments were passed, they were challenged in court. In January 1976, the U.S. Supreme Court ruled in *Buckley v. Valeo* that the provisions of the law limiting campaign expenditures made by candidates, by their campaign committees, or by others spending independently of the campaign violated their constitutionally-protected right to free speech.[8] The Court also ruled that the method used to appoint the members of the FEC violated the Constitution's separation of powers. Congress reacted by restructuring the commission and tinkering with other aspects of the law that had been found in violation of the Constitution. This second set of amendments, passed in 1976, was followed by a third set in 1979. The 1979 amendments to the FECA were passed in order to simplify reporting requirements, increase the role of state and local parties in federal elections, and change some procedural aspects of the enforcement process. The amended FECA currently regulates the financing of American federal elections.

The FECA's Impact

The FECA has restructured the financing of federal elections. Public funding has reduced the costs of presidential elections and minimized the influence of money in determining the outcomes of these contests. Under the FECA, candidates for a major party presidential nomination who accept matching funds must accept the spending limits that accompany those funds. Those who win the nomination and accept federal funding for the general election are prohibited from accepting money from any other sources.[9] The FECA has severely limited the growth in spending in presidential elections. In fact, the 1988 general election between George Bush and Michael Dukakis was the first presidential contest to break the $91.4 million spending record set in 1972 by Richard Nixon and George McGovern.[10]

The FECA's contribution limits have greatly reduced the sums of money wealthy individuals and groups can give to candidates for federal office. The FECA limits individuals to a maximum contribution of $1,000 per candidate for each primary, runoff, or general election. It caps at $5,000 a year the amount of money a person may give to a political action committee and places a $20,000 per year ceiling on individual contributions to the national committee of a political party. Moreover, the law sets an aggregate contribution limit of $25,000 per year for individual contributions. The FECA has put an end to the days when multi-millionaires like W. Clement Stone could give millions of dollars to federal candidates.[11] It has increased the emphasis that candidates and parties place on small contributions and led to the expansion and professionalization of the direct-mail fundraising industry.

The FECA, while having banned corporations, trade associations, and unions from contributing monies from their treasuries to federal candidates, has not diminished interest group activity in these races. Rather, it has transformed such activity. Following the FEC's advisory opinion to the Sunoco Oil Company (the SunPAC Advisory) in November 1975, which stated that corporations could give financial support to federal candidates provided that the money it gave came from voluntary contributions of employees and stockholders,[12] the number of PACs, especially business-related PACs, proliferated greatly (see Figure 2.1). By 1988 there were 4,828 PACs, roughly eight times more than existed in 1974. Fifty-three percent of these PACs were active in the 1988 elections, having spent some money in connection with at least one federal campaign. Yet, just over 22 percent of all PACs accounted for 89 percent of all PAC contributions given in that election cycle.[13]

The campaign contributions of corporation, association, and labor PACs have increased more than those of other types of PACs (See Figure 2.2). PACs now play a major role in the financing of congressional elections. They can each give up to $5,000 per election to a candidate and $15,000 a year to a national party committee. PACs account for more than half of the money raised by some congressional campaigns. The rapid proliferation and increased financial activity of PACs demonstrates the quickness with which American business and other organized interests can adapt to changes in the political environment.

22

FIGURE 2.1 Registered PACs by Type, 1974-1988

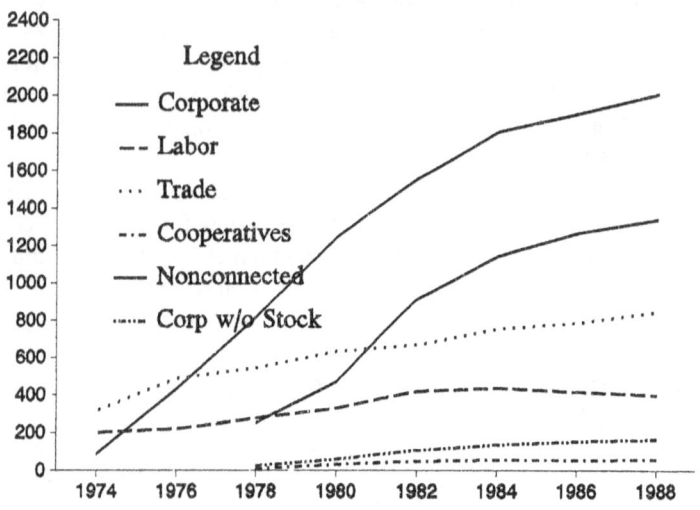

Source: Federal Election Commission

Political parties, like PACs, are limited in the amounts of money they can contribute to candidates. National and state party committees can each give $5,000 per election to a House candidate.[14] The parties' national and senatorial campaign committees can give a combined total of $17,500 to a Senate candidate.[15] Neither parties nor PACs can give contributions to presidential candidates who accept public funding. Parties also can spend limited amounts of money in direct coordination with their candidates' campaigns, while PACs can spend unlimited sums for or against a federal candidate just as long as that money is spent completely independent of the candidate's campaign. State and local party committees also can spend unlimited amounts on brochures, bumper stickers, registration and get-out-the-vote drives, and other grassroots activites designed to benefit a group of candidates running under the same party label.[16]

The immediate impact of the law was to weaken the political parties. The law's contribution limits hindered the parties' ability to collect the large sums of money they traditionally had received from wealthy individuals and groups. The FEC's SunPAC Advisory resulted in PACs supplanting party organizations as the major organized financiers of congressional elections. PACs have memberships, and some recruit House and Senate candidates and carry out many of the campaign functions traditionally associated with political parties. A

FIGURE 2.2 PAC Contributions to Federal Candidates by Type of PAC, 1978-1988

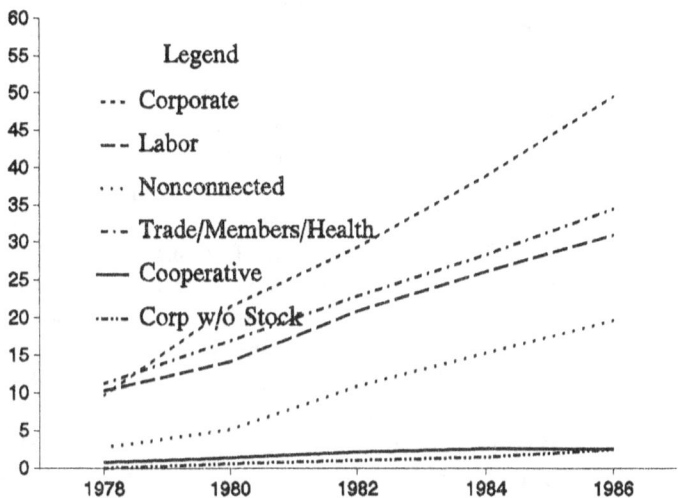

Millions of Dollars

Legend

··· Corporate
—·– Labor
··· Nonconnected
–·– Trade/Members/Health
—— Cooperative
···· Corp w/o Stock

Source: Federal Election Commission

number of political observers associate the rise of PACs with the decline of parties.[17]

The FECA's public funding provisions, party spending limits, and disclosure requirements had the immediate impact of severely restricting the roles of parties in presidential elections. The law reduced party influence in the 1976 presidential election because it forced the candidates to discourage state and local party committees from campaigning on their behalf out of a fear that their activities would be in violation of the FECA's contribution or spending limits.[18] Until the 1979 amendment to the FECA was enacted, state and local parties were effectively banned from conducting voter mobilization drives and distributing campaign buttons, handbills, and other election paraphernalia on behalf of their presidential candidates.[19]

At first, the FECA appeared to enlarge the already substantial gap that had grown between party organizations and their presidential and congressional candidates as a result of the emergence of the new-style politics. Yet, it is wrong to conclude that the FECA's impact on the political parties was entirely negative. During the late 1970s and early 1980s, Republican and Democratic party leaders responded to the technological and financial demands of the new-style politics by taking unprecedented steps to develop the organizational apparatuses of their respective party committees. Most of the party-building efforts were spearheaded by party organizations in Washington, D.C.[20]

The FECA helped shape the nature of the parties' organizational development. The ceiling on individual contributions encouraged the parties to develop direct-mail and telephone fundraising programs that could be effective in soliciting small and medium contributions from large numbers of donors. The result is that throughout the 1980s, national party organizations received most of the money in their federal accounts in the form of individual contributions of under $50.[21] Large contributions from wealthy individuals and PACs accounted for a relatively small portion of the parties' funds throughout most of the decade. By the decade's end, however, the overprospecting of small contributors and an industry-wide decline in direct-mail fundraising forced the parties to refocus their efforts on raising money from big givers and PACs.

Party contribution and spending limits, especially those restricting party activity in presidential elections, prevented the parties from spending all of their revenues in elections and encouraged them to reinvest substantial sums in further organizational development. The results of this investment are that the parties' national, congressional, and senatorial campaign committees are now institutionalized. They possess substantial budgets, employ large staffs, are located in party-owned headquarters buildings, and own state-of-the-art mass media studios, computers, and other campaign equipment.[22] Many state party committees have developed similar organizational characteristics.[23] The Republican party organizations are more highly developed than their Democratic counterparts, but both parties have adapted to the new regulatory environment created by the FECA and the capital-intensive nature of the new-style politics.

The FECA is believed by many to have played a critical role in stemming the tide of illegal contributions that traditionally have flowed to political campaigns. Although the FEC is often criticized for its inefficiency, it has written a number of important advisory opinions, pointed out questionable campaign finance practices to Congress and the general public, and recommended several useful changes in current campaign finance statutes.[24] Moreover, the mere existence of a watchdog agency to oversee the financing of federal campaigns has discouraged candidates, political parties, and PACs from straying from within the bounds of the law.

The FECA introduced a number of important changes in campaign finance, but it did not alter the basic pattern of federal elections. They remain candidate-centered. Congressional and presidential candidates continue to bear the responsibility for financing and waging their own campaigns. Parties and other groups continue to assist candidates, and candidates and their campaign committees remain the primary actors in federal election campaigns. By clarifying and strengthening the distinctions among different types of political committees and imposing stiffer regulations on the flow of campaign money, the FECA has helped to reinforce the candidate-centeredness of American elections.

Congressional Elections

General election candidates for the U.S. House and Senate raised a total of $426.1 millon in campaign money in 1988.[25] House incumbents raised just under $175 million, over four times more than House challengers (see Table 2.1). Senate incumbents raised approximately $98.3 million, almost twice as much as Senate challengers. The disparities between Democrats and Republicans are not particularly large, especially when the numbers of candidates running under each party label are taken into consideration.

Congressional candidates raise their funds from a variety of sources. In 1988, as in previous elections, individuals were the biggest source of campaign contributions to House and Senate candidates, followed by PACs, the candidates themselves, and party committees (see Table 2.2). Democratic incumbents in

TABLE 2.1 Net Receipts of House and Senate General Election Candidates, 1988 (in millions)

	Democrats		*Rebublicans*	
	House			
Incumbents	$102.5	(248)[a]	$ 72.5	(164)
Challengers	22.5	(154)	19.8	(194)
Open Seats	12.4	(27)	12.8	(26)
Total	$137.4	(429)	$105.1	(384)
	Senate			
Incumbents	$51.0	(15)	$47.3	(12)
Challengers	26.2	(12)	23.1	(15)
Open Seats	19.3	(6)	15.7	(6)
Total	$96.5	(33)	$86.0	(33)

[a] The number of candidates is in parentheses.
Source: Federal Election Commission.

the House were able to rely more on PAC money than any other group. Their majority status in the House gives the Democrats all of the chamber's powerful committee and subcommittee chairmanships and the ability to set the House's agenda. PACs recognize that Democrats possess control over the flow of legislative business in the House and most behave accordingly by giving

TABLE 2.2 Share of House and Senate General Election Campaign Funds Received by Source and Candidate Status,[a] (by percent)

Candidate status	Source				
	Individuals	PACs	Parties	Self	Other
House					
Democrats					
Incumbents	39	52	6	2	1
Challengers	47	32	6	14	0
Open seats	40	38	7	15	1
Republicans					
Incumbents	52	40	7	1	0
Challengers	57	10	14	19	0
Open seats	56	21	10	12	0
Senate					
Democrats					
Incumbents	64	30	5	1	0
Challengers	68	16	11	3	2
Open seats	39	17	8	37	0
Republicans					
Incumbents	65	27	8	0	0
Challengers	64	12	18	6	0
Open seats	57	28	13	2	0

[a] Includes loans received, offsets to campaign operating expenses, interests on deposits, transfers from House campaign accounts to Senate campaign accounts, proceeds from joint fundraisers, and contributions from members of Congress to other candidates.

[b] The figures in this row are significantly influenced by the campaign of Herbert Kohl (D-WI) who spent $6,920,071 of his own money.

Source: David B. Magleby and Candice J. Nelson, *The Money Chase* (Washington, D.C.: The Brookings Institution, 1990), p.60.

Democratic House members substantial campaign contributions. In 1988, House Democrats raised 52 percent of their funds from PACs, accounting for an average of $215,000 per candidate. The Democrats' control of the House also enables them to put the squeeze on PACs to give substantial sums of money to Democratic open seat candidates and challengers.

Although Republican House members raise significantly less from PACs than their Democratic counterparts, they were able to rely on PACs for 40 percent of their campaign funds, amounting to an average of $175,000 per candidate. Republican challengers and open seat candidates do not fare nearly as well, raising only 10 percent and 21 percent, respectively, of their money from PACs. Republican House candidates tend to rely more on individual contributions than do Democrats. Challengers and open seat candidates of both parties have to reach fairly deep into their own pockets in order to finance a bid for the House. Self-financing accounted for almost one-fifth of Republican challengers' receipts.

Republican candidates typically receive more party assistance than do Democrats. Many party contributions are given as an in-kind service, such as a poll, campaign advertisement, or the assistance of a professional campaign consultant.[26] Some political action committees, such as the American Medical Association's AMPAC, also give in-kind contributions. These services are subject to the same limits as are cash contributions.

The fundraising patterns for Senate candidates indicate they rely heavily on contributions from individuals. PACs are typically the next most important source of Senate campaign money, followed by parties and the candidates themselves. Republican candidates receive substantially more party money than Democrats.

Most party contributions are distributed by the Democratic and Republican congressional and senatorial campaign committees. The major goal of these committees is to maximize the number of seats they control in the House or Senate. The campaign committees give most candidates who are running in competitive districts the maximum legal contribution; lesser amounts are given to candidates who are expected to win easily or are thought to have little chance of electoral success. The match between competitiveness and contributions, however, is rarely perfect. A lack of information about the competitiveness of particular races and changes in the levels of competitiveness of individual candidacies introduce inefficiencies into the distribution of party contributions.[27] Broader strategic imperatives, such as a desire to shore up support in the South, and pressures from congressional incumbents, especially those who serve on the campaign committees, can have a similar impact.[28]

PAC contributions are guided by a different set of goals and imperatives. Most PAC giving reflects two general motives: the desire to influence a subset of public policies or the desire to influence the composition of Congress. PACs that seek to advance the first goal often give large contributions to incumbents who serve on committees that oversee legislative matters of importance to their parent organizations. Giving contributions to these members of Congress is believed to help a PAC gain or maintain access to them. PACs initiate some of these contributions, while incumbent solicitations lead to others. PACs may give money to incumbents who have supported their positions in the past as a form of reward. PACs also may give money to incumbents who have opposed their interests in an attempt to encourage favorable treatment in the future. Defensive giving is often practiced with the hope of minimizing the opposition that a representative or senator might express when legislation that is of importance to a PAC comes before the incumbent's committee.

Unlike the policy-oriented contributing described above, contributions that aim to influence the composition of Congress are guided primarily by considerations of candidate competitiveness. PACs that pursue this second goal may behave like party committees. They frequently give large contributions to incumbents, challengers, and open seat candidates who represent their parent committee's interests and are involved in close races.

Many PACs pursue both goals simultaneously. They give contributions to incumbents who serve on powerful committees and to challengers and open seat candidates who are sympathetic to their views. PACs that pursue both strategies have been known to give large contributions to incumbents and challengers who are seeking to win the same seats. Hedging one's bets by supporting both sides can be very expensive, and only the most wealthy PACs usually exhibit this behavior.

It should be noted that labor and nonconnected (often ideological) PACs often pursue behaviors that differ from those of other PACs. Labor PACs give most of their money to Democratic candidates, reflecting the labor movement's historical ties to the Democratic party. Nonconnected PACs give money to candidates who represent the views of the PAC's supporters. Both types of PACs have been known to give large contributions to candidates who are longshots in order to help advance the candidates' political careers or help the candidate publicize their mutually-supported causes.

In addition to the contributions, political parties and PACs also spend money on behalf of candidates. In 1988, parties could legally spend a maximum of $46,100 in coordination with a House candidate's campaign.[29] During that election cycle, the Democratic party spent over $2.6 million, or an average of $6,154 per candidate, on voter mobilization drives, polls, campaign advertisements, and other coordinated activities designed to help its House candidates. The Republican party spent over $3.9 million, or an average of $10,208, on behalf of its House contestants in 1988.[30] As one might expect, the largest coordinated expenditures were made in connection with competitive contests.

The limits for party spending in Senate elections vary by state. In 1988, the two major parties could each spend $92,200 in small states and just under

$1.88 million in the most populous state--California. Both parties routinely spend the legal maximum on coordinated activities in competitive Senate contests. The Democrats spent a total of $6.5 million dollars on behalf of their Senate candidates in 1988; Republican coordinated spending amounted to over $10.2 million during that same election cycle. Both parties spent the legal maximum in California.[31]

Independent expenditures by PACs differ from party coordinated spending in that there are no ceilings on independent expenditures and they legally must be made without a candidate's knowledge or consent. Independent expenditures, most of which are made by ideological PACs, can be made to help or harm a candidate's electoral prospects. They often take the form of television and radio advertisements, such as the negative campaign ads aired by "new right" groups during the 1980s. PACs made a total of $7.2 million in independent expenditures in connection with the 1988 congressional elections.[32]

Congressional candidates spend their money on a variety of campaign activities. Campaign staff, office space, polls, fundraising activites, and the need to travel all contribute to the expense of running a modern campaign. Advertising, however, accounts for the vast majority of campaign expenditures. Television, radio, and direct-mail advertisements account for about 60 to 75 cents of every dollar spent by a congressional candidate.[33] The increased reliance of candidates on the electonic media and the rapid escalation of broadcasting and production costs have helped to drive up the amount of money it takes to get elected to Congress.

The rising costs of campaigning have had unequal effects on different candidates. Incumbents typically need to spend much less to deliver their message to the general public. They use franked mail, congressional television studios, and other perquisites of office to familiarize constituents with their issue positions and accomplishments. These resources enable representatives and senators to build up high levels of name recognition and good will before the election season begins. Challengers and open seat candidates, especially those for the House, often begin the campaign virtually unknown to voters. They need to spend much more money than incumbents to get their message across. Campaign spending is believed to have a major impact on a challenger's level of name recognition and probability of getting elected, while incumbent spending is somewhat less influential.[34] The irony of this situation is that challengers usually have a great deal of difficulty raising money and frequently run underfunded, noncompetitive campaigns.

Low levels of name recognition and scarce resources make it difficult for nonincumbents, especially those running for the House, to get elected. These factors contribute to the high reelection rate of members of Congress and to the widely held perception that congressional incumbents are invincible. This, in turn, discourages highly qualified, potentially strong candidates from challenging incumbents.

Presidential Elections

Major party presidential candidates have the option of accepting public funds to finance their campaigns.[35] Candidates for the nomination may be able to qualify for partial public funding. Candidates who win the nomination are eligible to have their campaigns fully subsidized with money taken from the Presidential Election Campaign Fund. Party nominating conventions also receive a public subsidy.

The FECA requires candidates for the Democratic or Republican nomination who wish to receive federal matching funds to raise at least $5,000 in individual contributions in sums of $250 or less in at least 20 states.[36] Candidates who opt for public funding must abide by the FECA's spending limits.[37] They cannot spend more than $50,000 in personal or family money. They also must abide by an overall spending limit and separate spending limits for each state.[38] In 1988, the overall spending limit for a candidate for the Democratic or Republican presidential nominations was set at $23 million, with an additional $4.6 million allowed to be spent on fundraising. The state limits ranged from $461,000 in the smallest states to $7.5 million in California.[39] Collectively, the 16 candidates who competed for the nominations raised a $213.8 million and spent $210.7 million.[40] Sixty-six percent of these funds were raised from individuals, just over 31 percent came from the federal government, and a mere 1.4 percent was given by PACs.[41]

Candidates for the nomination use a variety of techniques to raise money. Fundraising dinners and other events designed to raise large contributions remain important, but the FECA's matching funds system places a premium on fundraising techniques that enable candidates to collect small contributions from large numbers of people. This is because only the first $250 of an individual's contribution counts toward meeting the matching funds requirement and, once a candidate has qualified for matching funds, only the first $250 of an individual's contribution is matched. The enhanced value of small contributions has encouraged the development of the direct-mail and telephone fundraising industries and increased the importance of building networks among upper-middle class and wealthy individuals who are in a position to call upon friends and associates to give $250 contributions. People and groups who have the ability to aggregate large sums of money have replaced those individuals who used to make large contributions as the new "fat cats" in financing American federal elections.

Spending limits for individual states and the scheduling of presidential primaries and caucuses have a major impact on how campaign money is spent. The Iowa caucuses and New Hampshire primary, for example, are important in establishing the field of front runners and helping them build momentum,[42] but because these states have relatively small populations candidates are not allowed to spend large sums of money in them. As a result, candidates routinely engage in a variety of machinations to circumvent the spending limits. Television and radio advertisements are taped and sometimes broadcast from neighboring states in order to reach people who live in Iowa, New Hampshire, and other targeted states without having the costs of these activities count fully against the spending limits for the targeted states. For the same reason, candidates and their staffs routinely sleep in neighboring states and commute across state borders in order to attend campaign events for the same reason.

Presidential nominating conventions also receive federal subsidies. In 1988, each major party committee received $9.2 million to help pay for sound systems, videotaped introductions and testimonials, and other forms of pageantry associated with contemporary nominating conventions. Other sources of convention funding include state and local governments, municipal corporations, private companies, associations, and individuals. The Republicans spent a total of $9.6 million to finance their 1988 convention, while the Democrats spent $9.4 million.[43]

Following the conventions, the two major party nominees are given lump sums from the federal government to finance their general election campaigns. In 1988, presidential candidates Michael Dukakis and George Bush each received $46.1 million. These were the only funds the two campaigns were allowed to spend.[44]

Broadcast media account for the largest expenditure made in contemporary presidential general elections. The amounts spent in the 1988 general election are typical of those in most presidential races. During that election, the Bush-Quayle campaign spent approximately $31.5 million (68.3 percent of its total funds) on televison and radio advertising, and the Dukakis-Bentsen campaign spent about $23.6 million (51.2 percent of its total) on broadcast media.[45] Travel expenses comprise the second largest expenditure, accounting for roughly one-quarter of the typical presidential campaign budget. Employee payroll, benefits, and office-related expenses typically comprise the next largest group of expenditures, followed by consulting contracts and polling. Candidates generally spend lesser sums on voter contact activities, printed campaign matter, and other forms of grassroots campaigning, relying on party committees to perform these.

The parties' national committees can spend additional sums on the presidential campaign. In 1988, the DNC and the RNC could each spend $8.3 million directly on behalf of their presidential ticket. Most direct party expenditures are allocated to mass media advertising. Voter contact activities typically comprise the next largest expenditure, followed by polling and public addresses by surrogate speakers.[46]

Although they are banned from giving contributions to candidates in the presidential elections or spending money in coordination with the candidates' campaigns, PACs and other organized groups can play a role in these contests.

A small number of PACs make independent expenditures in support of or against presidential candidates. The most visible form of PAC independent spending consists of television and radio advertisements aired by ideological PACs that advocate the election or defeat of a presidential ticket. In 1988, PACs spent just under $13.3 million in connection with the Bush and Dukakis campaigns. Roughly 96 percent of that money was spent to help George Bush: $9.7 million spent to advocate Bush's election and $3.0 million was spent for negative advertising designed to defeat Dukakis. Only $519,000 was spent in support of Dukakis and a mere $75,000 was spent to defeat Bush.[47] Many PACs, businesses, unions, and other interest groups also spend significant sums urging their members to vote for specific candidates and organizing nonpartisan campaigns to mobilize voters.[48]

Exemptions and Loopholes

The authors of the FECA purposefully included in the law certain privileges for party committees. In addition to the contributions and expenditures they can make directly to or spend on behalf of federal candidates, political parties also can spend unlimited amounts in a "coordinated party campaign." The 1979 amendment to the FECA allows state and local parties to make unlimited expenditures on grassroots political activities. These expenditures are exempt from the FECA's spending limits for individual federal races as long as they are made in conjunction with the campaigns of several candidates. Parties also are allowed to make unlimited expenditures on generic, party-focused campaign commercials that do not mention individual candidates by name. Throughout the 1980s, the parties broadcasted generic television and radio commercials in order to convey thematic messages about themselves and to attract support for their candidates.

Most of the money used to finance the coordinated campaign--commonly referred to as "soft money"--flows outside of the FECA's contributions and spending limits and is not subject to the law's reporting requirements.[49] Party committees have demonstrated the capacity to raise and spend substantial sums of soft money. In 1988, for example, the DNC and the RNC are each estimated to have raised between $20 million and $30 million dollars in soft money. Substantial portions of this money were collected in contributions of $100,000 or more. The Republican Party collected $100,000 donations from 249 corporate and individual contributors. The Democratic Party collected $100,000 donations from approximately 130 individuals.[50] These are impressive sums, even when compared to the $52.3 million and $91.0 million in "hard money" the national committees raised within the confines of the FECA's contribution limits.[51]

Soft money is collected primarily by party organizations located in Washington and distributed to state and local party committees in electorally competitive regions. State and local party committees use soft money to finance party-building activities, party-focused advertisements, and voter mobilization programs. During presidential election years, soft money is distributed in accordance with the strategy of the party's presidential nominee. During midterm election cycles, soft money is distributed primarily to states that are expected to host close congressional or gubernatorial contests or in which control of the state legislature is at stake.

Parties also have discovered loopholes that enable them to funnel large campaign contributions directly to their congressional candidates. The National Republican Senatorial Committee (NRSC), which has raised more money than it can legally spend in Senate elections during the last few election cycles, has taken the most initiatives in the search for ways to provide federal candidates with additional cash. In 1984, under its "conduit" role, the NRSC instructed potential contributors who wanted to give money to the committee instead to write checks to competitive Republican candidates and allow the committee to deliver the checks to them. During the 1990 election cycle, the NRSC expanded its conduit activities to include a joint fundraising committee to raise money for Republican Senate candidates. The joint fundraising committee, which was composed of 50 GOP senators and Senate candidates and NRSC staff, raised roughly $2 million for Republican Senate candidates from members of the Republican Inner Circle (a group of NRSC contributors who each give the committee $1,000 a year). NRSC staff arranged all of the joint committee's fundraising events, took one percent of the proceeds, and funneled the remainder of the money to Senate candidates using a formula that favored those involved in close elections. The NRSC's joint-fundraising program, which is perhaps the most innovative of its conduit activities, is currently under legal challenge.[52]

Candidates also have discovered a number of loopholes that enable them to increase their political activities. Prior to the launching of their official nomination campaigns, many candidates form personal PACs and foundations that enable them to build support by making speeches around the nation and giving contributions to state, local, and congressional candidates.[53] Candidate PACs and foundations frequently pay the salaries of campaign staff prior to the formation of a candidate's official campaign committee. Candidate PACs also can ease the costs of fundraising by developing direct-mail solicitation lists that can be used to raise money once a candidate formally begins campaigning for his or her party's nomination. Candidate PACs spent a total of $24.8 million in connection with the 1988 presidential nominating contests.[54]

Some members of Congress also form candidate PACs and political foundations. These members contribute money from their personal PACs to other members of Congress and promising nonincumbents in order to build up good will that they hope later to translate into support for their bids for congressional leadership positions or for their pet policies. Members also may use personal PACs as a legal subterfuge for channeling party money to other candidates. In 1990, for example, some members of the Senate who were not up for reelection accepted contributions from their party's senatorial campaign committee to their personal PACs and then had their PACs give the money to senatorial colleagues who were up for reelection.

Some representatives and senators use their political foundations to register sympathetic voters. The foundations are allowed to carry out unlimited voter mobilization programs, because these activities, like those conducted in coordinated party campaigns, affect several elections and are not directly connected with the campaign of any one federal candidate. The activities of political foundations have undergone intense scrutiny as a result of the adverse publicity surrounding the regulatory interventions made by five senators on behalf of financial investor Charles Keating and his failed Lincoln Savings and Loan. Keating's contributions to the Senators' campaigns and political foundations totaled over $1.3 million and led to a highly publicized scandal.[55]

Prospects for Further Reform

The Keating Five Scandal, highly publicized attempts to link PAC contributions to congressional roll call votes, the unaccountability of soft money, the tremendous increase in the costs of campaigning, and the decline in the competitiveness of congressional elections have encouraged many politicians, political observers, and "good government" groups, such as Common Cause, to call for reforming the federal election campaign finance system. Their recommendations include disclosure requirements for soft money transactions, higher ceilings for individual contributions, federal tax credits for individual donations to candidates or parties, higher ceilings for party contributions and coordinated expenditures, a ban on PAC contributions, expenditure limits for congressional campaigns, public funding for congressional elections, and postage and broadcast subsidies for federal candidates and political parties.

Towards the end of the 101st Congress, members of the House and the Senate debated legislation that proposed to further reform the financing of federal elections. Following intense partisan debate the chambers passed bills that were sponsored by Democratic leaders in the House and Senate. The bills were very dissimilar and the session ended before their differences could be resolved in a conference committee.

Campaign finance reform will almost certainly be debated in the 102nd Congress. Yet, significant obstacles will need to be overcome before a comprehensive reform bill can be enacted. Foremost among these are partisan disagreements. Most Democrats favor combining public subsidies with ceilings on the amounts that can be spent by individual congressional candidates.

Republicans tend to oppose spending limits because they believe these make it more difficult for challengers to defeat incumbents and could lock the GOP into its minority status. Many Republicans also have opposed public subsidies because of their philosophical opposition to increased government involvement in elections and concern about the costs of public funding. Instead, most Republicans would rather enact a bill that bans or severely limits PAC contributions, limits the amount of money a candidate may raise outside of his or her state, and increases the amounts that political parties can contribute to or spend on behalf of their candidates. Most Democrats, especially those in the House, perceive a ban on PAC contributions as a threat to one of their major sources of funding, have serious questions about the desirability of limiting out-of-state money, and believe it would not be in their party's best interest to increase party spending in congressional elections because Republican party committees have proven themselves to be far better fundraisers than their Democrat counterparts.[56] The major areas of agreement appear to be over the need to increase the disclosure of campaign transactions that influence federal campaigns, such as those made in connection with coordinated party campaigns, and the desirability of reducing the costs of televising campaign commercials either by providing candidates with vouchers or requiring local television stations to provide free broadcast time.[57] Reformers will most likely find it difficult to fashion the broad consensus needed to pass a comprehensive campaign finance reform package given the fundamental differences that exist between the parties, the opposition that most incumbents have against changes in the law that could threaten their reelection, and the personal animosities that currently exist between Democratic and Republican House leaders.

Conclusion

Federal election campaign finance reflects the candidate-centered nature of the American elections and the pluralist tradition of American politics. The system provides all groups--candidates, political parties, interest groups, individuals, and the federal government--a role in campaign finance. It gives political parties a few extra avenues for spending money that are not afforded to other organized groups, but it provides them with virtually no funding for routine party activities and does little to strengthen their stature. The FECA is much more favorable to individual candidates than to party committees.

Like its predecessors, the FECA regulates the flow of money in congressional and presidential elections, but it is not comprehensive enough to cover all of the election activities of those who participate in the campaign finance system. As was the case in earlier periods in American history, candidates, political parties, organized interests, and individuals have identified and exploited loopholes in the law. Some of the shortcomings of the law, such as those concerned with soft money, reflect the complexity of trying to regulate the flow of political money in a federal system that has several levels of elective office, each of which is governed by its own set of campaign finance statutes. Others, like the rights of political action committees and individuals to make unlimited independent expenditures advocating the election or defeat of a candidate, are rooted in the belief that such expenditures are a form of political expression that is protected under the U.S. Constitution.

Some of the criticisms levied against the FECA parallel those made in earlier periods. The complaint that wealthy individuals and interest groups are able to buy access to members of Congress spans most of American history. The complaint that elected officials are able to "arm twist" these same groups into giving money to their campaign committee or party has an equally long tradition. More recent criticisms focus on the skyrocketing high costs of getting elected to Congress. Some critics blame the huge war chests raised by incumbents, and the lopsided financing of congressional elections in general, for the lack of competitiveness in congressional races and the parties' inability to field good challengers. Others argue that the unprecedented amounts of time that incumbents devote to fundraising seriously distracts from their ability to focus on legislative work. Most critics believe that the campaign finance system contributes to a widespread distrust of government and politicians. Supporters of the system maintain that while revelations surrounding scandals like the Keating Five affair contribute to the decline in public trust, they also are evidence that the system is working because incidents of corruption or seemingly improper political conduct are finding their way into the public purview.

Several proposals for further campaign finance reform have been introduced in Congress and others loom on the horizon. Yet, the prospects for comprehensive reform are limited. Major barriers to reform exist in Congress, presidential leadership on the issue remains weak, and public pressure has yet to become great enough to force members of Congress and the president to come to an agreement. Unless a major scandal brings public outrage to a heated pitch, it is unlikely that the system of federal election campaign finance will experience comprehensive reform.

Notes

1. This estimate includes money spent by primary and general election candidates for the House, Senate, Presidency, funds spent by political parties (including convention and soft money expenditures) and political action committees (including independent expenditures), and communications expenditures made by interest groups to their members in order to advocate the election of candidates. Estimates commonly range from $1.4 billion to $1.65 billion, depending on whether one includes money raised but

not spent by candidates, parties, or political action committees (PACs), or whether one subtracts party and PAC contributions to candidates from the totals spent by these organizations in order to prevent these dollars from being counted twice (first when they are contributed to candidates and second when they are spent by candidates). For information about spending in 1988 federal elections see Federal Election Commission, "Independent Expenditures of $21 Million in '88, FEC Study Shows," Press Release, May 19, 1989; Federal Election Commission, "FEC Releases Final Report on 1988 Presidential Primary Campaigns," Press Release, August 25, 1989; Federal Election Commission, "Final Report on 1988 Congressional Campaigns Shows $459 Spent," Press Release, October 31, 1989; Federal Election Commission, "Final Report Shows Slower Growth of PAC Activity During 1988 Election Cycle, Press Release, October 31, 1989; Federal Election Commission, "Final Report Shows Republican Party Doubles Democrats' Effort 1987-88," Press Release, October 31, 1989.

2.   For discussions of the history of campaign finance reform see Herbert E. Alexander, *Financing Politics* (Washington, D.C.: CQ Press, 1984), ch. 2; Robert E. Mutch, *Campaigns, Congress, and the Courts* (New York: Praeger, 1988), chs. 1-3; and Frank J. Sorauf, *Money in American Elections* (Glenview: Scott, Foresman/Little, Brown, 1988), ch. 2.

3.   Prior to the passage of the Corrupt Practices Act, campaign treasurers were responsible for reporting campaign committee transactions.

4.   The Long Act, which was attached as a rider to an unrelated piece of legislation, actually became law on the last day of the 89th Congress. Shortly after the 90th Congress began, however, House members and senators voted to make provisions of the act inoperative, thereby preventing its provisions from going into effect without having to repeal the legislation. See Alexander, *Financing Politics*, pp.31-35.

5.   Alexander, *Financing Politics*, pp.35-36.

6.   The tax deductions and contributions were eliminated when the federal income tax code was reformed in 1986.

7.   For some useful discussions of the scandal and its impact on the regulation of campaign finance see Carl Bernstein and Robert Woodward, *All the President's Men* (New York: Warner, 1974) and Ralph K. Winter, *Watergate and the Law* (Washington, D.C., 1974).

8.   *Buckley v. Valeo*, 424 U.S. 1 (1976).

9.   Every major party nominee has accepted public funding in the general election.

10.   Bush and Dukakis each received $46.1 million in public funds for a total of $92.2 million, which barely breaks the 1972 spending record. If one adjusts the figures to control for inflation, however, the amount spent in 1988 falls short of that spent in 1972.

11.   In 1972, Stone contributed $2.8 million to Nixon's presidential campaign. See Alexander, *Financing Politics*, p. 59.

12.   Federal Election Commission, Advisory Opinion 1975-23, December 3, 1975.

13.   Federal Election Commission, "Final Report Shows Slower Growth of PAC Activity."

14.   Primaries, runoffs, and general elections are each considered separate elections under the FECA. Party committees, however, usually give contributions to general election candidates only.

15. The limits for Senate elections are higher than those for House elections presumably because the authors of the FECA believed that parties should be allowed to spend more in Senate elections since they typically involve larger constituencies than House elections.

16. As will be discussed later, activities that solely benefit one federal candidate must be reported as a contribution or coordinated expenditure and cannot exceed the FECA's contribution or spending limits.

17. William J. Crotty, *American Political Parties in Decline* (Boston: Little, Brown, 1984), p. 172; and Larry J. Sabato, *The Rise of the Political Consultants* (New York: Basic Books, 1981), p. 274.

18. Richard B. Cheney, "The Law's Impact on Presidential and Congressional Election Campaigns," in Michael J. Malbin, ed., *Parties, Interest Groups, and Campaign Finance Laws* (Washington, D.C.: American Enterprise Institute, 1980), pp. 240-241.

19. Prior to the 1979 amendment, these activities had to be counted against either the party's spending limits or paid for out of the candidate's treasury. It is worth noting that some local parties did not carry out these grassroots activities in the 1980 presidential election because they were either unaware of the contents or status of the 1979 amendment to the FECA.

20. John F. Bibby, "Party Renewal in the National Republican Party," in Gerald M. Pomper, ed., *Party Renewal in America* (New York: Praeger, 1981), pp. 102-116; Joseph A. Schlesinger, "The New American Political Party," *American Political Science Review* Vol. 79, 1985, pp. 369-400; and Paul S. Herrnson and David Menefee-Libey, "The Dynamics of Party Organizational Development, *Midsouth Political Science Journal*, Vol. 11, 1990, pp. 3-30.

21. As will be discussed later, national party organizations also have nonfederal accounts which are not subject to the FECA so long as the money in these accounts is not spent in direct connection with elections for federal office.

22. Paul S. Herrnson, *Party Campaigning in the 1980s* (Cambridge, Mass.: Harvard University Press, 1988), ch. 2.

23. Cornelius P. Cotter, James L. Gibson, John F. Bibby, Robert J. Huckshorn, *Party Organizations in American Politics* (New York: Praeger, 1984), esp. ch. 2; and John F. Bibby, "Party Organization at the State Level," in L. Sandy Maisel, ed., *The Parties Respond* (Boulder: Westview Press, 1990), pp. 21-40.

24. David B. Magleby and Candice J. Nelson, *The Money Chase* (Washington, D.C.: Brookings Institution, 1990), ch. 7.

25. This includes money raised during the nomination stage of the election. The figure for all 1,792 candidates, including those who lost in a primary or runoff, is $477.6 million. See Federal Election Commission, "Final Report on 1988 Congressional Campaigns."

26. Herrnson, *Party Campaigning*, esp. chs. 3-4.

27. Gary C. Jacobson, "Party Organization and Distribution of Campaign Resources: Republicans and Democrats in 1982," *Political Science Quarterly* vol. 100, 1985-1986, pp. 603-625.

28. Paul S. Herrnson, "National Party Decision Making, Strategies, and Resource Distribution in Congressional Elections." *Western Political Quarterly* vol. 42, 1989: 301-323.

29. The coordinated expenditure limits for states with only one House member were set at $92,200 for each committee during the 1988 election cycle. See Federal Election Commission, "FEC Releases Final Report on 1988 Presidential Primary Campaigns."

30. Federal Election Commission, "Final Report on 1988 Congressional Campaigns."

31. Ibid. and Federal Election Commission, "Final Report Shows Slower Growth of PAC Activity."

32. Federal Election Commission, "Final Report Shows Slower Growth of PAC Activity."

33. Edie N. Goldenberg and Michael W. Traugott, *Campaigning for Congress* (Washington, D.C.: CQ Press, 1984), p. 86; and Magleby and Nelson, *The Money Chase*, p. 62.

34. Gary C. Jacobson, *The Politics of Congressional Elections* (Boston: Little, Brown, 1987), pp. 122-125; and Donald Philip Green and Jonathon S. Krasno, "Salvation for the Spendthrift Incumbent: Reestimating the Effects of Campaign Spending in House Elections," *American Journal of Political Science* vol. 32, 1988, pp. 884-907.

35. Independent and third party candidates also may be eligible for lesser amounts of funding, depending on the share of the vote they receive in the current or previous election.

36. Once candidates qualify for federal funding, they lose their eligibility for additional public funds if they win less than 10% of the vote in two consecutive primaries in which they compete. In the event that a candidate loses his or her eligibility, he or she can requalify for public funds by winning at least 20% of the vote in a subsequent primary.

37. Since the law went into effect only one candidate, Republican John Connally of Texas, chose not to accept public funds.

38. The state spending limits originally were set in 1974 at $200,000 or 16 cents per eligible voter, whichever was greater, and have been increased to allow for inflation prior to each election cycle.

39. These ceilings do not include legal and accounting expenses, which do not count toward the FECA's spending limits. See Federal Election Commission, "FEC Announces Spending Limits for 1988 Presidential Race," Press Release, February 5, 1988.

40. These are "adjusted" receipts and expenditures. The total figures, which include accounting and legal expenses, were $253 million in expenditures and $250 million in receipts.

41. Federal Election Commission, "Independent Expenditures."

42. Larry M. Bartels, *Presidential Primaries*. (Princeton: Princeton University Press, 1988), pp.7,27,130-270.

43. Federal Election Commission, "Final Report Shows Republican Party Doubles Democrats' Effort."

44. The FEC has predicted that the declining numbers of taxpayers who donate one dollar of their federal income tax to the Presidential Election Campaign Fund and the increasing subsidies allocated to presidential campaigns (the subsidies are adjusted for inflation) may cause a shortage that will make it impossible for presidential candidates

to receive full federal funding during the 1992 presidential election (see Federal Election Commission, "FEC Testifies on Status of Presidential Election Fund: Primary Candidtaes Could be Shortchanged, "Press Release, March 1, 1991). This has the potential to result in a major party presidential candidate rejecting federal funding for the first time since the FECA was enacted.

45. Herbert E. Alexander and Monica Bauer, *Financing the 1988 Election* (Boulder: Westview Press, 1991), p. 36.

46. See, e.g., ibid., p. 41.

47. Federal Election Commission, "Independent Expenditures."

48. Alexander and Bauer estimate that $21.4 million was spent on these activities during the 1988 election, see *Financing the 1988 Election*, pp. 84-85.

49. Soft money is regulated by state statutes but these vary tremendously. See Elizabeth Drew, *Politics and Money: The New Road to Corruption* (New York: Macmillan, 1983), esp. p. 15; and Sorauf, *Money in American Elections*, pp. 148-149, 320-324.

50. Common Cause, "Federal Election Commission Allows 'Soft Money' Millions to Flood 1988 Presidential Races," Press Release, September 1988; and Common Cause, "Soft Money Activities in '88 Election Spur New Controversies, Reform Proposals," Press Release. September 1989.

51. Federal Election Commission, "Final Report Shows Republican Party Doubles Democrats' Effort."

52. Chuck Alston, "If Money Talks, Mr. Smith Won't go to Washington," *Congressional Quarterly Weekly Report*, November 3, 1990, p. 3758; and Federal Election Commission, "Republicans Maintain 4-1 Spending Edge Despite Fundraising Decline over Prior Cycles," Press Release, November 1, 1990.

53. Individuals are not officially considered candidates for the Presidency until they file with the FEC.

54. Anthony Corrado, "Honored in the Breach: The Rise of Presidential Candidate PACs and their Impact on the Federal Election Campaign Act," paper presented at the 1990 Annual Meeting of the American Political Science Association; and Clyde Wilcox, "Financing the 1988 Prenomination Campaigns," in E. Buell and L. Sigelman, eds., *Electing a President in 1988* (Knoxville: University of Tennessee Press, forthcoming 1991).

55. The Senators under investigation are Alan Cranston (Democrat of California), Dennis DeConcini (Democrat of Arizona), John Glenn (Democrat of Ohio), John McCain (Republican of Arizona), and Donald Riegle (Democrat of Michigan). See Helen Dewar, "Cranston Intervention Called 'Unusual,'" *Washington Post*, December 5, 1990.

56. It should be noted that Democratic Senate Majority Leader George Mitchell favors legislation that bans PAC contributions to federal candidates.

57. Chuck, Alston, "Image Problems Propel Congress Back to Campaign Finance Bills," *Congressional Quarterly Weekly Report*, February 21, 1991, pp. 275-281.

3

Campaign and Party Finance
in the American States

Ruth S. Jones

United States electoral activities with which the majority of readers are familiar are those of candidates and party organizations involved in federal elections and discussed elsewhere in this volume by Paul Herrnson. Yet, there are almost 500,000 elected officials in the U.S. and 99 percent of them hold state or local offices which they have won through state or local election campaigns. Federal, state and local elections have many things in common, yet each possesses unique characteristics. Elections for U.S. President, U.S. Senate and U.S. House of Representatives are different from elections for governor, state legislatures and state-wide offices such as treasurer, attorney general, school superintendent, and insurance commissioner; these, in turn, are different from elections for local offices such as. mayor, city council, school board, or cultural arts council. The purpose of this chapter is to provide an overview of the roles of parties and elections at the state and local level because they are central to a comprehensive understanding of campaign and party finance in the United States.

There are many historic structural forces that have shaped the context for contemporary elections in the U.S., but three in particular stand out. The first, and perhaps most important, is the significance of U.S. federalism for state and local elections. Each state is charged with the creation and administration of its own electoral laws, processes and procedures. If there is a conflict with federal law in areas related to federal offices, federal law takes precedent; but there is minimal overlap in laws governing federal and state elections.[1] For example, some states purposefully hold major state elections in the non-presidential or odd-numbered years just to insulate them from national forces. In effect, there are fifty very different sets of regulations that govern the selection of state officials, define the role and activities of state-level political parties, and shape the raising and spending of money in political campaigns.

A second structural feature that shapes electoral campaigns in the U.S. is the predominantly single-member district, plurality vote decision rule of the electoral system. This contrasts sharply with a list system with some form of proportional representation as is widely used in Europe. In the majority of cases in U.S. general elections, there is only one candidate per party per office on the ballot, each candidate must reside in the district, and to win, a candidate need get only a plurality of the votes cast for that particular office. The consequence is that most candidacies are geographic specific, in an all-or-nothing, one-on-one competition. This has promoted the dispersion and decentralization of elections and of the institutions related to elections, such as the political parties.

The third historic feature of the electoral system that influences campaign finance in the 1990s is the role of political parties. Almost all state elections are partisan elections (the state of Nebraska provides the major exception), and many, although certainly not all, local elections have partisan dimensions. Yet, in contrast to the European experience, the role of political parties is not always central to the electoral campaign. Two important differences focus on the degree of party control over the selection of candidates (and therefore, officeholders) and the coordination or cohesion among different units of the same party.

It is important to note first that not all elected officials are aligned with a political party. At the turn of the century, reformers sought to weaken U.S. party organizations by instituting non-partisan electoral systems in some state legislatures, many large cities and a host of smaller communities throughout the country. Over the years, the enthusiasm for non-partisan elections has ebbed and flowed, but many non-partisan elections in which there is no evidence of party involvement still take place each year. Hence many officials in policy-making positions have no party-based relationships to other, partisan, policy makers in the state.

At the same time, many party organizations have adapted to the non-partisan systems that surround them so that many "non-partisan" elections have all the trappings of partisan elections, except that no party is mentioned on the ballot. Thus, it is not uncommon, for example, for a "non-partisan" mayor to become a party's standard bearer for state-wide office. The reverse is also true. In 1990, "Independents" were elected as governors in Alaska and Connecticut. In point of fact, Walter Hickel had been Alaska's Republican governor in 1966-1969 and Interior Secretary in the Nixon administration. Lowell Weicker, Jr., was a Republican U.S. Senator from Connecticut from 1971-1989. While the 1990 ballot label for each was that of "Independent," their public image was clearly that of an established, albeit maverick, Republican partisan running against a "newcomer" who happened to win the Republican primary.

Second, to say that most elections remain partisan does not necessarily mean that parties are dominant or control the selection of candidates, the themes and policy proposals articulated during a campaign or the campaign strategy. In addition to the decentralization forced by single member legislative districts, the party primary system that was widely adopted as part of the turn of the century progressive movement severely limits the power of party leaders to determine who the party standard bearers will be or what their platforms will advocate. Moreover, there are different types of primaries, some of which even deny the party the opportunity to identify who the voters in the party primary are likely to be.

For example, in an open-primary system citizens need only to be registered voters. They do not have to indicate a party preference, and can participate in the primary of any party on the ballot. This limits the ability of the parties to establish a roster of "members" or even citizens potentially sympathetic to their party. And they certainly cannot restrict participation to party faithful who have the party's best interest at heart. Open primaries also can lead to instances of cross-over voting in which loyalists of one party participate in the selection of the candidates for another, often the strongest, opposition party.[2] But the most significant point is that in any primary system the party leaders cannot *ipso facto* determine who the party candidates will be because the primary system leaves the selection of general election candidates to rank and file voters.

Although the Democratic and Republican parties are the major political parties in all fifty states, this does not mean that either of these two parties is necessarily organizationally cohesive or highly centralized. Moreover, the parties at the national, state, and local level may or may not interact regularly, may or may not share common positions on current political issues, and may or may not coordinate fund raising, campaign strategies and expenses or other election-related activities. The absence of a clear hierarchy of organization, a fully integrated, coordinated campaign strategy or a common philosophy means that for each major national party there may be fifty state parties and hundreds of local parties, and each one may be different from its counterpart in another state or city. To know only that state or local candidates are Democrats or Republicans does not necessarily convey a great deal of information about the support they have from party organizations.

The 1990 Republican race for the U.S. Senate in Louisiana provides an extreme example of the intersect of electoral federalism, single-member districts with plurality vote needed for election, and a decentralized party with limited control over ballot access. Louisiana law provides for a non-partisan primary election. If no candidate gets over 50 percent of the vote, there is a run-off election between the top two candidates, regardless of party. In 1990 the Republican candidate who received the second highest number of primary votes, which qualified him to participate in the run off, was a leader of the Ku Klux Klan and an avowed white supremacist. Both national and state Republican party organizations disavowed his Republican candidacy and openly supported the election of the Democratic opponent who won the general election with 54 percent of the vote.[3] Electoral structures established by state law frequently place contemporary political parties in a very awkward position relative to the traditional party role of providing political leadership, including providing assistance in the funding of election campaigns.

Information About State Elections

The federal nature of the electoral system and the lack of a national party hierarchy means that the collection of comparative data essential to scholarly inquiry is often difficult. There are numerous private, nationally distributed journals and unofficial reports that record electoral data for federal offices.[4] And the Federal Election Commission (FEC) collects, maintains records of and disseminates all campaign finance data associated with federal election campaigns.

At the state level, each state is the official record keeper of its election results, but public dissemination of final vote tallies is unofficially left up to the major newspapers in the state.[5] Because there is no counterpart to the FEC at the state level, campaign finance data must be collected from each individual state. Not only is this a laborious task, but there also are no shared reporting conventions among states, and data available from one state are not necessarily available from another. Moreover, the reporting categories, even when apparently the same across several states (e.g., campaign expenses) do not always include the same information (i.e., repayment of bank loans, cross-transfers among candidates, outstanding debts). Consequently, research on state-level campaign finance most frequently takes the form of a single-state case study or modest cross-state analyses.[6]

The story is much the same for gathering detailed information about the organizational structure and roles of the various units of the political parties. With a few notable exceptions, information on state and local party organizations is unlikely to be comprehensive or even comparable across units within a single state let alone across states.[7]

These problems of data availability, collection and analysis are compounded many fold when the inquiry shifts to local elections. Instead of fifty states from which to seek information, there are almost 100,000 local government entities engaged in various forms of election politics. Moreover, local governments often have specific election laws, unique partisan organizational structures, and detailed campaign-related norms and regulations. With the noticeable exception of the herculean effort by the California Commission on Campaign Financing to document campaign finance in seventeen California cities, there are few comparative analyses of the role of money in local elections.[8] Consequently the remainder of this chapter focuses almost exclusively on state level campaigns. Even then, what we report here is an incomplete synthesis of information provided by multiple sources. The reader who seeks more in-depth analysis would be well served to consult individual state governments.

The Context of State Elections

The relationships between the different party units and the coordination or independence of campaigns has varied over the 200 year history of the country. And in each state, the events of the past have helped shape the present. However, several general observations can be made about the status of political parties and electoral campaigns in the states in the 1990s.

Parties

The popular description of all-powerful political party machines associated with the Hague, Tweed or Pendergast eras may once have been accurate for a substantial portion of state and local governments, just as the Daleys and Rizzos have made more recent contributions to the lore of strong party organization. Since the early 1950s, however, political parties largely have been electorally focused organizations which in fact are open to all citizens even though in practice they are run by a small cadre of politically motivated citizens.

Party influence within and between states has changed noticeably over the last half century. States such as those of the Southern Confederacy that were once solidly Democratic now boast three Republican governors as well as more than 400 Republican state legislators. Various indices of party strength suggest a range of states along a continuum from the most solidly Republican (Wyoming and Vermont) to most solidly Democratic (Alabama and Mississippi) with an increasing number of "competitive" states in between.[9] Similarly, divided government is not a new phenomena in state government. Jewell and Olson (1988) found that between 1965 and 1988 in only five states was there solid Democratic dominance and in only two was there a consistent Republican majority.[10] In 1990 the Democrats controlled the governorship and a majority of both legislative chambers in 17 states; the Republicans controlled only three states and there was divided government in the other 29 (Nebraska is non-partisan). And it follows that for voters, split-ticket voting is as much the rule as the exception in more than half the states. In sum, the direct impact of political parties on election outcomes is far from universal.

There has been continuing concern over the health of state and local party organizations during the last two decades. The research literature, in fact, documents great variability in the professionalism and current functions of political parties across the states. Moreover, the role of state party organizations has changed vis-a-vis local candidates, other political organizations and the national party committees. In some states, interest groups and political action committees are more visible than are the state parties. In others, the coordination of party effort with the national party committees is sizeable and quite visible. And yet in still other states the autonomy and independence of the party have not changed noticeably in twenty years.

It remains true that the two major political parties continue as the most persistent, visible actors across all election campaigning. And while some parties have grown stronger (Republican parties in the southern states) and some have grown weaker (Democratic parties in the New England states), what parties do and how they behave has changed across all states. Parties now are the facilitators, the coordinators, the behind-the-scenes partners rather than the visible "king-makers" of past years.

Campaign Context

There is even greater variation in campaign activities and techniques across state and local elections than there is in the status and function of party organizations. Characteristics associated with federal campaigns--candidate centered, media oriented, high cost, incumbent dominated--are more or less applicable to a large number of state-level campaigns, especially for offices such as governor. On the other hand, it is also true that the majority of state and local elections continue to be relatively low-key, low cost, grass roots campaigns compared to congressional campaigns.

Campaign technology has been readily exported from the national to the state arena, and there is little state or party officials can do to halt the increased use of expensive technology. There is great variation across states and even within states in the use of media consultants, professional fund raisers and polling firms. Most gubernatorial campaigns are heavily dependent on these modern campaign techniques, increasingly other state-wide office seekers are utilizing such technology, and it is not at all unique for state legislative and mayoral candidates to employ external consultants, polling experts and even mass mail technology.

The opportunities and techniques of "modern" campaigning have placed states in a reactive mode rather than a proactive, leadership role in terms of legislation that shapes the campaign arena. This is nowhere more evident than in the area of campaign finance.

Financing Campaigns

Many of the features associated with the financing of campaigns for Congress also apply, in varying degrees, to financing campaigns for state and local offices. The costs of campaigns have risen, open-seat races tend to be more competitive and expensive, incumbents spend more money than challengers, candidates who spend the most usually, but not always, win and yet electoral outcomes are often affected by the unique, idiosyncratic nature of particular campaign contexts and candidate characteristics. Similarly, raising campaign funds dominates the activities of state-level candidates and party activists. However, the sources of funds for state and local campaigns do not directly parallel those of federal campaigns because each state has different campaign finance regulations.

Campaign Expenditures

With the exception of Arkansas, Montana, North Dakota, Oklahoma and Wyoming, all states require candidates to report the amount of expenditures, paid to whom, and for what purpose.[11] A pioneering report by the Washington Public Disclosure Commission demonstrated that the costs associated with the use of more elaborate campaign techniques have risen faster than the general consumer price index, suggesting that technology is part of the reason for sharp increases in some campaign costs.[12] Nevertheless, it remains true that very little attention has focused on expenditures in state campaigns. Hence we cannot speak in any detail to the specific use of campaign funds. We can, however, address aggregate trends in the magnitude of expenditures and the distribution of expenditures among types of candidates across states and campaigns.

In general, the cost of running for elected state office has increased far in excess of inflation. Between 1958 and 1986, for example, the cost of California state legislative elections increased by a factor of 40 (4000 percent), and total costs reached $68 million by 1987-88. Prior to 1980, no California state legislative race had cost as much as $1 million. In 1986, twelve legislative races cost over $1 million (and five exceeded $2 million)! In 1990 the median cost of a California Senate race was $713,974; the median cost of an Assembly race was $341,324.[13]

California represents an extreme case in terms of the absolute amounts of money involved, but sharp increases have been experienced in many other states. In the state of Washington, the total costs for legislative races increased from $2.07 million to $8.38 million between 1976 and 1988, an increase of over 300 percent. In New Jersey, just between 1987 and 1989, expenditures for campaigning for the legislature increased 38 percent to more than $7.5 million. Jewell and Miller (1988) analyzed the costs of state legislative races in Kentucky and concluded that the expenditures in state legislative campaigning quadrupled between 1975 and 1988 while the cost of living approximately doubled.[14] In Alaska and Oregon, the median cost of legislative elections more than doubled between 1982 and 1988. Although increasingly there are state legislative races within one state that are more expensive than gubernatorial campaigns in another state, the costs of gubernatorial campaigns everywhere also have skyrocketed. Between 1978 and 1986, gubernatorial spending in Maine increased from just over $900,000 to $5.6 million. In 1990, all gubernatorial spending records were broken when expenditures topped $53.1 million in California and $50.6 million in Texas.[15] Yet over time there is great variation among states as well as within a single state. In 1988, governors were elected in North Dakota (the 8th smallest state) and North Carolina (the 10th most populous state). The total costs in these two races were $673,000 and $11,300,000, respectively.

Part of the difference in the cost of campaigns across states is attributable to the great variation in the size of state populations. In terms of absolute dollars, smaller states tend to spend less (See Table 3.1). But there are numerous exceptions. For example, reported expenditures for the most recent gubernatorial campaign in West Virginia ($8.5 million) were greater than for the most recent campaign in New York ($7.2 million) even though the voting age population of New York is more than nine times that of West Virginia. When expenditures are considered in terms of cost per registered voter, gubernatorial candidates in Montana and Rhode Island, the sixth and ninth *smallest* states, respectively, spent at a rate considerably higher than their counterparts in California, the most populous state.

The factors affecting campaign expenditures obviously are quite complex. Yet, as at the federal level, campaign financing appears to play an increasingly important role in election outcomes. In California, for example, 96 percent of candidates who had the most money won. A recent study by Gierzynski and Breaux suggests that the impact of state level campaign expenditures "appears to vary with state partisan trends, whether or not there is an incumbent in the race, media market congruence, party organization strength, and district population."[16]

Historically, there has been considerably more turnover in state legislatures than in the U.S. Congress.[17] In part this was because there were more voluntary retirements from the state legislatures. However, as state legislatures have become more professionalized and many public policy issues have been redirected to the state level, a trend toward reelection of state legislators has emerged.[18] In 1988 only one incumbent, defeated in the primary, failed to win reelection to Alaska's state legislative chambers. In 1990, 92 percent of California legislative incumbents seeking reelection won, and they outspent their challengers by a margin of eight-to-one. Incumbency and spending are usually but not always related.

In the 1989 New Jersey legislative races, winners spent 116 percent more than losers and incumbents outspent challengers almost two-to-one. Seventy-six incumbents were candidates for the New Jersey legislature and only three lost. In two of these races, the winning challengers spent twice as much as the incumbent; in the third case, the losing *incumbent* outspent the challenger two-to-one in his futile effort. Among the 32 New Jersey legislative candidates who contrast, two of the three highest spending legislative candidates were challengers who lost.

TABLE 3.1 Gubernatorial Campaign Costs in Selected States by Size of State Population Cost per Registered Voter

State	Year	Total Costs[a]	Voter[b]
Small States (under 1 million)			
Delaware	1988	$318,362	$2.78
New Hampshire	1988	1,520,086	2.34
Montana	1988	3,225,864	6.38
North Dakota	1988	673,000	1.42
Rhode Island	1988	5,037,168	9.18
Utah	1988	3,513,294	4.35
Vermont	1988	1,139,676	3.27
West Virginia	1988	8,533,441	8.80
Medium States (1 to 6 million)			
Indiana	1988	$8,239,770	$2.88
Kentucky	1987	18,366,985	9.06
Louisiana	1987	13,142,072	6.08
Mississippi	1987	8,702,740	5.45
Missouri	1988	4,292,387	1.46
Washington	1988	2,240,429	.90
Large States (over 6 million)			
California	1990	$53,100,000[c]	$3.79
Florida	1990	14,517,000[d]	2.40
Illinois	1990	14,758,759[c]	2.32
New Jersey	1989	25,976,697[c]	7.02
New York	1990	7,220,000[c]	.84
North Carolina	1988	11,275,234	3.29
Texas	1990	50,610,000[c]	6.17

[a] Cost figures are from Thad L. Beyle, "Costs of Gubernatorial Elections in 1987"; "Costs of Gubernatorial Elections in 1988," in *Comparative State Politics*, February, 1990, pp. 28-31; Washington State Public Disclosure Commission, *1988 Election Financing Fact Book*; and the New Jersey Election Law Enforcement Commission.

[b] Source for registered voters is Michael Barone, *The Almanac of American Politics 1990* (Washington, D.C.: National Journal 1989).

[c] Unofficial expenditures. Obtained from individual state offices relevant to elections or state offices of Common Cause.

[d] Unofficial expenditure. *Campaigns and Elections*, Vol. II, No. 5, December/January 1991, pp. 22-25.

spent less than $2,000, only two were incumbents and both were reelected. In

In Washington, one contested incumbent senator spent only $18,500 to win; a fellow legislator spent over $200,000 but still lost while a challenger spent over $237,000 to defeat an incumbent. In New York, the average senate incumbent spent slightly less than $50,000, while the average challenger spent just under $20,000.

Whereas state legislative contests often parallel those of the U.S. House of Representatives in terms of incumbency advantage, the importance of incumbency for governors is more akin to that of U.S. Senators.[19] That is, incumbent governors are less assured of reelection. Between 1977 and 1990, only 75 percent of incumbent governors seeking reelection won.[20] In 1990, six governors failed in their quest to retain the executive mansion and several others survived only after very competitive campaigns. Thus 1990 fit the pattern of recent years with victories by only 74 percent of incumbents seeking reelection. Most incumbent governors are able to spend more than their opponents,[21] and, to be successful, challengers often find it necessary to come close to matching, if not exceeding, incumbent spending. In 1988, for example, in the costly West Virginia race ($8.80 per registered voter) the victorious Democratic challenger outspent the Republican incumbent $4.6 to $2.4 million in the general election. On the other hand, in 1990, former U.S. Senator Lawton Chiles spent only half as much as the Republican incumbent Bob Martinez and yet won the Florida governorship with 57 percent of the vote. Joan Finney became the first woman governor of Kansas in 1990 after defeating the incumbent governor in the Democratic primary, although she spent only $50,000 compared to Governor Carlin's $400,000.[22]

Such exceptions to the general rule that challengers must spend more to win helps underscore the importance of specific electoral contexts to the outcome of state-level races. The most recent New York and West Virginia gubernatorial campaigns provide yet another useful contrast. The New York incumbent, Governor Mario Cuomo, went into the campaign with a high level of popularity and had minimal opposition in the primary as well as the general election. In West Virginia, incumbent governor Moore was a much more controversial candidate, and was eventually defeated by an aggressive, well-financed challenger.

In 1986, there was a three-person contest for governor of Arizona--the Republican and Democratic primary winners and an "Independent" (who had been a major contender in the Democratic primary before withdrawing). Although the Republican candidate spent just over half of what each of the other two candidates spent, he won a simple plurality as the other two split the Democratic vote. The result was that Evan Mecham became a minority governor, and two years later became the first governor of Arizona to be impeached.

In 1990, the gubernatorial campaigns in Texas and California were the focus of national attention. In part this was because these were open seat races (i.e., no incumbent) and were expected to be very competitive. But these races also are illustrative of the influence of "external" forces on state-level elections. Because Texas and California are among the largest as well as most rapidly growing states, each will gain several additional U.S. congressional seats as a result of reapportionment based on the 1990 U.S. Census. Under the conventions of U.S. federalism, it is the *state* legislature and the governor who generally determine, either directly or indirectly, how new electoral district boundaries will be drawn. Hence, governors elected in 1990 will play an important role in shaping new electoral districts for the state legislature. They also will, in turn, shape the districts for the *U.S. House of Representatives* for the next decade. It was not surprising, therefore, that national party organizations of both major parties wanted desperately to win these gubernatorial races. Such "external" interests only served to exacerbate campaign costs in already high-spending open-seat races.

Changing electoral contexts make it impossible to predict the cost of the next campaign based on the last campaign. For example, a 1980 rematch between two Missouri gubernatorial candidates cost over 200 per cent more than their first contest just four years earlier. In the next election, with a different, more popular incumbent in the office, the total cost of the gubernatorial campaign decreased by one-third ($4 million instead of $6 million). This fluidity of state-level campaign forces makes long-term financial planning for campaigns very difficult. As a result, most candidates assume a worst-case scenario (i.e., strong competition) and set about to raise as much money as they can.

Sources of Money

Historically, the states have been more active and innovative than the federal government in experimenting with issues of campaign finance.[23] Sunshine laws, emphasizing accountability, are not new to the states, and the idea of centralized reporting of campaign funding has long existed in many states. Today, all states require state-wide and state legislative candidates to file campaign finance reports. Consequently, it is possible to learn a great deal about the sources of campaign money.

State records, like state politics, vary. Wyoming requires only one post-primary and one post-general election report, while Virginia requires as many as three pre-primary, five mid-campaign, and a series of post-general election reports until all unreported obligations and financial issues are resolved. Alaska even requires that contributions over a specific dollar amount made within a week of the election be reported within 24 hours. The general assumption is that the more comprehensive and timely the reports, the greater the likelihood that information about the sources of campaign funds will be relevant to the electoral process.

Usually, however, campaign finance laws come into public view only after the campaign when most instances of alleged misconduct are investigated and hearings are held. Nevertheless, political parties and candidates are mindful of the laws even before the campaign begins because the laws define who can contribute, how much and when. Contribution regulations define the legal sources of campaign funds, and thus greatly influence the resources available to the campaign.

Similarly, the stricter the enforcement mechanisms and the greater the sanctions imposed for not filing financial reports or for other violations of the law, the greater the probability that disclosure laws will have their intended effect. Many states will not certify candidates for the ballot or for holding elected office until campaign finance reports are filed. In Rhode Island, failure to file a report is a petty misdemeanor and subject to a fine of not more than $500. In contrast, failure to file an accurate report in Wisconsin could mean criminal penalties (fines of up to $10,000 and up to 3 years imprisonment). In Texas, failure to file a report is a misdemeanor; in addition, candidates are civilly liable to opposing candidates for double the amount of any unlawful contribution or expenditure they fail to report, and liable to the state for triple the amount. Over half of the agencies responsible for overseeing campaign finance reports have the power to subpoena witnesses and almost one-fifth have the power to file independent court actions (Table 3.2).

State regulation of campaign money is often the focus of great disagreement. Those who view political contributions as the equivalent of political speech believe there should be no limitations on individuals or groups that want to contribute to the electoral process.[24] On the other hand, reformers have two concerns with a system that permits unlimited contributions. First, they argue that some individuals and groups are in a position to give exceptionally large contributions which create obligations for the candidates who receive them. Second, when wealthy individuals and groups give vast amounts they tend to crowd out the small contributors and thereby diminish the role of rank and file voters in the campaign process. The debate has been waged in every state, and thus there is great variation in how states treat contributions from individuals, political parties, special interests and other sources.

Although the ultimate sources of campaign funds are the same as at the federal level--private individuals, political parties, interested groups, and government--each state defines specific parameters for the flow of funds from these sources. Examination of the sources of funding for campaigns suggests that state regulations interact with contributing preferences of individuals and groups to create very different profiles of state campaign financing. For example, in Michigan individual contributors provide only about a quarter of the money for state representative races (interest groups and parties provide the

TABLE 3.2 Summary of State Regulation of Contributions

Regulation	# of States with Regulation
Financial reporting	50
Agencies can subpoena	27
Agencies initiate court action	18
Expenditure itemization	45
Name of recipient of expenditure	46
Amount paid to recipient	48
Limit on Contributions	
By candidate's family	22
By individual contributors	29
By corporations (prohibit or limit)	33
By labor (prohibit or limit)	28
By parties	13
By regulated industries	29
By PACs and committees	30
Limit parties and PACS equally	5
Limited amount from all PACS	3
Disclose occupation of contributor	20
Limit loans to campaigns	26

Source: *COGEL Blue Book 8th Edition 1990*, Council on Governmental Ethics Laws, (Lexington, KY: Council of State Governments); K. Kebschull et. al., *Campaign Disclosure Laws*, North Carolina Center for Public Policy Research (Raleigh, North Carolina, 1990); and *The Book of the States: 1990-91*, Vol. 28 (Lexington, KY: Council of State Governments, 1990).

remainder) whereas in North Carolina, individual contributors (including the candidates themselves) provide almost two-thirds of the funding for state legislative races. In Ohio half of the contributions to House candidates come from individuals, almost 40 percent from PACs and about 10 percent from political parties, whereas in Wisconsin 70 percent of political contributions are from individuals, 13 percent from PACs, 10 percent from public funds, 3 percent from party sources and the remainder from miscellaneous sources including the candidates themselves.

Individual Contributors

State laws differ in terms of how much individuals are permitted to give to individual candidates, political parties and special interest groups. Over one-half of the states place limits on the amount of money an individual can give to particular campaigns. The modal contribution limit is $1,000 per campaign, but actual limits run from as low as $220 for a state legislative candidate in Arizona to as high as $60,000 for the gubernatorial slate in Minnesota.

In contrast, in California, which does not limit contributions, an individual contribution to a single legislative race has exceeded $200,000 and contributions of $50,000 are not unusual. The task of fund raising in states with low contribution limits on individual contributors is obviously quite different from fund raising in states where it is legitimate to obtain the entire campaign war chest from three or four wealthy supporters.

As at the federal level, "independent expenditures" provide a loophole from state-level contribution limitations. While limiting "contributions" has been upheld as constitutional, states cannot limit "expenditures" made by individuals to influence a campaign directly. It is increasingly common for wealthy individuals who have given the maximum under the state's contribution limits to make sizeable expenditures "independent" of the party or campaign organization to assist a candidate's electoral prospects. In the first election after Arizona imposed strict limits on contributions, 20 percent of all expenditures for winning legislative candidates was through independent expenditures. The fact that many "independent expenditures" often are the source of funding for negative media campaigns has become a particular concern in many states.

States have responded to the rise of independent expenditures largely by enacting regulations designed to make the source of such expenditures more visible. Two-thirds of the states have either requirements for full disclosure of sponsorship of political ads or campaign materials, call for disclaimers that the materials are not approved by or made in cooperation with any political campaign or candidate, or mandate registration and reporting by *all* individuals (and groups) who raise or spend any money related to a political campaign. It remains true, however that these regulations only make the sources of independent expenditures more visible; they do not directly restrict how much an individual can *spend* to assist a state-level candidate.

Almost half of the states put restrictions on contributions from the candidate's immediate family, but only a few states place expenditure restrictions on how much candidates can give to their own campaigns. Consequently, in Delaware, the gubernatorial candidate can contribute only $5,000 to his/her campaign whereas in Texas, where there are no contribution limits at all, Clayton Williams was able to "contribute" more than $11 million of his personal fortune to his unsuccessful 1990 campaign for governor.

While there is limited research on the contribution patterns of state-level contributors, there is ample evidence to suggest that individual contributors tend to give to candidates directly. In Arizona and Tennessee, for example, 47 and 57 percent, respectively, of all contributors report giving to individual candidates. However, political contributions tend to be cumulative. About 30 percent of Arizona contributors report giving to political parties, and almost as many report giving to politically active groups as well.[25]

Political Parties

Forty-five states (excluding Arkansas, Maine, Nevada, New Hampshire and Texas) require both state and local political parties that are significantly engaged in funding campaigns to make campaign finance reports to the state. Thirteen states specify contribution limits for direct contributions by the political parties to particular candidates. Hawaii and West Virginia are among the handful of states that do not distinguish between individuals and political parties when setting contribution limits. Both parties and individuals are limited to maximum contributions of $2,000 in Hawaii and $1,000 in West Virginia. In Minnesota, on the other hand, an individual may not give more than $60,000 to the gubernatorial slate in an election year while political parties may contribute up to $300,000. In Arkansas, individuals may give up to $1,500 while parties may contribute a maximum of $2,500.

Some states, including Maine and Montana for example, distinguish between individual and party contributions but do not distinguish between political parties and other politically-oriented groups. In these states political parties are subjected to the same direct contribution limits as any other recognized campaign-oriented group. On the other hand, Arkansas, Minnesota and Utah place limits on what political parties may contribute but set higher limits for parties than for other groups. Florida's 1991 law limits all contributions by individuals to candidates for the legislature to $500 per election; but the law permits direct contributions by national, state or local political parties that aggregate up to $50,000 per candidate. (No more than $25,000 may be accepted prior to 28 days before the general election.)

Several states, including Alaska, Connecticut, Delaware, Kansas and Vermont, limit what contributors may give to individual candidate committees, but not to political parties. This creates a situation in which large contributors who "max out," i.e., give the maximum to a given candidate, use the party as a conduit through which to funnel additional money which often is informally earmarked for that specific candidate. Although earmarking of this type occurs in states with relatively high contribution limits to parties, it is most prevalent where individuals are unlimited in what they may give to parties. Some states have specifically addressed earmarking, or targeting, through legislation but enforcement of such regulations is difficult. Clearly, the status of political parties in the overall financing of political campaigns differs markedly from state to state, in part, because of state regulations.

As a further complication, most states recognize a difference between direct contributions, coordinated expenditures, and in-kind contributions on behalf of a candidate. Massachusetts, for example, limits parties to $1,000 in cash contributions but places no restrictions on in-kind contributions. Other states explicitly identify in-kind contributions which are not subject to contribution limits. Hence, most states do not include voter registration efforts or get-out-the-vote drives as contributions to candidates, although such activities benefit candidates. On the other hand, states differ as to how printed literature, polls, and media spots supporting several candidates are apportioned and reported as contributions.

In recent years, the federal system has contributed to one of the primary sources of money for state political parties. Funding has taken the form of "soft money," channeled, directly or indirectly, through the national party organizations. This represents a switch from early party history. Previously, the national party organizations were dependent upon the state party units to provide dues or assessments with which to finance national party activities.

Once *federal* law put restrictions on how much any one individual may contribute directly to a candidate, party or political action group, "excess" contributions began to find their way into *state* party coffers. Recent FEC regulations require that both federal and state political party accounts must now specify the sources and amounts of soft money. But as long as state law permits extremely high or even unlimited general contributions to parties, state party organizations can be expected to utilize legitimate funds provided by the national party groups to fund state-level electoral activity--up to the allowed limits for direct contributions to a candidate's campaign or for in-kind or coordinated expenditures. To advocates of strong state political parties, this is seen as a way of strengthening the political parties. To critics who resist organizational centralization and control of campaigns, the "outside" funding of state parties is simply one more example of pass-through money influencing state and local politics.

Special Interests and PACs

Although students of American politics most readily identify interest group representation with Washington lobbyists, states have a long history of interest group involvement in electoral campaigns. And state campaign finance regulation, in part, reflects the influence of these special groups. Ten states prohibit labor unions from making direct contributions to candidates from union treasury funds. Twenty states prohibit direct contributions from corporate treasuries. In no state is the regulation of union funds more restrictive than for corporations, but the reverse is true in several states. Twenty-nine states have explicit regulations (23 outright prohibit) on contributions from industries (banks, insurance companies, utilities, etc.) regulated by the state. In general, however, in half of the states, regulations governing the use of corporate and labor treasury funds for campaign purposes are far less restrictive than at the federal level.

Consequently, in states where direct contributions from unions or corporations are permitted or are only minimally restricted, the growth of political action committees (PACs) has been relatively slow. However, all states have experienced an increase in the number of PACs involved in state and local electoral campaigns. In New Jersey, for example, the number of state-level PACs increased 118 percent and the total amount of PAC contributions increased 87 percent between 1983 and 1987. Between 1976 and 1984 there was a 68 percent growth in PACs in Washington and, contrary to recent trends in federal PAC activity, PAC activity in the state of Washington is still increasing and PACs are raising and spending more money.

Recent state legislative sessions across the country have wrestled with the very controversial topic of limiting special interest group (i.e., PAC) electoral activity. Most have adopted a strategy based on limiting PAC contributions, although several have gone so far as to discuss legislation prohibiting all PAC contributions. Although several states have a history of treating labor union and corporate political activity differently, only a few differentiate between union and labor PAC regulation. Because PACs represent the full spectrum of special interests--from economic interests to single-issue groups to ideological organizations--current state-level PAC legislation tends to be quite generic.

Montana and Arizona pioneered a different strategy for limiting the amount of PAC money in campaigns that several states are watching carefully. These states limit the total amount of money that candidates may take from all PACs combined. The 1986 Arizona law limits candidates for statewide office to a total of $50,000 from PACs (adjusted each election cycle for inflation). However, challengers faced with an incumbent contributing significant amounts from his/her personal funds are released from the PAC limitations. In the first election in which this new law was in effect, PAC contributions to winning legislative candidates dropped 62 percent (whereas they had increased 46 per cent during the preceding election).

Public Funding

Even before the 1976 *Buckley* decision in which the U.S. Supreme Court ruled that it was constitutional to limit campaign expenditures if public money were used in financing the campaign, several states, including Iowa, Minnesota, Utah and Rhode Island, had instituted public funding programs. Since 1976, more than two dozen states and several cities have initiated programs in which public agencies and/or tax dollars are involved in financing state or local campaigns. In some states, i.e., Oregon and Maryland, the programs were operative for a short time and then faded away. In others, the programs have been firmly established although they have been modified over time (i.e., Minnesota, Kentucky, North Carolina). And in yet others (such as Illinois, New York, and Washington), legislation has been passed in at least one chamber of the legislature but, for a variety of reasons, has not been enacted into law. At the beginning of the decade, almost two-thirds of the states either have enacted or have seriously considered public funding programs.

State-level public financing programs are funded by one of three general mechanisms. One is a tax add-on program in which the only government involvement is the use of state agencies to collect voluntary contributions from taxpayers. Once collected, the agency transfers money to the appropriate political parties or candidates. Seven states (Alabama, California, Maine, Massachusetts, Maryland, Montana, Oregon and Virginia) have experimented with add-on programs. Although these programs differ in specific details, they have been singularly unsuccessful as mechanisms for raising significant amounts of campaign funding. Because few taxpayers are eager to *increase* their tax liability by adding on a political contribution, taxpayer participation rates in add-on programs generally do not exceed one per cent of all state taxpayers. Hence add-on programs generate very little money and consequently have little impact on the electoral campaign.

The most common public funding programs employ a tax check-off whereby taxpayers indicate that a small fraction ($1 to $5) of their tax liability be channelled to electoral campaigns. Some states (Michigan, Wisconsin, New Jersey, and Hawaii) put these check-off dollars in a central fund that is then apportioned among candidates for specific offices who meet the eligibility criteria.[26] In other states (Kentucky, Utah, Ohio, Idaho) the check-off tax dollars are allocated to political parties, either as designated by the taxpayer or according to a preestablished formula. Minnesota, Iowa, Rhode Island and North Carolina are among the states that combine programs to fund various levels of state political parties or allocate money to both parties and candidates.

The check-off programs have made an impact on the state electoral process. First, taxpayer participation rates, although dwindling in recent years, have been high enough to provide significant amounts of money for state-level campaigns. Second, states have set limits on campaign spending for candidates who voluntarily participate in the public funding programs. Third, states have variously specified how funds will be allocated (flat grant or matching) and how they may or may not be spent (for media expenses but not for personal salaries), or, as in New Jersey, have mandated that candidates receiving public funds take part in such campaign activities as public debates.

New Jersey and Wisconsin have the ability to draw on funds from the state treasury if the tax check-off does not produce sufficient campaign funds. However, when state general revenue funds are severely limited, legislators find it politically very difficult to appropriate money for subsidizing electoral campaigns. Florida enacted a public funding program that depended totally on a general appropriation from the legislature. Before a single election could be held, the state ran into financial difficulty, and the legislature declined to appropriate funds for the 1990 campaign. However, in 1991, Florida revisited the concept of public campaign funding and adopted a new program. The 1991 program first draws on funds provided by a tax on political parties and PACs, increased candidate filing fees and a variety of voluntary add-on fees and taxes. If these do not provide sufficient funds, money will automatically be transferred from the general revenue fund to the campaign fund.

The details of public funding programs are different in every state. But there are some common features. Participation in all public funding programs is optional--no party or candidate must participate. Programs that fund parties do not include expenditure limits on the parties; all states that fund candidates, with the exception of Montana's add-on program, establish expenditure ceilings for candidates accepting public funds. Several states use an added incentive to encourage candidates to accept public money and thereby accept expenditure limits. For example, Florida's law provides that if one candidate does not agree to participate in the public financing system, the expenditure ceiling is doubled as is the public match of dollars for the candidate who opts for public funding. Wisconsin's program, which has been reasonably successful in recent years, includes a feature designed to discourage candidates from taking PAC money. Candidates who accept both PAC money and public subsidy funds have the amount of their public subsidy reduced by the amount of the PAC contributions accepted.

State Activities in the 1990s

In an area as volatile as campaign finance, it is difficult to predict future actions and trends. As states enter the last decade of the 20th century, they are being pulled in several directions. For example, the efforts of several Republican administrations to reduce the role of the federal government is now being felt in almost every state. Activities and services that once were funded and regulated by the federal government have been pushed back to the states. This means that states need more revenue, must implement more and different types of legislation, and must create administrative structures to take on new responsibilities.

At the same time, most states have experienced recession and severe economic downturns at the very time they are asked to provide more leadership and service. Hence states are being asked to do more with less. And, with many more policy decisions being made at the state level, there are more interests involved in the political process--often out-of-state interests that have a stake in how states choose to regulate certain businesses, activities and organizations. The arena of state government has become more complex and the political battles for power and influence more intense--and no state is exempt from these developments.

Under these circumstances, it is easy to see why issues of campaign finance might not have the highest priority on state political agendas. However, other forces will combine to keep campaign financing in the forefront of policy makers' concerns. Support for democratic values--open access to the political system, an informed electorate, and competitive elections with meaningful choices--runs very deep in the United States. The ever increasing amount of money being spent in state races is becoming more visible and is seen by many as undermining these basic values. Hence, concerned citizens and politicians are engaged in serious examination of ways to ensure a viable, participatory democratic electoral system.

This concern has been reinforced by recent scandals that have rocked more than half the states. In New York, California, Arkansas and Tennessee, for example, public officials have been accused of serious misconduct resulting in felony charges, criminal and civil convictions, fines, and imprisonment. In Arizona, seven legislators were forced to resign when a major "sting" operation revealed misuse of campaign contributions, conflict of interest violations, bribery, and general misuse of the public trust. In the wake of "AZscam," campaign finance legislation was reviewed, ethics regulations revisited and the level of legislative consciousness heightened. A significant piece of legislation was passed almost immediately, and a study commission was established to report to the legislature in special session within six months. Similarly, a sting known as "Operation Lost Trust" resulted in the indictment of 17 South Carolina legislators, three of whom served on the House Ethics Committee. Fellow legislators moved quickly to prepare legislation on public ethics, campaign finance and lobby disclosure.

These recent scandals have served to underscore the fact that the focus of change includes not only campaign finance but closely related issues of public ethics, lobbying, and financial disclosure. Because these issues are increasingly understood to be tightly interconnected, policy makers in the future are much more likely to take an inclusive approach that deals with this "package" of related issues rather than a piecemeal approach that focuses on only one dimension of the package. Yet, because these issues are both complex and controversial, it will take more time for new legislation to work its way through the process. At a minimum, three basic questions remain to be answered before we can predict the status of state-level campaign finance at the beginning of the 21st century.

Will States Respond to Recent Scandals?

Based on past experience, the expectation would be that states directly affected by major scandals will move quickly to address issues raised by the scandals and to ensure public confidence in the political system. Other states, mindful of the potential damage such scandals inflict, can be expected to design programs or to fine-tune, if not overhaul, existing legislation in hopes of averting similar scandals. All things being equal, the prediction should be for significant change in many states.

However, all things are not equal. State leaders are besieged by economic problems, crises in social service delivery and demands for attention to the quality of the environment, education, and public safety. Consequently, issues of campaign financing and long-term political and electoral viability may appear less pressing than a host of other issues before the legislatures. Moreover, regulations governing campaign finance are seldom perceived as neutral. Whatever the change in regulations, some group or interest is generally seen as gaining; another set of groups or interests as losing. And since the political futures of policy makers are involved, campaign finance legislation is always controversial, partisan and difficult to achieve. In the short run, in spite of recent scandals, it is unlikely that major changes will be made except in a few states where forceful, persistent and skillful leadership makes the package of campaign related reforms a top priority.

Leadership by Whom?

The second unknown is who will provide the leadership for change. In the immediate post-Watergate flourish of state campaign reforms, the legislatures were the prime movers. In the early 1980s citizen groups and individual "reform" legislators were the chief spokesmen for state-level issues related to campaign finance. Finally, governors, for example, Mario Cuomo of New York, Buddy Romer of Louisiana, Bill Clinton of Arkansas, became the driving force for change during the last part of the decade.

But throughout the past twenty years, state initiative processes have played an important role in campaign finance reform, just as the initiative is the vehicle that recently created legislative term restrictions in Oklahoma, Colorado and California. Enactments of limits on how long legislators can remain in office have caught the attention of state legislators everywhere and have reminded them of the potential force of citizen initiatives. It also has reminded other public groups that the initiative is a vehicle of recourse when elected leaders decline to act.

It is not unlikely, therefore, that in the 21 states in which the initiative is an alternative to legislative policy-making, campaign finance reform will be the focus of future initiatives. It is also probable that governors and gubernatorial candidates will continue to be central to enacting new regulations related to campaign finance. Governor Lawton Chiles of Florida not only voluntarily limited all campaign contributions to $100 or less during his 1990 campaign but once in office proposed a strict code of conduct for himself and his staff that prohibits acceptance of anything from special interests valued over $2.00. Regardless of where strong leadership comes from, it will be a prerequisite for forging new campaign finance policies.

What Will Be the Targets for Change?

In the past, some states have focused on campaign finance by regulating political parties and interest groups; others look at financial disclosure by office holders/candidates and greater public access to such information; others have put their hopes on public financing of campaigns. Common to all, however, has been an emphasis on greater "regulation" which we predict will continue to increase.

The state political parties can expect to be caught in a cross current. On the one hand, there has been a growing tendency for state legislatures to increase (and for courts to uphold) regulation that specifies what parties must publicly report, how much parties may give to specific candidates, under what circumstances a party activity is a coordinated, in-kind or direct contribution, and what constitutes party building as opposed to candidate support. The new FEC rules on allocating expenses that jointly benefit both federal and non-federal candidates is a unique example of a federal agency mandating financial reporting regulations for *state* political parties.[27] In short, parties are losing autonomy over their own activities.

On the other hand, state parties increasingly show signs of reasserting their role, albeit somewhat redefined, in state electoral politics. They are responding to the extra-party initiatives that have accompanied the rise of candidate-centered politics. Parties now serve as coordinators and facilitators rather than as king-makers. Their current activities range from providing mailing lists, voter profiles, and joint phone banks, to state-wide polls, telethon fund-raisers and joint TV spots. And as more state-level candidates seek to take advantage of modern campaign technology, the state party will be the logical unit to provide continuity for campaign infrastructures and economies of scale for these high priced campaign activities.

This renewed role for parties will mean a different kind of party organization with leadership provided by technologically sophisticated, organizational managers rather than veteran politicians skilled in the politics of one-on-one negotiation. And as the requisite skills for day-to-day party managers grow, so too will the party expenses increase in order to secure the quantity and quality of skilled leadership required. One of the indirect effects of more intense and more sophisticated campaigns will be the very different and much more expensive party machinery which is needed to wage today's campaigns.

Legislative activity will continue, not only to regulate political parties, but also to look at the full range of campaign finance issues. Future regulation will recognize the relationships between financial disclosure, contribution and expenditure regulations, lobby regulation, and conflict of interest legislation. The post-Watergate experience has taught legislators that these issues cannot be viewed in isolation. Thus, legislation that establishes or strengthens a state ethics agency will come to be viewed as directly related to campaign finance. Moreover, as ethics agencies identify and publicize conflicts of interests, influence peddling, bribes, extortion and other forms of misconduct, the link between campaign finance and public ethics will become clearer to everyone involved, including aroused citizens.

States will differ over which aspects of the total "package" to approach first. Consequently, the state-level picture will probably continue to look chaotic as states pick and choose targets for action. However, current trends suggest that states are most likely to target the following areas:

Lobby regulation. Emphasis will be on greater disclosure of what lobbyists and their employers give to candidates and public officials, either as direct campaign contributions or as gifts. Some states even include income from PACs; however, few states willgo as far as Wisconsin in prohibiting legislators from taking anything of value from a lobbyist. More states can be expected to enact "revolving door" legislation that prohibits a legislator from leaving the legislature and immediately beginning work as a lobbyist. And as three-party lobbying (where a lobbyist is hired and paid by a middleman) increases, states will revise registration and reporting requirements accordingly.

Contribution limits. States will continue to review who can give what to whom under what conditions. Particular emphasis will be given to limiting PAC contributions, restricting transfers among candidates, tightening regulations on "loans" to campaign committees by candidates as well as supporters, and limiting PACs established by legislative leaders. More states can be expected to restrict fund-raising during the legislative sessions and give serious consideration to the proportion of campaign funds raised out-of-state or out-of-district. Finally, states will seek to expedite disclosure of large contributions and expenditures made during the last days of a campaign.

Voluntary codes of campaign conduct. Several states have already enacted legislation that calls for candidates to sign pledges agreeing to abstain from character defamation and fact distortion involved in negative campaigning. Others have called for voluntary agreements to limit campaign expenditures, to engage in public debates or to limit special interest contributions. More states can be expected to design programs to encourage candidates to take the moral high road, but some will use carrots and others will use sticks to motivate participation by candidates.

Public funding. Even in times of severe financial difficulties, states continue to explore public subsidy programs as means of leveling the electoral playing field and stemming the sky rocketing costs of elections. Some states are being very creative. Minnesota, for example, recently extended its public funding program to include congressional candidates; but if both candidates agree to the spending limits, neither will receive public funds. However, if one candidate accepts public funds (and the expenditure limits) but the other does not, the participant will be *released* from the expenditure limits *and* will also receive the opponent's public subsidy as well as his/her own. Learning from the experience of more than twenty unique state programs, legislators can be expected to propose very innovative public funding programs.

Independent expenditures. As more groups and individuals attempt to circumvent contribution limits through independent expenditures, states will mandate fuller disclosure of the sources of independent expenditure funds. In addition, more states will require that all ads and political activities be identified with the source funding supporting them. In the case of independent expenditures, the disclaimers of the future will also indicate that the activity is not endorsed by the candidate or party it seeks to help. States with public financing for candidates already are exploring ways to provide enhanced public subsidies to offset independent expenditures as one way to discourage independent spending.

Surplus campaign funds. One of the ironies associated with ever increasing campaign costs is that more and more candidates, especially incumbents, are ending campaigns with a large surplus of funds. Therefore, states are looking carefully at how such surplus funds may be used. The most popular restriction is to prohibit converting excess campaign funds to personal use. But many states specify how the funds must be disposed of (given to charity, contributed to the party, returned to contributors) and several prohibit certain uses (financing a different campaign, contributing to other candidates, using for office-holder expenses). States also have begun to look at limiting the time frame in which candidates can raise or spend campaign money as a means of stopping the accumulation of excessive campaign war chests.

Many of the fifty states are geographically larger, have more heterogeneous populations, and manage larger public budgets than many independent nations around the world. Some of the most vexing problems and greatest domestic challenges the U.S. faces involve issues that fall within the jurisdiction of state governments: tax restructuring, abortion, drugs, crime, affordable housing, mental health, education. These are issues that affect citizens directly and about which sentiment runs high. Thus, the immediate future will include more politics--of all kinds--at the state level. And the issues of campaign finance are likely to loom larger as state and local political parties, private interests and candidates adjust their campaign strategies. In the last decade of the twentieth century campaign finance will provide opportunities and challenges for the states to remain effective partners in the U.S. federal system. And the odds are that the states will succeed in meeting these challenges.

Notes

1. Likewise, cities are creatures of the state and must abide by state regulations. However, local governments are often given the power to design campaign and electoral laws as long as they do not conflict with state laws in areas in which the state has retained supremacy. The federal-state jurisdictional issue should not, however, be confused with the ability of the U.S. Supreme Court to invalidate state regulation of parties, campaigns and campaign financing. See, for example, *Cousins v. Wigoda; Tashjian v. Republican Party of Connecticut*.

2. Ronald D. Hedlund, "Crossover Voting in a 1976 Open Presidential Primary," in *Public Opinion Quarterly*, Vol. 41, No. 4, Winter 1977-78, pp. 498-514; Malcolm Jewell, *Parties and Primaries: Nominating State Governors* (New York: Praeger Publishers, 1984).

3. In 1988, Buddy Romer was elected governor of Louisiana on the Democratic ticket. In 1991 Governor Romer decided to switch parties, and overnight Louisiana gained a Republican governor.

4. *Congressional Quarterly, America Votes, The Almanac of American Politics, National Journal* all provide comprehensive electoral returns for federal elections after each election cycle.

5. Recently, a major step has been taken by the Comparative State Election project which has collected recent state primary and general election data for all states. These data are stored and distributed by the Inter-university Consortium for Political and Social Research at the University of Michigan. Thus, there now is a readily accessible source of state electoral data available to the scholarly community. There is no comparable archive of local election data, however. One of the ironies of U.S. electoral politics is that there is no definitive source for determining even the *number* of elections held each year.

6. The annual *Blue Book* of the Council on Governmental Ethics Laws (Council of State Governments, Lexington, Ky); Sandra Singer, "The Power of the Purse--It Costs to Run for Legislative Office!!" Western Political Science Association paper, Salt Lake

66

City, Utah, 1990; and Kim Kebschull, *Campaign Disclosure Laws* (Raleigh: The North Carolina Center for Public Policy Research, 1990), are notable exceptions.

7. But see Sarah McCally Morehouse, "The Politics of Gubernatorial Nominations," in *State Government*, Vol. 53, 1980, pp. 125-28; Malcolm E. Jewell and David M. Olson, 3rd edition, *Political Parties and Elections in American States* (Chicago: Dorsey Press, 1988); and Cornelius P. Cotter, James L. Givson, John F. Bibby and Robert J. Huchshorn, *Party Organization in American Politics* (New York: Praeger, 1984).

8. California Commission on Campaign Financing. *Money and Politics in the Golden State* (Los Angeles: The Center for Responsive Politics, 1989).

9. James D. King, "Interparty Competition in the American States: An Examination of Index Components," in *Western Political Quarterly*, Vol. 42, 1986, pp. 83-92; Austin Ranney, "Parties in State Politics," in Herbert Jacob and Kenneth Vines (eds.) *Politics in the American States*, 3rd ed. (Boston: Little Brown, 1976), pp. 51-92.

10. Jewell and Olson, *Political Parties*, p. 29.

11. But there is little comparability in expenditure reporting categorization across states. Even within a state, the data may be of limited utility. For example, if an expenditure is reported as a lump sum to a consulting firm, there is no way to disaggregate how much money went for television, postage, direct mailing, radio commercials, tracking polls or issue-position consultation.

12. Paul Gilley, "The Increased Cost of Legislative Campaigns: 1974 to 1982," (Olympia: Washington Public Disclosure Commission, 1984).

13. California Common Cause, "Money Can't Buy You Love," February 26, 1991.

14. Malcolm Jewell and Penny Miller, *The Kentucky Legislature* (Lexington: University of Kentucky Press, 1988), p. 27.

15. Observers often note the irony in these huge campaign costs to win positions with such low salaries. The salaries for governors of California ($85,000) and Texas ($93,000) are among the highest (New York is at the top paying $130,000) while Arkansas pays only $35,000. Source: Daryl Theobald, "What Governors Earn," in *State Government News*, June, 1989, p. 25.

16. Anthony Gierzynski and David Breaux, "The Role of Money in Legislative Elections," paper presented at the annual meeting of the Midwest Political Science Association, Chicago, Illinois, April 18-20, 1991, p. 8.

17. Alan Rosenthal, "Turnover in State Legislatures," in *American Journal of Political Science*, Vol. 18, 1974, pp. 609-616.

18. David Ray, "Membership Stability in Three State Legislatures, 1893-1969," *American Political Science Review*, Vol. 68, 1974, pp. 106-112, and Malcolm Jewell and David Breaux, "The Effects of Incumbency on State Legislative Elections," in *Legislative Studies Quarterly*, Vol. 13, 1988, pp. 495-514.

19. Malcolm Jewell and David Breaux, "The Effect of Incumbency on State Legislative Elections," in *Legislative Studies Quarterly*, Vol. 13, 1989, pp. 495-514.

20. Thad Beyle, "Gubernatorial Elections: 1977-1990," in *Comparative State Politics*, Vol. 12, April, 1991, pp. 18-21.

21. Thad Beyle, "Costs of Gubernatorial Elections in 1987" and "Costs of Gubernatorial Elections in 1988," in *Comparative State Politics*, Vol. 11, February, 1990, pp. 28-31.

22. Diana Carlin and Joe Pisciotte, "Unusual Politics of Gubernatorial Elections in Kansas," in *Comparative State Politics*, Vol. 11, December, 1990, pp. 22-29.

23. James K. Pollock, *Party Campaign Funds* (New York: Alfred A. Knopf. 1926) and Alexander Heard (Chapel Hill: University of North Carolina Press, 1960).

24. The Supreme Court ruling in *Buckley vs. Valeo* distinguished between "contributions" which can create the impression of impropriety and therefore can be limited without infringing on freedom of speech, and "expenditures" which cannot be limited.

25. Ruth S. Jones and Anne H. Hopkins, "State Campaign Fund Raising," in *Journal of Politics*, Vol. 47, 1985, pp. 427-449.

26. The cities that have established public funding (Seattle and King County, Tucson, New York City) allocate public funds to candidates. They have devised very unique methods of collecting monies for the campaign fund however. See Herbert E. Alexander and Michael C. Walker, *Public Funding of Local Elections, 1990* (Los Angeles: Citizens' Research Foundation, 1990).

27. See the *Federal Register*, Vol. 55, No. 123, June 26, 1990, pp. 26058-26073, for details of this regulation.

4

Financing Federal
Politics in Canada
in an Era of Reform

William T. Stanbury

Money is essential to conduct election campaigns and to finance the operation of political parties between elections. Joseph Israel Tarte, who was Prime Minister Wilfrid Laurier's chief organizer and fundraiser in Quebec between 1894 and 1896, and who also organized election campaigns in Quebec and New Brunswick until 1902, wisely observed that "les elections ne se font pas avec des prières" ("prayers do not win elections"). Jesse Unruh, who was speaker of the California legislature in the early 1960s, used a different metaphor when he observed that "money is the mother's milk of politics." More recently, Norman Atkins, who was chairman of the federal Progressive Conservative Party's highly successful general election campaigns in 1984 and 1988 stated that "you can't run national campaigns on [the proceeds from] selling fudge."[1] Political parties need funds for at least three purposes: "first, to fight election campaigns; second, to maintain a viable inter-election organization; third, to provide research and advisory services for the party's leadership and elected representatives at various levels."[2]

As the fuel for political activity, money, like gasoline, is a volatile substance. Because it can corrupt the people and the political process, the raising and spending of money by parties and candidates is usually subject to government regulations. Canada is no exception.

The focus of this chapter is on the financing of federal parties and candidates since 1 August 1974 when the *Election Expenses Act* came into effect.[3] It is organized as follows. Section 1 describes the regulatory regime put in place effective 1 August 1974 and the subsequent amendments made to it. Section 2 analyzes the pattern of party revenues and expenditures between 1974 and 1990, including the four general elections in 1979, 1980, 1984 and 1988. Contributions from individuals and corporations are examined in some detail. Section 3 analyzes the revenues and expenditures of candidates for Parliament in the last four general elections. Section 4 describes and estimates the amount of public financing of federal parties and candidates which has been an integral part of the regulatory regime since 1974. Section 5 focuses on the problems/issues for public policy. It includes some of the many recommendations by the Royal Commission on Electoral Reform and Party Financing whose report was released in February 1992.

Regulatory Policy

The important elements of federal regulatory policy in respect to the financing of parties and candidates *prior* to the reforms embodied in the *Election Expenses Act* of 1974 can be summarized as follows.[4] The *Canada Elections Act:*

- provided for registration of parties since 1970;
- required candidates to name an official agent to receive all contributions and pay all expenses (except the personal expenses of the candidate up to $2000);
- forbade private expenditures by the candidate's supporters, but the candidate or his/her agent could not be held responsible;
- required that campaign expenses be presented for payment within one month of voting day and paid within 50 days (after the latter, payment required the approval of a judge);
- required the agent to present a detailed sworn statement of the candidate's finances (form 61) to the constituency returning officer (election official) within two months of voting day. The returning officer had to publish a summary of the report in a newspaper circulated in the constituency. The penalties for failure to submit a report was a fine of up to $500 or imprisonment for up to one year. Falsification of the report with an intent to mislead was also an offense--the offender could be disqualified from being elected;[5] and
- did not specifically assign responsibility for enforcement of its provisions.

The 1974 reforms, which form the bases of the current policy, were the product of a complex series of events including innovative legislation introduced in Quebec in 1963, a series of political scandals linked to party financing, and the election of a minority Liberal Government in 1972 in which the New

Democratic Party (NDP) held the balance of power. Robin Sears, then federal secretary for the NDP, states that the 1974 reforms

> came out of the Barbeau Commission in the mid-60s which produced some very thoughtful research on how expenditures affect decisions, how public financing in other jurisdictions affects electoral outcome, and so on. Then there were three closely related phenomena in the early 70s: the Quebec election in 1970, the Ontario election in 1971 and the American presidential election in 1972, in which election expenditures mushroomed beyond anything anyone had conceived of previously. Then there were all the ramifications of Watergate following the 1972 election. These built up a head of steam about the impact of those expenditure levels on democracy.[6]

The present federal regulatory policy stems largely from the *Election Expenses Act* which came into effect on 1 August 1974. In outline, the legislation contained the following important provisions:[7]

Party Registration and Agency. The legislation requires the appointment of a chief agent and auditor responsible for filing information with the chief electoral officer. Only a person authorized by a party or candidate may incur election expenses. The Act, however, specifically exempted interest groups or individuals who engage in advertising during election campaigns, provided they promoted discussion of public policy and did not directly support or oppose a specific party or candidate (see the section on problems/issues below).

All contributions to a candidate or a party in excess of $25 must be made to the chief agent of the candidate or registered agent of the party. It was also made an offense to make a contribution of money that does not belong to the donor. All expenditures by registered parties or candidates of $25 or more must be made through its registered agent and must be vouched for by a bill stating the particulars and by a receipt.

Spending Limits. The 1974 legislation provides that each registered *party* could spend on "election expenses" no more than 30 cents for each elector in each constituency in which it had an official candidate in the sixty-day period prior to election day. This provision was modified in October 1983 by "indexing" the maximum allowable expenditure by the increase in the Consumer Price Index (CPI) retroactive to 1980. Party "election expenses," however, exclude the value of volunteer labour, grants by the parties to candidates, and other items (see also the section on problems/issues below).

Candidates are also subject to a ceiling on their "election expenses." It was set at $1 per elector for the first 15,000 electors plus $.50 for the next 10,000 plus $.25 for each elector in excess of 25,000. This ceiling was also indexed in October 1983 in the same way as the limit on party expenditures.

"Election expenses" are defined in Section 2 of the *Canada Elections Act* as amounts paid; liabilities incurred; the commercial value of goods and services donated or provided, other than volunteer labour; and amounts that represent the differences between amounts paid and liabilities incurred for goods and services, other than labour, and the commercial value of such goods and services where they are provided at less than their commercial value. This applies to such amounts paid, incurred or provided "for the purpose of promoting or opposing, directly and during an election, a particular registered party, or the election of a particular candidate...."[8] The word "directly" is very significant for in practice it has been used to exclude from the definition some important types of expenditures including polling--see the last section on problems/issues below.

Reimbursement of "Election Expenses." All candidates who receive at least 15% of the votes cast and who comply with the requirements for submitting their report on "election expenses" are entitled to be reimbursed for a part of their election expenses by the federal government. The formula established in 1974 set the reimbursement as the sum of (1) the cost of a first-class letter to all electors; (2) $.08 for each of the first 25,000 electors, and (3) $.06 for every elector above 25,000. This was changed in October 1983 to reimburse candidates for one-half of their actual expenses (not to exceed 50 per cent of the maximum allowable expenses) provided that the candidate obtained 15% of the votes cast and had filed the appropriate forms with the Chief Electoral Officer (CEO). Note that between 1974 and 1983 the price of a first-class stamp rose from eight to 32 cents.

When the reforms were enacted in 1974, parties were entitled to be reimbursed for one-half their expenditures on *electronic* media during the election campaigns. This was changed in 1983 to 22.5% of total "election expenses" up to the legal limit (which was $8 million in 1988 if a party ran a full slate of 295 candidates).

Advertising. Under the 1974 legislation, radio and television stations must make available up to 6.5 hours of prime time for paid advertising or political broadcasts by the *parties* during the last four weeks of the election campaign.[9] This time is now allocated among the parties by the Broadcasting Arbitrator (a position created in 1983), according to a formula based on the number of seats held and the party's popular vote in the previous general election. This amount (in minutes) becomes the maximum each party can purchase. The formula was modified in 1983 to include the number of candidates in the previous election and to provide that no party can receive more than one-half the total time. Broadcasters are required to charge for political ads and programs the same rate they would charge to any other person for an equivalent time on the facilities. There is, however, no limit on the amount of advertising that may be purchased in other media (e.g., print), although expenditures must stay within the party's or candidate's overall limit.

Network operators are required to make *free-time* programming periods available to registered parties during the period from 29 to two days before polling day.[10] This time must be in network reserved time periods, but need not be in prime time. The free time is allocated among the parties in the same proportions as the *paid* time, but the total amount is to be determined after consultation between the parties and the Broadcasting Arbitrator.

Disclosure. Under the 1974 legislation, every registered party must submit annually a detailed statement of revenues and expenditures to the CEO. Candidates must do the same after a by-election or general election. The name of every person or organization who has donated more than $100 in cash or in kind to the party or to a candidate must be reported to the CEO who publicly discloses the information.[11]

Each party's annual return must be filed with the Chief Electoral Officer within six months after the end of the fiscal year. The return provides information in four categories: identity of donors; amount of donations over $100; operating expenditures of the party; all other expenditures. A separate return must be filed by each party and each candidate within six and four months respectively of an election.

Where a candidate receives a contribution of more than $100 from his/her local party association, the sources of the association's funds must be reported for each contributor giving more than $100.

Tax Credits. In addition to reimbursing parties and candidates for a substantial fraction of their official "election expenses," the federal government provides a tax credit for individuals and corporations (deduction against taxes payable, not income) as follows:

- 75% of amounts contributed up to $100, plus
- 50% of amounts contributed between $100 and $550, plus
- 33.3% of amounts contributed exceeding $550--up to a total tax credit of $500.

Therefore, the maximum credit of $500 is achieved with a donation or a number of donations totalling $1150 per year. There is no statutory limit, however, on the total amount a person or corporation (or trade union) may give to a party or candidate.[12]

A candidate's agent may issue a receipt for tax credit only *after* the individual has been nominated. Therefore, between elections, local district party organizations can receive funds but cannot themselves issue receipts for the tax credit. However, if the contribution is made through the official agent of the national party, a tax receipt may be issued.[13]

Attempts at Reform. Efforts were made to change the regulatory policy between 1983, when the last amendments were enacted, and when the last general election was called[14] on 1 October 1988. The main one was Bill C-79 (extensive amendments to the *Canada Elections Act*) which was given first reading in June 1987, but died on the Order Paper when the general election was called. No changes, except those embodied in the CEO's *Guidelines*, have been made since.[15] However, in November 1989 the federal government established the Royal Commission on Electoral Reform and Party Financing, some of whose recommendations are discussed in the last section.

Party Revenues and Expenditures

The Big Picture: Total Revenues and Expenditures

The annual revenues and expenditures (including election years) of the three main federal parties between 1974 and 1990 are set out in Table 4.1 in both nominal and constant 1989 dollars using the Consumer Price Index (CPI) which rose from 34.9 in 1974 to 104.8 in 1990. While the CPI may not be the best possible deflator, there is no better one available that reflects the changing prices of those goods and services purchased by political parties.[16]

The fiscal strength of the Progressive Conservative Party can easily be seen by looking at the average revenue in the three inter-election periods. From 1976 to 1978, the party averaged $9.8 million annually in revenue (in 1989 dollars). This increased by 40% to $13.7 million annually during the period 1981-83. Financing, then increased again--to $16.7 million annually--in the period 1985-87 (Table 4.1).

While the Liberal Party raised more money than the Conservative Party in the period 1976-78 ($11.5 million in 1989 dollars), its average revenue in the next two inter-election periods was substantially below the 1976-78 period: $9.20 million annually in the period 1981-83 and only slightly better in 1985-87, $9.75 million annually in 1989 dollars. The point is that the Conservatives, in real terms, were able to raise $4.5 million annually more than the Liberals in the period 1981-83 and $6.9 million annually more in the period 1985-87. The gap was even larger in 1989--see Table 4.1. There was a doubling in Liberal Party revenues in 1990 over 1989. Much of this is attributable to the 1990 party leadership race and convention. The party imposed a 20% tax on candidate's expenditures over $250,000 but below the limit of $1.7 million. This generated almost $608,000 for the party. Second, some $1.95 million of the $6 million contributed to the candidates was routed through the Party in order to obtain the tax credit. Third, the convention generated several millions in the form of delegate fees classified as contributions so as to make them eligible for the tax

TABLE 4.1 Federal Political Parties' Revenues and Expenditures, 1974-1990 in Nominal and Real (1989) Dollars ($000)

	1974/75	1976	1977	1978	1979E	1980E	1981	1982	1983	1984E	1985	1986	1987	1988E	1989	1990
Progressive Conservative																
Revenue[a]																
- Nominal	2,924[c]	4,084	3,774	5,465	9,170	8,542	6,950	8,521	14,767	23,417	15,073	15,63	13,058	27,013	14,521	11,298
- Real	7,556	9,817	8,405	11,153	17,140	14,527	10,499	11,625	19,030	28,909	17,901	17,832	14,271	28,375	14,521	10,781
Expenses																
- Nominal	2,486[c]	3,497	4,233	5,470	8,929	9,330	7,542	8,521	13,199	27,165	11,654	14,141	13,490	29,046	12,824	10,635
- Real	6,424	8,406	9,428	11,163	16,690	15,867	11,393	11,625	17,009	33,537	13,841	16,124	14,743	30,511	12,824	10,148
Excess over E																
- Nominal	438[c]	587	(459)	(5)	241	(788)	(592)	0	1,568	(3,748)	3,419	1,498	(432)	(2,033)	1,696	663
- Real	1,132	1,411	(1,023)	(10)	450	(1,340)	(894)	0	2,021	(4,628)	4,060	1,708	(472)	(2,136)	1,696	633
Liberal Party																
Revenue[a]																
- Nominal	2,217[d]	5,823[e]	4,587	5,018	7,020	8,367	5,592	6,747	7,736	13,014	6,163	10,719	8,882	17,897	6,397	13,778
- Real	5,729	13,998	10,216	10,241	13,122	14,230	8,447	9,205	9,969	16,067	7,320	12,222	9,707	18,799	6,397	13,147
Expenses[b]																
- Nominal	1,963[d]	4,707[e]	4,187	5,283	6,684	7,548	5,116	6,781	6,277	18,292	8,149	11,166	9,274	7,016	7,115	13,327
- Real	5,072	11,315	9,325	10,782	12,494	12,837	7,728	9,251	8,089	22,583	9,678	12,732	10,136	17,874	7,115	12,717
Excess of R over E																
- Nominal	254[d]	1,116[e]	400	(265)	336	819	476	(34)	1,459	(5,278)	(1,986)	(447)	(392)	881	718	451
- Real	657	2,683	891	(541)	628	1,393	719	(46)	1,880	(6,516)	(2,358)	(510)	(429)	925	718	396
New Democratic Party I[g]																
Revenue[h]																
- Nominal	4,017[f]	2,925	3,525	4,184	6,517	6,778	6,003	7,108	8,669	11,577	10,152	14,639	12,608	20,343	13,865	15,439
- Real	10,380	7,031	7,851	8,539	12,181	11,527	9,068	9,697	11,171	14,293	12,057	16,692	13,779	21,369	13,865	14,732

(continues)

Table 4.1 (continued)

	1974/75	1976	1977	1978	1979E	1980E	1981	1982	1983	1984E	1985	1986	1987	1988E	1989	1990
Expenses[b]																
- Nominal	3,840[f]	2,381	3,105	3,514	6,867	9,078	6,491	4,872	8,009	12,138	11,071	15,188	14,012	21,994	12,507	14,262
- Real	9,922	5,724	6,915	7,171	12,836	15,438	9,805	6,647	10,321	14,985	13,149	17,318	15,314	23,103	12,507	13,609
Excess of R over E																
- Nominal	177[f]	544	420	670	(350)	(2,300)	(488)	2,236	660	(561)	(919)	(549)	(1,404)	(1,651)	1,358	1,177
- Real	458	1,307	936	1,368	(655)	(3,911)	(737)	3,050	851	(692)	(1,092)	(626)	(1,535)	(1,734)	1,358	1,123
New Democratic Party II																
Revenue[a]																
- Nominal	1,175[f]	547	656	642	3 315	3,780	1,185	1,058	1,716	6,880	1,922	2,114	1,803	8,962	2,565	na
- Real	3,117	1,315	1,461	1,310	6,196	6,429	1,790	1,443	2,211	8,494	2,283	2,411	1,971	9,414	2,565	na
Expenses[b]																
- Nominal	1,100[f]	476	688	714	3,343	4,224	984	1,055	1,130	6,663	1,720	1,973	2,522	11,459	1,530	na
- Real	2,918	1,144	1,532	1,457	6,249	7,184	1,486	1,439	1,456	8,226	2,043	2,250	2,789	12,037	1,530	na
Excess of R over E																
- Nominal	75[f]	71	(32)	(72)	(28)	(444)	201	3	586	217	202	141	(719)	(2,497)	1,035	na
- Real	199	171	(71)	(147)	(53)	(755)	304	4	755	268	240	161	(818)	(2,623)	1,035	na
CPI Index 1974 =	34.9															
(1989=10) 1975 =	38.7	41.6	44.9	49.0	53.5	58.8	66.2	73.3	77.6	81.0	84.2	87.7	91.5	95.2	100.0	104.8

E = Election Year; [a]Includes election reimbursement; [b]Includes election expenses; [c]1/8/74 - 31/12/75 (17 months); [d]1/8/74 - 31/12/75 (17 months); [e]1/8/75 - 31/7/75 (12 months); [f]1/8/74 - 31/12/76 (17 months); [g]NDPI = NDP figures as reported to CEO plus certain adjustments; [h]Includes provincially recepted revenue and provincial government subsidies and reimbursement; [i]NDP II = federal office revenue and expenditures plus election revenue and expenditures.

Sources: Chief Electoral Officer, *Report of the Chief Electoral Officer Respecting Election Expenses, 1979, 1980, 1984, 1989* (Ottawa: Ministry of Supply and Services, 1980, 1981, 1985, 1989); Registered parties fiscal period returns (1974-1989); NDP financial statements as provided to the author.

credit. The result was that the Liberal Party's' total revenues in 1990 exceeded the Conservative Party's for the first time since 1977--see Table 4.1.

The extraordinary performance of the Conservative Party in election years and its capacity to spend far more than the Liberals (and the NDP) can be seen when we look at election year expenditures in real terms *other* than official "election expenses" (which are very similar for the PCs and Liberals). The Conservatives were able to outspend the Liberals in terms of outlays other than "election expenses"[17] in election years by $4.5 million in 1979 and $2.1 million in 1980. However, in 1984 the "gap" was $10.8 million and in 1988 it was $11.5 million. To put these two figures in perspective, note that the official "election expenses" of both parties were about $7.9 million in 1984 and $8.3 million for the PCs and $7.2 million for the Liberals in 1988 (as measured in 1989 dollars).

The NDP presents a serious problem if its federal activities are to be compared to the other main parties. The "NDP I"[18] figures in Table 4.1 are for the party as a whole including most of its provincial sections. Like the federal PC party, the NDP has been able to increase its revenues and expenses in real terms. For example, expenditures averaged $6.6 million annually in the period 1976-78 while in the last inter-election period, 1985-87, they averaged $15.26 million (Table 4.1). These figures, however, include a large component of provincial activity.

The "NDP II" figures include only the revenues and expenditures of the *federal office*, including the revenues associated with elections and the federal office's figures for "election expenses" (which are slightly larger than those reported to the CEO). NDP II is most closely comparable to the figures for the Liberal and Conservative parties. While the federal wing's revenues and expenditures have grown substantially in real terms, they were always far below the levels of the other two main parties. For example, the NDP federal office average annual expenditures in inter-election years grew from $1.38 million in the period 1976-78 to $1.46 million in the 1985-87 period. Recall that the comparable figure for the Liberals in the last period was $9.75 million while that for the Tories was $16.7 million. While the NDP's federally-receipted revenues (*not* the revenues of the federal office) exceed the expenses of the federal office, typically by several million dollars, the difference is used to finance provincial political activities.

Party Election Expenses

There have been four general elections since the *Election Expenses Act* of 1974 came into effect: 1979, 1980, 1984 and 1988. The "election expenses" of all registered parties increased from $10.1 million in 1979 to $17.6 million in 1984 to $22.4 million in 1988--see Table 4.2. In real terms (1989 dollars), the increase was much smaller--from $18.9 million in 1979 to $21.75 million in

TABLE 4.2 Election Expenses by Parties on Federal General Election Campaigns, 1979, 1980, 1984 and 1988 ($000)

	1979	1980	1984	1988
Election Expenses:				
●Prog. Conservative	3845	4407	6389	7922
●Liberal	3913	3846	6293	6840
●NDP	2190	3086	4731	7061
Total	9948	1339	17413	21823
●Other parties	166	202	205	604
All Parties	10,115	11,541	17,618	22,426
Total Election Expenses in 1989 Dollars	18,907	19,628	21,751	23,557
Party Election Expenses as Percentage of the Statutory Limit				
●Prog. Conservative	87.7%	96.9%	99.96%	99.95%
●Liberal	86.2	84.6	98.5	85.7
●NDP	49.1	68.1	74.0	88.2

Source: Report of the Chief Electoral Officer Respecting Election Expenses, 1979, 1980, 1984, 1988 (Ottawa: Minister of Supply and Services, 1980, 1981, 1985, 1989).

1984 to $23.56 million in 1988. Parties other than the "big three" have never accounted for more than 2.6% of total expenditures.

In nominal and real terms, the NDP has had the greatest increase in the level of "election expenses"; it has been spending a higher fraction of the statutory limit on "election expenses": from 49.1% in 1979 to 74.0% in 1984 to 88.2% in 1988.[19] Indeed, in 1988 it went closer to the limit than did the Liberal Party (85.7%) because of the Liberals' financial straits. Even in 1979 the Tories (87.7%) were closer to the limit than the Liberals (86.2%), and they went even closer in 1984 (99.96%) and 1988 (98.85%). Given the practical problems of controlling and coordinating party spending in a general election, it is a remarkable achievement to be able to get so close to the limit and not exceed it. Officials of all three main parties indicated that budgeting for anything over 95% of the limit is very risky. Advertising costs (print, radio and TV) have consumed more than half of each party's total outlay, except for the NDP in 1984 and 1988.[20] For the Conservative Party, advertising absorbed 70 and 71% in 1979 and 1980 respectively, but this category fell to 50% in 1984 and rose to 60% in 1988. For the Liberal Party, advertising accounted for 62% of total "election expenses" in 1979, 68% in 1980, but only 56% in 1984 and 1988. For the NDP, advertising accounted for 60% of "election expenses" in 1979 and 1980, but only 38% in 1984 and 44% in 1988.

Broadcast or "electronic advertising" accounts for the bulk of each party's expenditures on advertising. Print advertising accounted for from only 3.2% of total "election expenses" in 1984 to 13.1% in 1980. The comparable figures for the Liberals were 10.4% (1980) to 14.7% (1979), while those for the NDP were 2.2% (1984) and 14.4% in 1979. Within the electronic advertising category, television is far more important (in terms of expenditures) than radio. In 1988, for example, the Conservative Party spent $2.4 million on TV versus $1.56 million on radio. However, the NDP spent slightly *more* than the PCs on TV ($2.5 million), but only $477,000 on radio.

For the PCs and Liberals, travel costs typically absorb one-sixth to one-seventh of total election expenses. For the NDP, the percentage is somewhat lower. The NDP's figure for 1984 ($148,000) is suspect for internal party data put the cost of the leader's tour at $531,000.[21] In 1988 the NDP leader's tour cost $1,258,000, and the "travelling" expenses reported to the CEO was $1,037,000. On a proportionate basis, therefore, it appears that the "travelling" figure for 1984 should be over $430,000 or about 9% of total election expenses, not the reported 3.1%.

In real terms (1989 dollars) party outlays on radio and TV advertising grew from $5.4 million in the 1965 election to $9.2 million in the 1972 election, and then fell to $7.8 million in the 1974 election--the last one in which election expenses were not subject to a limit.[22] In the last four elections, expenditures on radio and TV ads were between $9.1 million (1984) and $10.5 million (1980 and 1988). In other words, it appears that party outlays on electronic advertising have doubled between the 1965 and 1988 general elections.

In terms of total party election expenses, electronic advertising absorbed a much larger percentage in the 1979-1988 period than the 1965-1974 period. However, in the earlier period, a much larger fraction of party (or national campaign) expenditures consisted of transfers from headquarters to individual candidates. For example, in 1974 the Liberal Party spent $5.5 million on the election of which $2.6 million consisted of transfers to candidates. In 1979, the party spent $3.9 million, but transfers to candidates amounted to about

$300,000.[23] In the past two elections, the Tories transferred very little to candidates.

Three Main Parties: Liberal, PC and NDP

Since the *Election Expenses Act* of 1974 has been in force, the Liberal Party held power as a majority government from 1974 to the spring of 1979 when the Tories, led by Joe Clark, formed a short-lived minority government. Early in 1980 the Liberals under Pierre Elliott Trudeau were returned to power. John Turner replaced Trudeau as leader in June 1984. Then the Tories won a massive victory under Brian Mulroney in September 1984, and won re-election in November 1988. In summary, the Liberals held power for two-thirds of the 17-year period for which we have data on the financing of parties (and candidates) under the reforms instituted effective 1 August 1974.

Yet while it was in power the Liberal Party did not dominate the Conservative Party in terms of its ability to raise and spend money on non-election activities. As noted earlier, the parties have been fairly evenly matched on official "election expenses." In terms of *total* party revenues in 1989 dollars (Table 4.1), the two parties raised the following amounts while the Liberals were in power:

Period	Liberal	Progressive Conservative
1974-1978	$40.2 million	$36.9 million
1980-1984	$57.9	$84.6

In 1979, the party spent $3.9 million, but transfers to candidates amounted to These figures indicate that in the period after the *Election Expenses Act* came into effect and before the Clark Government came to power, the Liberal Party raised some 9% more than the Conservative Party. However, during the last Trudeau Government (1980-84) the Liberal Party raised only 68.4% of the amount raised by the opposition Conservative Party. Moreover, in absolute terms, the difference was almost $27 million in 1989 dollars.

Then, when the Liberals under John Turner's leadership fell from electoral grace in September 1984, matters got worse in terms of raising and spending money between election years and on operating expenses other than official "election expenses" in election years. Indeed, the Liberals' fiscal problems were such that in 1988 its "election expenses" were only 85% of the statutory limit and in absolute terms were below those of the NDP. Between 1985 and 1990 the Liberal Party's total revenues in 1989 dollars were $67.6 million versus $103.7 million for the Tories (Table 4.1). The Liberals' expenditures, excluding "election expenses" over the same period, were $63.5 million in 1989 dollars versus $90.5 million for the Conservative Party.

The Liberal Party's failure to dominate the Conservatives in terms of party financing even while in power reflects a number of structural features of the party and its assumption that as the "natural governing party" it had little need to change its methods of raising money. Party officials have suggested that the weaknesses of the old fund raising structure (which relied on large corporations) were not real but simply apparent when the party was in power.[24] Moreover, the party failed to appreciate the implications of the new technologies and how much they were relying on being in power. Specifically, the party failed to expand its funding base, most notably by failing to create a major direct mail effort before 1986.

While there are clear signs that the renewal phase was well underway with new policies instituted in 1987-1989,[25] it is not clear that the party has the capability of raising money between election years on a scale that is closely comparable to the Tories. The superior performance in 1990 is largely attributable to the *extra* revenues generated by the leadership race and party convention (about $6.4 million).

The provisions of the *Election Expenses Act* of 1974 have benefitted the New Democratic Party a great deal. However, much of the benefit--for example in the form of higher revenues--has *not* gone to the *federal* wing of the party except during elections. The federal tax credit for political contributions has been used to raise far more money for the NDP as a whole than is spent by the federal office outside official "election expenses." The NDP, as an integrated party, has chosen to use the federal tax credit as a vehicle to help to finance its provincial ambitions. In most years between 1974 and 1990, the federal office's budget (all sources of revenue) to promote the election of a federal government was less than the amount of money flowing to provincial or territorial sections (PTSs) for the purpose of electing *provincial* governments from money raised using the *federal* tax credit.[26]

While the federal office of the NDP receives 15% of revenues generated by its PTSs using the federal income tax credit for political contributions to registered parties, the federal office's other sources of revenues generate only modest amounts of money and some of these sources depend upon the generosity of the PTSs. In contrast, in the Conservative Party there is a clear separation between federal and provincial politics. When the federal Conservative Party (PC Canada Fund) retains 25% of the money raised by riding associations (local district organizations) between elections in "exchange" for the use of its (federal) tax receipting authority, it is dealing with a local organization *solely* devoted to electing a *federal* government. Moreover, the Ottawa headquarters of the federal Conservative Party has complete autonomy from provincial parties and has exclusive control over all of the various methods of raising funds.[27]

Trade unions through affiliation dues, cash contributions and contributions of goods and services continue to be an important source of revenue for the NDP. However, their importance in financing federal elections has declined from 43-44% of the total revenue in 1979 and 1980 to 34% in 1984 to 25% in 1988.[28] In large part, this decline is due to the increase in party spending on election expenses: from 49% of the statutory limit in 1979 to 88% in 1988 and the fact that union contributions have not been raised accordingly.

While the federal wing of the NDP is now spending as much as its main rivals on general elections, it remains far behind in expenditures between elections.[29] The expenditures of the NDP's federal office in 1977 were less than one-sixth of the Liberal and Conservative parties. In 1989 this had fallen to 12% of the Conservatives' expenditures, but it had increased to 21.5% of the Liberals' expenditures.

Officials in the three main parties and many citizens see the roles of trade unions in financing the NDP as closely analogous to that of corporations in the Conservative and Liberal parties. The analogy, in fact, is not a close one for several reasons. First, trade union locals that are affiliated with the party pay annual affiliation dues that provide a regular source of income for the NDP; there is no corresponding relationship between corporations and the PC or Liberal parties. Second, it appears that a higher fraction of trade union locals give money or services to the NDP[30] than do corporations (although 40% of the 500 largest non-financial corporations contribute to one or both parties). Third, except in the 1979 and 1980 elections, the resources provided by unions have been a smaller fraction of the NDP's revenues than corporate contributions are of the Liberal or Conservative parties' revenues. However, union contributions that are centralized through the Canadian Labour Congress (CLC) might give that body more influence. Fourth, a much greater fraction of the unions' contributions to the NDP's federal election campaigns consists of goods and services than is the case for corporate contributions to the Liberal or Conservative parties. Indeed, in 1979, 1980 and 1984 the value of unions' contributions in the form of goods and services greatly exceeded their cash contributions. (In 1988, union cash contributions were double their contributions in kind.)

Number and Importance of Individual Contributions

Number of Contributions. Within three years after the *Elections Expenses Act* of 1974 had come into effect, all parties were receiving over 109,000 contributions from individuals-- see Table 4.3. In fits and starts the number of contributions rose to almost 149,000 in 1982. Then it jumped sharply to 205,000 in 1983. The total rose to 211,000 in 1984, an election year, and stayed almost at that level in 1985 (203,000). Then the total number of contributions by individuals to all parties fell to 159,000 in 1987, but, as expected, it rose sharply in 1988, an election year, to over 208,000. Then the number of contributions dropped to 166,700 in 1989, but rose to a record 218,300 in 1990. Forty percent of the increase was attributable to the "minor parties," notably the Reform Party. It obtained 23,500 contributions from individuals in 1990, up from 7400 in 1989. Note that in 1990 the Reform Party's total was 85% of the number of contributions to the faltering Conservative Party from individuals. (Throughout 1990 the personal popularity of the Prime Minister declined and reached an all-time low in mid-1991.)

The total number of contributions by individuals to *candidates* in the four elections since the new legislation came into effect rose from 67,323 in 1979 to 104,807 in 1988 (Table 4.3). The figure for 1979 amounted to 56.4% of the number of individuals contributing to parties. In 1984, the ratio of the number of individuals contributing to candidates to the number contributing to parties fell to 41.5%, but it recovered to 50.3% in 1988.

The pattern of the total number of contributions by individuals to the three largest parties is somewhat surprising given the growing intensity of direct mail fund raising by the three main parties (NDP, PC and Liberal) after 1984. If we take the three-year period straddling the 1984 election we find the average total number of contributions was 200,600. However, the average for the three years straddling the 1988 election was 177,900. This pattern should be disturbing to the parties because the drop in the *real* value of the tax credit (described below) should affect the average size of contributions in real terms, but not the number. Indeed, in light of the strenuous efforts by all three major parties to use the direct mail technique, it would seem reasonable to expect more individual donors in recent years, not fewer.

The contrast in the NDP and Liberals' pattern in obtaining money from individuals can easily been seen in the following data on the *average* number of contributions from individuals in four-year intervals:

Period	Liberal	PC	NDP[31]
1974-77	14,204	14,191	50,778
1978-81	19,445	37,853	62,440
1982-85	29,805	80,069	77,420
1986-89	28,738	46,548	96,524

The total number of contributions by individuals to federal parties peaked in election years 1984 and 1988, but the number in 1990 exceeded both years--reflecting the growth in the Reform Party as noted above. The percentage of potential electors contributing to a federal party was 1.26% in 1984 and 1.18% in 1988.[32] If we add the number of contributions by individuals to candidates, the percentage rises to 1.78% in 1984 and 1.77% in 1988.

TABLE 4.3 Number of Contributions by Individuals to Federal Parties and Candidates, 1974-1990

	Number of Individual Donors to				
Year	PC, NDP and Liberal parties	Other parties	All parties	All Candidates[c]	Total Indiv. Donors
1974(5 mos)	34,703	7,796[a]	42,499		42,500
1975	82,603	2,007[b]	84,610		84,611
1976	97,812	11,432	109,244		109,244
1977	101,571	2,754	104,325		104,325
1978	125,098	5,040	130,138		130,138
1979(E)	111,632	7,701	119,33	67,323	186,656
1980(E)	112,908	3,865	116,773	70,528	187,301
1981	129,405	1,600	131,005		131,005
1982	147,327	1,538	148,865		148,865
1983	198,537	6,556	205,093		205,093
1984(E)	202,282	8,700	210,982	87,456	298,438
1985	201,026	1,622	202,648		202,648
1986	178,642	2,442	181,084		181,084
1987	156,219	2,603	158,822		158,822
1988(E)	202,925	5,410	208,335	104,807	313,142
1989	149,451	17,443[d]	166,894		166,683
1990	180,511	37,912[c]	218,423		218,423

E = Election year; [a]1/8/74 - 31/7/75; [b]1/8/75 - 31/12/75;
[c]More precisely it is the number of contributions from individuals. Obviously, an individual can make more than one contribution to a candidate and/or contributions to several candidates. There is no way of knowing how much double counting occurs.
[d]Includes 7541 for the Christian Heritage Party (Oct. 22/88 to Dec. 31/89) and 7360 for the Reform Party.
[e]Includes Reform Party, 23,462; Christian Heritage Party, 9226; and Confederation of Regions Party, 2956.

Sources: *Report of the Chief Electoral Officer Respecting Election Expenses, 1979, 1980, 1984, 1988* (Ottawa: Minister of Supply and Services, 1980, 1981, 1985, 1989) and the parties annual returns filed with the CEO.

Average Size of Contributions. To some degree the Liberals' weakness in getting money from larger numbers of contributions by individuals has been made up by the larger average contribution the party has received. In 11 of the 17 years between 1974 and 1990, the average contribution to the Liberals exceeded the Tories and in all 16 years the Liberals' average exceeded that of the NDP--see Table 4.4. From 1987 through 1989 the Liberals fell behind the Tories but staged a remarkable recovery in 1990--due largely to the leadership campaign won by Jean Chretien. The average annual contribution from individuals to the Liberals, in nominal terms, ranged from $85 in 1981 to $205 in 1990. The comparable figures for the Tories were $75 (1978) and $189 (1988), while those for the NDP were $32 (1976) and $76 (1983). Even though the average contribution to the Tories and NDP increased substantially (Table 4.4), it did not keep up with the rate of inflation. While the average contribution in terms of 1989 dollars "bounces around" in the period 1974-1990, the trend for all parties is clear: in real terms average contributions have fallen.

Importance of Contributions by Individuals. In *real* terms, it is clear that contributions from individuals to the three main parties have increased when we group the annual data into four-year periods and compute the annual average during each period as follows:

1974-77	$13.2 million
1978-81	13.9 million
1982-85	20.4 million
1986-89	19.0 million

The figure for 1990 was $17.3 million in 1989 dollars.

Contributions from individuals vary in their importance to each of the three main parties as measured by the percentage of total party revenue for which they account.[33]   In non-election years, individuals typically accounted for three-quarters of the NDP's federal revenues.[34]   In 1979, 1980 and 1984 the percentage dropped to about 50%. (It was 57% in 1988.) The percentage dropped in election years for several reasons. First, the party receives the rebate of 22.5% of its "election expenses." Second, trade unions make substantial cash contributions and contributions in kind in election years. Third, the NDP raises money from its provincial sections (PTS) to fight elections. If this money comes from contributions for which federal receipts have been issued, the money is an intra-party transfer not a contribution to the party.

In most years over the period 1974-1990 the Conservative Party was more dependent on contributions from individuals than the Liberals. Prior to the 1979 election, from 44% to 49% of PC revenues came from individuals. This dropped to about 35% for the election years of 1979 and 1980, then it rose to

TABLE 4.4 Number and Average Size of Contributions by Individuals to Federal Parties, 1974-1990[a]

Year	Progressive Conservative Party[c] No.	Avg. Nom.$	Avg. 1989$	Liberal Party[b] No.	Avg. Nom.$	Avg. 1989$	New Democratic Party No.	Avg. Nom.$	Avg. 1989$
1974 (5 mos)	6,423[b]	$99[b]	$284	4,117	$112	$321	27,910	$46	$132
1975	10,341	98	253	13,373	113	292	58,889	35	90
1976	23,409	82	197	18,261	114	274	56,142	32	77
1977	20,339	86	192	21,063	94	209	60,169	37	82
1978	35,615	75	153	22,350	94	192	67,133	38	78
1979(E)	34,952	91	170	13,025	91	170	63,655	43	80
1980(E)	32,720	98	167	17,670	141	240	62,428	52	88
1981	48,125	90	136	24,735	85	128	56,545	51	77
1982	52,694	98	134	27,968	114	156	66,665	57	58
1983	99,264	92	119	33,649	97	125	65,624	76[d]	98
1984(E)	93,199	109	135	29,056	178	220	80,027	52[e]	64
1985	75,117	105	125	28,545	110	131	97,364	47	56
1986	52,786	149	170	35,369	163	186	90,487	56	64
1987	39,320	154	168	28,972	120	131	87,927	54	59
1988(E)	53,893	189	199	30,642	155	163	118,390	66	69
1989[f]	40,191	170	170	19,970	119	119	89,290	67	67
1990	27,702	169	161	36,361	205	196	116,448	52	50

[a]In nominal dollars. The number does not include individuals contributing to *candidates* in election years.

[b]The original figures for the Liberal Party were for 1 August 1974 to 1 July 1975 and 1 August 1975 to 31 December 1976. They were recomputed on a pro rata basis to fit the calendar years.

[c]The original figures for the Conservative Party were for 1 August 1974 to 31 July 1975 and 1 August 1975 to 31 December 1975. They were recomputed on a pro rata basis to fit the calendar year.

[d]If the $453,365 donation of Irene Dyck is eliminated, the average is $69.

[e]If the $215,767 donation of Irene Dyck is eliminated, the average is $49.

[f]Note that the average for the nine *other* parties was $154, including an average of $333 for the Communist Party.

(E) Election year.

Sources: *Report of the Chief Electoral Officer Respecting Election Expenses, 1979; 1980; 1984;1988* (Ottawa: Minister of Supply and Services, 1980, 1981, 1985, 1989); and annual returns of the parties filed with the Chief Electoral Officer.

61%-62% during the early 1980s. The ratio dropped to 43% in election year 1984. Individual contributions rose to 52% in 1985, but then declined gradually to only 38% in 1988, an election year. They rose to 47% in 1989 but dropped to 41.5% in 1990. Almost all of the decline in the relative importance of individual contributions in the case of the PCs in election years is due to the growth of corporate contributions.[35]

The Liberal Party obtained one-half their total revenues from contributions from individuals in the mid-1970s. Then the percentage began to fall, reaching a low of only 17% in 1979, an election year.[36] The percentage rose to 27% in 1980, another election year, and then increased sharply to 38% in 1981 and 47% in 1982. While it fell slightly thereafter, it was still 40% in the election year of 1984. It then rose to a peak of 54% in 1986 only to decline sharply to only 26.5% in 1988, another election year. In 1989, the Liberals obtained 37% of their total revenue from individuals, but this rose to 54.0% in 1990--due to the leadership race and convention.

Large Contributions by Individuals. While large contributions[37] by individuals may make the headline of the odd newspaper story, they are not an important source of revenue for Canada's three largest political parties. Between 1983 and 1990 the largest single contribution to the Liberal Party ranged from $3000 in 1985 (from three persons) to $40,000 in 1988. For the Tories, the comparable figures were $15,000 in 1983 and 1987 to $54,919 in 1989. Note that in 1988 the former chairman of BCE Inc. (which owns Bell Canada) gave $40,000 to the Tories *and* $25,000 to the Liberal Party. Interestingly, all of these contributions pale beside the contributions to the NDP by Mrs. Irene Dyck, a Calgary widow: in 1983 she gave $453,365. Thereafter the amounts ranged from $23,165 (1985) to $215,767 (1984). Her contributions might be compared to that of Tory leader R.B. Bennett in 1950 who gave $750,000 to the Conservative Party's election campaign.[38] That is the equivalent of roughly $4.2 million in terms of 1989 prices.

The number of contributions of $2000 or more in the period 1983-1990 to the PCs ranged from 45 in 1983 to 295 in 1988.[39] The Liberals fared less well: their range was from 15 in 1985 to 101 in 1990. The NDP usually received 10 or 11 large contributions in each year. However, the NDP did better in 1983 (n=21), 1988 (n=39), 1989 (n=26), and 1990 (n=19). In every case, virtually all of the contributions to the NDP were in the $2000 to $4000 range. While the Tories received a total of 963 contributions of $2000 or more between 1983 and 1990, the Liberals received 396 and the NDP received only 146.

Between 1983 and 1990 "large" contributions (i.e., > $2000) from individuals accounted for between 1.1% and 7.9% of total contributions by individuals to the Liberal Party.[40] For the Tories, such contributions accounted for from 1.5% to 11.3% of all contributions from individuals. These data strongly suggest that neither of these parties is heavily dependent upon a fairly small number of individuals who make large contributions to finance the party. Even in 1984 and 1988 when 278 and 295 individuals contributed an average of $3900 each, they accounted for only about 11% of the Tories' revenues from individuals. But individuals accounted for only about one-half the Tories' total party revenues.

Importance of Income Tax Credits

Taxpayers, through the income tax credit, paid for about one-half the value of political contributions made by individuals to parties and candidates. In election years, perhaps because a larger number of people made a contribution the percentage was lower, typically 46% versus 52% in the period 1985-87.[41] Note that between 1980 and 1988 no more than 1.4% of all tax filers claimed the tax credit for political contributions.[42] Hence the vast majority of taxpayers are subsidizing parties and candidates.

A substantial fraction of individuals did *not* claim the tax credit for their political contributions but the fraction appears to be rising. For example, while only 45% of individuals making a contribution between 1974 and 1977 claimed the tax credit, just over half did so in 1979 and 1988 when a much larger number made a contribution to a party and/or candidate.[43]

In constant 1989 dollars, the value of tax credits for political contributions totalled $145.1 million between 1974 and 1988. The amount exceeded $10 million in all four election years and in 1983 and 1986.[44]

Manitoba and Saskatchewan electors' use of the tax credit for political contributions was 5.7 times that of Quebec in 1984 and 4.4 times in 1988. However, the average contribution (and tax credit) of Quebecers was 41% higher than Prairie electors in 1984 and 53% higher in 1988.[45]

Importance of Contributions from Corporations

Corporate contributions as a percentage of total Conservative Party revenue was 56.6% in 1974/75; they then fell in an irregular fashion to only 32.6% in 1983.[46] Corporate contributions then rose in an irregular fashion to 53.2% in 1988 and 56.2% in 1990. For the Liberal Party corporate contributions rose from 42.4% in 1974/75 to 55.2% in 1979, then they fell to 37.4% in 1982. They then rose and fell, and went as high as 60% in 1987 and 1989, but dropped to 33.2% in 1990 largely due to "other revenues" amounting to 12.6% of the total. (They appear to relate to the tax imposed on leadership candidates' expenditures and a levy imposed on local associations.)

Only a tiny fraction of business enterprises make political contributions, typically less than 3% except in election years.[47] Even among the 500 largest non-financial enterprises in Canada, only 40% made a contribution to any political party in the period 1983-89.

Number and Size of Corporate Contributions. As noted above, prior to the *Election Expenses Act* of 1974 the Liberal and PC parties obtained virtually all their funds from less than 500 corporations. Table 4.5 makes it clear that both parties have been able to broaden greatly their corporate fundraising base. The Liberal Party typically obtained donations from 5000 to 6000 corporations between 1974 and 1990. The Tories did even better. From only 2000 corporate donors in 1974/75, they were able to increase the number to 21,000 in 1984. While the number fell off to about 9000 in 1987 and 1989, and to 7200 in 1990, the Conservatives were able to tap several thousand more corporations than the Liberals--see Table 4.5.

In nominal dollars, the average contribution from corporations to the Liberal Party ranged from $352 (1983) to $1167 (1988) between 1974 to 1990. The comparable figures for the Tories were lower: from $232 (1983) to $1023 (1988). Table 4.5 indicates that, ignoring the election years of 1979 and 1980, the average corporate contribution in real terms *declined* from the mid-1970s to 1983. Then the average contribution increased unsteadily to the late 1980s. However, the level in 1989 was below that of 1974/75. Further, the average in the 1979 and 1980 elections was well above either 1984 and 1988, the last two elections.

Importance of Large Corporate Contributions. Despite the sometimes heated rhetoric about large contributions from corporations, the largest contribution to the Liberal or Conservative party between 1983 and 1990 was $150,000.[48] Between 1983 and 1989 the largest corporate contribution to the Liberal Party (in nominal dollars) ranged from $51,958 (1983) to $80,501 (1988).[49] The comparable figures for the Progressive Conservative Party were $50,000 (1983) to $150,000 (1984).

The number of "large" contributions[50] from corporations to the Conservative Party has increased markedly, from 43 in 1983 to 198 in 1984, an election year, falling to an average of 106 annually in the inter-election years, and then rising to 299 in election year 1988 and falling again to 118 in 1989 and 107 in 1990.[51] Overall, from 1983 to 1990 the Tories received 45% more large contributions from corporations than the Liberals, although in 1983 the latter received two more than the Tories. The greatest differences occurred in election years, i.e., 198 for the Tories in 1984 versus 113 for the Liberals and 299 vs. 171 in 1988.

The average size of these corporate contributions of $10,000 or more changed very little between 1984 and 1990 for either party: about $22,000 for both parties.[52] Between 1984 and 1990, large corporate contributions accounted for about 45% of total corporate contributions to the Liberal Party.

TABLE 4.5 Contributions by Corporations to the Federal Liberal and Progressive Conservative Parties, 1974-1990

Year	Liberal Party			Progressive Conservative Party		
	Number[a]	Average		Number[a]	Average	
		Nominal Dollars	1989 Dollars[d]		Nominal Dollars	1989 Dollars[e]
1974/75[b]	2,430	$410	$1111	2,046	$477	$1293
1975/76[c]	5,173	510	1,253	7,045	341	838
1977	5,685	404	900	4,501	386	860
1978	5,026	495	1,010	8,105	325	663
1979(E)	3,737	1,037	1,938	7,752	651	1218
1980(E)	4,420	844	1,435	5,011	872	1483
1981	6,039	448	677	7,312	352	532
1982	5,652	446	608	9,432	310	423
1983	7,536	352	454	18,067	232	299
1994(E)	6,494	822	1,015	21,286	517	638
1985	3,775	644	765	15,789	424	504
1986	6,221	779	888	12,680	576	657
1987	6,073	880	962	9,198	729	797
1988(E)	7,238	1,167	1,226	14,032	1,023	1075
1989	3,857	1,019	1,019	9,435	736	736
1990	5,598	816	779	7,183	884	845

E = Election year
[a]From 1974 to 1979 the number is the sum of "private corporations" plus "public corporations," and "corporations without share capital." It excludes "unincorporated organizations." From 1980, the category is "business and commercial organizations."
[b]1/8/74 to 31/7/75 (12 months); [c]1/8/75 to 31/12/76 (17 months).
[d]Deflated using the Consumer Price Index.

Source: Tabulation by the author from *Report of the Chief Electoral Officer Respecting Election Expenses, 1979; 1980; 1984; 1988* (Ottawa: CEO, 1980, 1981, 1985, 1989); and annual returns of the parties filed with the Chief Electoral Officer.

The comparable figure for the Tories was more variable, ranging from 29.6% in 1985 to 48.0% in 1988.[53]

Contributions from the Financial Post 500. Despite their enormous importance to the corporate sector and to the economy as a whole, the 500 largest *non-financial* enterprises in Canada (FP 500) typically accounted for only about one-fifth of all contributions from corporations to the Liberal and PC parties. For example, in 1989 the FP 500 accounted for 18.9% of the total amount of corporate contributions to the Tories and 23.1% to the Liberals. These percentages were somewhat *lower* in election year 1988, although that for the Liberals was higher in election year 1984 (26.0%). It seems extraordinary that the FP 500, which account for 68% of all corporate assets, should provide only one-fifth of the value of contributions by corporations to the Liberal and PC parties. It is perhaps understandable that senior officials in both parties are are frustrated with the top management of the FP 500 firms. In their view: too fewmake *any* contribution to either party (as we have seen, typically only 40% of the FP 500 made an annual donation in the period 1983-1990); the contributions of the largest firms are seldom commensurate with the firms' size (as we shall see, the largest among the FP 500 give less relative to their size than lower ranked firms); too many large firms fail to support *both* the Liberal and Conservative parties with contributions of the same amount; and contributions from the FP 500 have failed to keep up with the rate of inflation. These are strong criticisms and most have empirical support.[54]

Contributions by the F 155. In six of the seven years between 1983 and 1989, the 155 largest *financial* enterprises in Canada (F155) have provided more than 10% of the Liberal Party's revenue from all corporations, but in no year was this true for the Tories. For example, in election year 1984, the Liberals received 11.6% of total contributions from corporations from F155 firms versus 6.3% for the Tories. In the next election year, 1988, the comparable figures were 10.9% and 8.0% respectively.[55]

Contributions from the F155 have never accounted for more than 8.6% of either party's *total* revenue in the period 1983-1990. In most years, the figure is 4% to 5%. Contributions from the F155 to both parties have increased in real terms (1989 dollars) between the early 1980s and the late 1980s.

Financing Candidates

This section provides an overview of the revenues, "election expenses," personal expenses, and surplus/deficit of the candidates of all parties who sought to become Members of Parliament in the past four elections.

Revenues

Total revenues[56] of all candidates rose from about $15.6 million 1979 and $15.4 million in 1980 to $24.3 million in 1984 and $32.5 million in 1988 (Table 4.6). However, in constant 1989 dollars (using the Consumer Price Index as the deflator) total candidates' revenues were as follows:

1979	$30.8 million
1980	26.2 million
1984	30.0 million
1988	34.1 million

In real terms, therefore, total contributions to candidates *fell* by 8.5% between 1979 and 1980 (probably due to the short period between these general elections), rose to the 1979 level in 1984 and then rose by 13.7% between 1984 and 1988.

It is obvious that the lion's share of revenues goes to candidates of the three main parties. However, the average revenue of candidates of other parties rose from $1155 in 1979 to $1438 in 1984 to $3899 in 1988. Turning to the three main parties, it is clear that NDP candidates have had the highest rate of increase in total contributions: from $2.3 million in 1979 to $6.8 million in 1988, an increase of 195%, well above the rate of inflation of 78%. PC candidates' revenues increased from $6.1 million in 1979 to $13.4 million in 1988, an increase of 120% also well above the increase in the CPI. Contributions to Liberal candidates grew more slowly: from $6.56 million in 1979 to $9.63 million in 1988, an increase of only 47%. Hence in terms of constant 1989 dollars, the Liberals raised $12.26 million in 1979 but only $10.12 million in 1988. However, in 1988 Liberal candidates raised, on average, 41% more than their NDP rivals, but only 72% of their PC rivals.

"Election Expenses"

For at least two reasons, the inter-party differences are less when official "election expenses" are concerned. First, while contributions are not limited, election expenses are constrained and a larger fraction of candidates of all parties are spending a higher fraction of the limit. On average, NDP candidates spent only 34% of the limit on "election expenses" in the 1979 election, but in 1988 this had increased to 53%. For the Tories, the fraction increased from 77.6% in 1979 to 89.0% in 1984, but dropped slightly in 1988 to 85.6%. The recent weakness of the Liberal party can be seen in the fact that its candidates (as a group) spent only 70% of the limit on "election expenses" in 1988, a drop of eight to nine percentage points from the previous three elections.[57] Second, candidates of parties like the NDP, which are less able to raise contributions,

TABLE 4.6 Candidates' Revenues, Expenses and Reimbursement in the General Elections of 1979, 1980, 1984, and 1988 ($000s)

	No. of Candidates	Contributions (C)	Election Expenses (E)	Personal Expenses (P)	Campaign Surplus (S) C-E-P[b]	Reimbursement (R)	Post Reimbursment Surplus/ Deficit (S)[b] C-E-P+R
1988							
PC	295	13,392	11,864	709	819	6,056	6,875
LIB	295	9,631	9,677	495	(541)[a]	4,656	4,115
NDP	295	6,807	7,306	368	(867)	2,839	1,972
3 main	885	29,830	28,847	1,572	(589)	13,551	12,962
Others	693[c]	2,702	2,494	161	47	184	231
Total	1578	32,532	31,341	1,733	(542)	13,735	13,193
1984							
PC	282	11,345	9,951	775	619	5,117	5,736
LIB	282	8,391	8,836	611	(1056)	4,081	3,025
NDP	282	3,724	4,227	252	(755)	1,917	1,162
3 main	846	23,460	23,014	1,638	(1192)	11,115	9,923
Others	603[d]	867	860	123	(116)	56	(60)
Total	1449	24,327	23,874	1,761	(1308)	11,171	9,863
1980							
PC	282	5,888	5,680	542	(334)	2,871	2,537
LIB	282	6,293	6,074	494	(275)	3,656	3,381
NDP	282	2,674	2,987	180	(493)	1,885	1,392
3 main	844	14,855	14,741	1,216	(1100)	8,412	7,312
Others	653[e]	541	628	123	(210)	112	(98)
Total	1497	15,396	15,369	1,339	(1310)	8,524	7,214
1979							
PC	282	6,087	6,016	488	(417)	2,868	2,451
LIB	282	6,558	6,186	527	(155)	3,594	3,439
NDP	282	2,307	2,665	186	(544)	1,671	1,127
3 main	846	14,952	14,867	1,201	(1116)	8,133	7,017
Others	581[f]	671	1,055	185	(569)	385	(184)
Total	1427	15,623	15,922	1,386	(1684)	8,518	6,834

[a]Numbers in parentheses indicate negative sums, i.e., deficit.
[b]This calculation omits "other expenses," but this figure is not published by the CEO. (Table notes continued)

can rely on the reimbursement of about half of their "election expenses" (provided they receive at least 15% of the popular vote).

In nominal dollars, total "election expenses" for all candidates rose from $15.9 million in the 1979 election to $31.34 million in the 1988 election (Table 4.6). In 1989 dollars, the increase was much smaller, from $29.76 million in 1979 to $32.96 million in 1988 (recall that in 1983 the limits on candidates' "election expenses" were indexed to the Consumer Price Index retroactively to 1980). Therefore, as more candidates spend closer to the limit, total "election expenses" will rise in nominal dollars, but not increase in real terms.

The decline in financial strength of the Liberal Party can be seen in its candidates' "election expenses" over the past four general elections. In 1979 the 282 Liberal candidates spent slightly more than their PC rivals. However, the growth in Liberal spending between 1979 and 1988 (56%) was less than the rate of inflation (78%). The result is that Liberal candidates, on average, have fallen well behind the Tories, and their lead over the NDP has been reduced 132% in 1979 to 32% in 1988.

Personal Expenses

The *Canada Elections Act* distinguishes "personal" from "election" expenses and does not impose limits on the former, although only certain types of outlays are specified by the CEO as properly falling into the category of "personal expenses," largely the candidate's travel and accommodation expenses to, from and within the local party organization during the campaign. As Table 4.6 indicates, such expenses have never exceeded 9% of "election expenses" over the past four elections and have grown less than the rate of inflation over the past four general elections.[58]

Reimbursement and Surplus/Deficit

How important is the federal government's reimbursement of 50% of a candidate's "election expenses"[59] in terms of the financing of campaigns at the constituency or riding level? To answer this question we sought to determine

---

(Table 4.6 notes continued)

[c]9 parties with 539 candidates plus 154 other candidates.

[d]8 parties with 519 candidates plus 84 other candidates.

[e]6 parties with 543 candidates plus 110 other candidates.

[f]6 parties with 511 candidates plus 70 independent candidates.

Source: Chief Electoral Officer, Report of the Chief Electoral Officer Respecting Election Expenses 1979, 1980, 1984, 1988 (Ottawa: Ministry of Supply and Services). "Election Expenses"

if contributions covered "election" and "personal" expenses. Hence we defined the term "campaign surplus"[60] (or deficit) as contributions minus election expenses and personal expenses. The data in Table 4.6 yield several important conclusions. First, for all the approximately 1500 candidates in each of the past four general elections, contributions just about cover both "election" and "personal" expenses. The "campaign *deficit*" fell from $1.7 million in 1979 to $1.3 million in 1980 and 1984 to $542,000 in 1988. In other words, even *before* reimbursement, in the aggregate, candidates take in enough money to cover their "election" and "personal" expenses.

Second, the 500 to 700 candidates not running under the banner of one of the three main parties turned their "campaign deficit" of $569,000 in 1979 into a slight *surplus* in 1988 ($47,000). No doubt, they have been driven to raise more money in contributions to cover their expenses because very few get 15% of the popular vote and therefore are not eligible for the reimbursements (see below). Indeed, Table 4.6 indicates that the total amount of reimbursement going to these candidates fell between 1979 and 1988 even in nominal terms.

Third, in 1979 and 1980 all of the three main parties had a "campaign deficit." However, in 1984 and 1988 Tory candidates as a group had a surplus while the NDP and Liberals continued to have a slight deficit. The key point is that in 1988, taking all 1578 candidates as a group, contributions covered all but 1.7% of their "election" and "personal" expenses. Hence, it could be claimed that virtually all of the federal reimbursement of $13.74 million was "unnecessary" in the sense of seeing that all candidates *as a group* had sufficient funds to cover the two categories of expenses specifically recognized in the *Canada Elections Act*.

Table 4.6 indicates that the "post-reimbursement surplus" for all candidates rose from $6.8 million in 1979 to $9.9 million in 1984 and then to $13.2 million in 1988. Note, however, that the CEO puts the "true" surplus for candidates at over $8.0 million in 1984 and $9.6 million in 1988.[61] His figures take into account part of the "other expenses" (estimated by the author to be $4.7 million in 1988) not recorded in his report on election expenses after each general election.

These figures strongly suggest that, in the aggregate at least, the 1974 reforms which established the reimbursement and the tax credit for contributions have proven a cornucopia for candidates. However, the Liberal Party and the NDP have forced virtually all of their candidates to sign over part (or even all in the case of the NDP in B.C. in 1988) of their reimbursement to the party. Their "stick" is the fact the party leader must sign every candidate's nomination papers. Much of the reimbursement flows through to the candidate's surplus (or reduces their deficit). Candidates must dispose of their surplus by transferring it to the party or to *a* local association. It appears that the surplus usually goes to the local party organization.

Public Financing

We turn now to the considerable role of the federal government in financing parties and candidates. As noted in the first section, the government provides financial assistance in three ways: reimbursement of 22.5% of parties' official "election expenses," reimbursement of 50% of each candidate's "election expenses" (provided he/she gets 15% of the votes), and the income tax credit on contributions by individuals and corporations to parties and candidates. Over the last complete four-year electoral cycle ending with the 1988 election, the federal government provided, directly and indirectly, $66.7 million to parties and candidates, of which the value of tax credits amounted to $47.96 million (Table 4.7). In 1988 alone, the value of such income tax credits was $18.85 million. Government funding for the previous electoral cycle, 1981-1984, totalled $51.5 million. In constant 1989 dollars, the costs of the last two cycles were $63.6 million (1981-84) and $70.0 million (1985-88) respectively.

Michaud and Laferriere estimate the value of tax credits to be equal to 30.7% of the income of federal parties in the electoral cycle 1981-1984 ($118.9 million) and 29.0% for the cycle 1985-1988 ($165.3 million).[62] They also estimate that for the four-year cycle ending in 1988, the federal government's *total* contribution to the financing of federal parties and candidates (tax credits plus reimbursement) amounted to 31.4% of parties', and candidates' expenditures. About two-thirds of this support took the form of tax credits.

Overall, the reimbursement amounted to 19.9% of the total "election expenses" of all parties in 1979 and 22.2% thereafter. As indicated in Table 4.7, the amount of reimbursement received by parties other than the three main parties has been minuscule. All candidates who obtained 15% of the total votes in their riding were reimbursed for one-half their election expenses. In 1988, 293 PC, 264 Liberal and 170 NDP candidates (out of 295 in each case) received reimbursement. However, only 12 of the 689 candidates of other parties were eligible for reimbursement.[63]

Michaud and Laferriere estimate the market value of free media time (required by federal law) in the 1988 election to be $169,500 for radio (excluding the CBC-AM English and CBC-AM French networks) and $4.1 million for television (excluding the CBC English network).[64] These amounts represent subsidies by the private radio and television networks.

Policy Problems/Issues and Recommended Reforms

In this section, I outline the policy problems/issues that are the subject of debate regarding the regulation of the financing of federal political parties and candidates in Canada. At the end of each section I indicate the recommendations of the Royal Commission on Electoral Reform and Party Financing whose report was released in February 1992.

TABLE 4.7 Major Sources of Federal Government Funding of Political Activity in Canada ($000)

	General Election of			
	1979	*1980*	*1984*	*1988*
Reimbursement of Parties				
● Prog. Conservative	794	978	1,437	1,782
● Liberal	718	910	1,416	1,539
● NDP	496	678	1,064	1,589
● Others	8	2	0	49
Total	2,016	2,567	3,917	4,959
Reimbursement of Candidates				
● Prog. Conservative	2,868	2,871	5,117	6,056
● Liberal	3,594	3,656	4,081	4,656
● NDP	1,671	1,885	1,917	2,839
● Others	385	112	55	184
Total	8,518	8,524	11,171	13,735
Tax credits paid to	1974-79	1980	1981-84	1985-88
● Individual	19,593	6,379	33,003	43,733
● Corporations	2,835[a]	1,247	3,454	4,231
Total	22,428	7,626	36,457	47,964
Total Government Funding Per Electoral Cycle[c]	32,959	18,717[d]	51,545	66,658
Amount in 1989 $[b]	61,606	31,832[c]	63,636	70,019

[a]Data available only for 1976-1979; the previous election was in 1974.

[b]Deflated using the year of the election, i.e., the tax credits in the years after the previous election were accumulated to the election year in nominal terms and then adjusted for changes in the CPI from the election year. This procedure slightly understates the cost in 1989 dollars.

[c]Includes the year of the election and the years preceding it. The cost of the electoral cycle ending in 1988 includes the reimbursements for the 1988 election plus the tax credits for 1981 through 1988.

[d]1980 only.

(Table notes continued)

At the outset, it is important to appreciate that while Canadians have become somewhat cynical about politicians and government in general, they support the central provisions of the regulatory system currently in place. For example, a telephone survey of 2947 adults conducted between 13 September and 5 November 1990 indicates that a majority (or plurality) of citizens believe that corporations, unions and interest groups have a right to give money to political parties.[65]   At the same time, 55% believe that unions/corporations should get the approval of members/shareholders before making political donations.   Three-quarters of those interviewed believe that parties should be required to disclose who contributes money to them.   Forty-three percent believe there should be *no* limit on the amount of contributions a person can make while 35% favour a limit of $1000 or less.   At the same time, 55% "basically agree" with the statement, "It is impossible to control what political parties receive and spend in an election."[66]

Activities of Advocacy Groups During Election Campaigns

The 1974 legislation prohibited individuals or groups other than candidates and registered parties from incurring "election expenses."   However, section 70.1(4) of the *Canada Elections Act* stated that if the spending was for the purpose of gaining support on an issue of public policy and was done in "good faith," the accused would not be convicted.   According to Seidle, this defense "had received a broader application than may have been intended and prosecutions were not assured."[67]   In 1983, with all party support and with almost no debate, the "good faith" defense was eliminated by Parliament (Bill C-169).   MPs were particularly concerned about single-issue groups "pushing a very emotional issue to the extent that it clouds the real political issues of a campaign."[68]

On 16 January 1984 the National Citizens Coalition (NCC) challenged the constitutional validity of the 1983 amendments.   The NCC claimed that the amended sections 70.1(1) and 72 prohibited them from using the print or electronic media to promote or oppose a candidate or registered political party during an election without their permission.   Hence, the NCC argued this infringed or violated its rights to freedom of thought, belief, opinion, and expression, including freedom of the press.   Alternatively, NCC argued that the sections denied the right to freedom of speech and expression, and the right to

(Table 4.7 notes continued)

Sources: Chief Electoral Officer of Canada, Report of the Chief Electoral Officer Respecting Election Expenses, 1988, 1984, 1980, 1979 (Ottawa: Ministry of Supply and Services, 1980, 1981, 1985, 1989); and Department of National Revenue data supplied to the Royal Commission on Electoral Reform and Party Financing.

participate freely in democratic elections guaranteed in the 1982 *Charter of Rights and Freedoms* (which is embedded in Canada's *Constitution Act*).

On 25 June 1984 Mr. Justice Medhurst of the Alberta Court of Queen's Bench held that S.70.1(1) and S.72 of the *Canada Elections Act* as amended were inconsistent with section 2(b) of the *Charter*, hence were of no force or effect.[69] Moreover, the ban on advocacy group activities during election campaigns did not meet the test in S.1 of the *Charter* which provides that the rights and freedoms it protects may be "subject only to such reasonable limits prescribed by law as can be demonstrably justified in a free and democratic society." The judge found there was very little evidence to suggest that section 70.1 had been abused by third parties in the 1979 and 1980 elections. Moreover, Parliament had not chosen the alternative of rewriting the "good faith" defense to make it more specific so that it preserved the right of freedom of expression while maintaining the intent of the 1974 legislation. Justice Medhurst held that "fears or concerns of mischief that may occur are not adequate reasons for imposing a limitation. There should be actual demonstration of harm or a real likelihood of harm to a society before a limitation can be said to be justified."[70] The Crown did *not* appeal. Although the decision applied only to Alberta, the Commissioner of Canada Elections decided not to enforce these sections elsewhere in Canada. It should be emphasized that, even in light of the *NCC* decision, advocacy groups' cannot *directly* support or oppose the election of a specific candidate or party. They are free, however, to advocate causes, issues or specific public policies.

In 1988 the proposed Free Trade Agreement (FTA) with the U.S. stimulated both the creation of groups for and against the FTA, but it also saw such groups spend large sums advertising their views. During the 1988 general election, advocacy groups spent about $4.73 million on advertising in 14 newspapers.[71] This figure amounted to 8% of the total "election expenses" of parties and candidates, but 40% of the three major parties' outlays on advertising. Most of the groups' advertising dealt with the free trade issue: four times as much was spent in support of the FTA as was spent opposing it. The amount of pro-free trade advertising amounted to 30% of the Conservative Party's advertising expenditures, while anti-free trade advertising amounted to 5% of the Liberal and New Democratic parties' (who opposed the FTA) advertising expenditures. The focus of the debate over free trade was at the national party, rather than candidate, level. Hiebert found that the pro-free trade groups spent 77 cents for every $1.00 of the Conservative Party advertising budget, while the anti-free trade forces spent only 13 cents for the total advertising budgets of the two parties opposing free trade."[72] Moreover, about 65% of the advocacy groups advertising space was purchased in the last week of the campaign,[73] with 25% in the final full-circulation day. Econometric research indicates that "the principal effect of the advertisements was to mobilize those Free Trade Agreement supporters intending to vote for the Liberal party to support the Conservative party."[74]

Proposals for Reform. The Royal Commission on Electoral Reform (pp. 350-356, V.1)[75] recommends that expenditures by individuals or advocacy groups during election campaigns be limited to $1000 and that the amounts not be pooled. It argues that such a limit will permit a significant amount of electoral activity. The Commission notes that 98% of contributions from individuals in 1988 were less than $1000 while 72% of those from business and 71% of those by unions were less than $1000. The Commission recommends that there be no restrictions on the ability of corporations, unions or other groups to communicate directly and exclusively with their bona fide shareholders/members on election issues. The Commission believes that its recommendations will survive a constitutional challenge.

Leadership Campaigns

Even though they can involve raising and spending millions of dollars and are often financed in part by contributions for which a tax receipt is issued, campaigns for the leadership of federal parties are not regulated under the *Canada Elections Act*. Expenditures on leadership campaigns have grown rapidly: Robert Stanfield spent $150,000 on his campaign to become leader of the Conservative Party in 1967; in 1983 the three leading candidates each spent more than $1 million.[76] Pierre Trudeau spent about $300,000 to win the leadership of the Liberal Party in 1968; in 1984 John Turner and Jean Chretien each spent almost $1.6 million, the limit set by the party on campaign expenditures. For the Liberal Party's 1990 leadership race, the two top contenders each spent $2.4 million and all candidates spent more than $6 million. To put these amounts in perspective, recall that the statutory limit on "election expenses" for a *party* running a candidate in every riding in the 1988 federal election was $8 million, and the average limit for a candidate was $46,900.

Wearing suggests that "the potential impact of high expenditure and secretive money-gathering on what is supposed to be an open and democratic process raises serious questions about leadership selection in Canada's major political parties."[77] Specifically, he asks "could unregulated, undisclosed campaign fund-raising ultimately undermine the democratic nature and integrity of the leadership selection process?"[78]

Public money is used in leadership campaigns in two ways: where contributions benefit from the federal income tax credit;[79] and where publicly-paid staff of the candidate work on his/her campaign instead of their regular jobs. Further, when a cabinet minister is a candidate, part of their travel and related expenses (government phone lines, mailing privileges) might well benefit their campaign for the leadership.

Recently, the Liberal and New Democratic parties have imposed their own regulations on leadership campaigns. In the case of the 1990 Liberal leadership race, the provisions for disclosure--except for contributions routed through the Federal Liberal Agency--were less rigorous than now apply to contributions of more than $100 made to a registered party or candidate. Columnist Jeffrey Simpson pointed out that

> The Liberals have given themselves a system superficially transparent but fundamentally opaque. Anyone who earmarks a donation for a candidate, but sends it through the Liberal Party, becomes eligible for a tax deduction. Those donors' names, with the amounts they gave and the candidates they financed, will be made public. But anyone not wishing a tax receipt can give money to a candidate. The party will then publish only a list of those donors' names, identified as contributors to the party. There will be no link to a candidate or report of the amount donated.[80]

Wearing argues for both the formal extension of tax credits for contributions to leadership campaigns and for more and better disclosure. To ensure full disclosure of revenues and expenditures, he suggests that candidates not be allowed to mail out tax receipts until disclosure has been made. "What candidate could resist the pressure coming from contributors who wanted their tax credits?" he asks.[81] I concur with Wearing's suggestion.

Proposals for Reform. The Royal Commission on Electoral Reform (pp. 273-285, V.1) made a series of recommendations in respect to leadership campaigns: (i) each candidate's campaign expenses should be limited to 15% of the party's limit in last election (this would amount to $1.89 million based on new definition of party limits and assuming the party ran a full slate of candidates); (ii) candidates (through the party) will be able to use the tax credit for contributions to their campaigns; (iii) any surplus will have to be transferred to the party or party foundation (see below) or registered constituency; (iv) there must be full disclosure of revenues and expenditures, including the names and addresses of donors of $250 or more; and (v) the selection of delegates would be subject to certain rules. Each party could place a lower limit on leadership candidates' expenditures than that provided in the legislation.

Nomination Campaigns

While the amount of "election expenses" a candidate (or party) may incur during an election campaign is limited under a formula in the *Canada Elections Act*, expenditures to obtain a party's nomination as its candidate are not regulated. The important point is that such expenditures can be substantial--

even more than the average limit on "election expenditures" of $46,900 in 1988. Gray notes that in Metro Toronto some of the winners of Liberal Party nominations in 1988 spent from $50,000 to $100,000.[82] Frank Stronach almost certainly spent much more to obtain the Liberal Party nomination for York-Simcoe than he was allowed to spend on the election campaign itself.[83] In the Toronto riding of Broadview-Greenwood, it is reported that Liberal challenger Dennis Mills had already spent $130,000 by the time the election was official announced.[84] During his seven-month "pre-writ campaign," Mills worked almost full-time in the riding. Yet Mills spent only $38,268 on official "election expenses" (89% of his limit) in 1988.

Carty and Erickson, however, note that in 65.2% of federal ridings in 1988, the candidate won by acclamation.[85] One-third of the winners reported they spent nothing on their nomination campaign, while 70% spent $500 or less and one-fifth spent over $1000. In contested nominations, winners spent an average of $4555 for seats rated as "safe" by riding officials. The author's own research on the 277 candidates spending the largest amount on "other expenses" found that the average spending prior to the issue of the writs of election was $2090.[86] Note, however, that this period could include more than the nomination process and it could exclude it because one-fifth of nominations were made after the writs were issued.[87]

In any event, the central issue is whether expenditures on nomination campaigns and pre-writ expenditures should be regulated even if large sums are spent in only a small percentage of cases.

Proposals for Reform. The Royal Commission on Electoral Reform (pp. 358-362, V.2) made a number of recommendations concerning nomination races: (i) contributions to the agent of each nomination contestant are to be eligible for the income tax credit up to the limit on expenses; (ii) there should be a limit on nomination expenses (defined in the same way as "election expenses") equal to 10% of the candidate's limit on "election expenses" in effect at that time (if an election were held in 1992, the average limit would be $6920); (iii) each contestant must submit to the constituency association a preliminary report on their revenues and expenditures by the day of the nomination meeting; (iv) each contestant must, within 30 days of the nomination meeting, submit a report on their revenues and expenses (except if the nomination meeting occurs during the election period; then the contestant who became the candidate may file it with his/her election revenue and expenses return); and (v) candidates are to be selected at an open convention. The Commission emphasized that expenditures on nomination process can promote a person who subsequently becomes a candidate--hence there is "a serious gap in the regulation of electoral spending."

Riding or Constituency Associations (District Party Organizations)

Constituency associations (CAs), as district party organizations are called in Canada, are not registered entities under the *Canada Elections Act* and this fact has a number of important implications for the regulatory system. Very little information about the financial activities of CAs is required to be made public. When a CA transfers money to a candidate (more precisely to his agent), the sources of those funds must be made public but since funds are not earmarked this is difficult to do. When the CA routes contributions to itself through the national party in order to provide the donors with receipts so they can claim the tax credit, the names of the donors (if over $100) must be reported by the party's agent, e.g., the PC Canada Fund in the case of the Conservative Party.

CAs are free to fund pre-nomination activities of would-be candidates and pre-writ activities of their candidate without limit or without public disclosure. They can also financially assist an incumbent MP between elections without limit or without public disclosure. CAs--unlike parties or agents for candidates--need not disclose the identity of donors if no receipts are issued between election campaigns.

CAs are the major recipient of candidates' surpluses (which totalled some $8 million in 1984 and $9.6 million in 1988). Once this money is put into the CA's bank account, all public accountability ends--except if part is "recycled" back to the candidate's agent at the next election. The absence of registration and public disclosure has meant that the national offices of all parties know very little about the financial operations of their CAs. Party officials indicate that some CAs have set up charitable foundations with money raised by a popular MP who has been able to raise a great deal of money for the local association. The foundation then distributes funds in a way that is likely to be politically beneficial to the MP.

Section 232 of the *Canada Elections Act* permits a candidate to transfer surplus funds to a local association or to the registered party. However, the *Act* does not define a local association,[88] and an association does not report on its activities, although a large portion of the funds expended by a local association have been provided out of public funds. Presently, anyone can organize a local association in a district and receive the candidate's campaign surplus.

In summary, constituency associations are the "black hole" of campaign financing which need to be made a registered entity (as they are in Ontario) which must file a revenue and expenditure statement and list of contributors annually.

Proposals for Reform. The Royal Commission on Electoral Reform (pp. 251-255, V.1) made a series of recommendations in respect to riding or constituency associations: (i) each constituency association must register with the new Canada Elections Commission (see below) and be part of a registered party; (ii) registered constituency associations are to be able to issue receipts for the tax credit for contributions; (iii) the constituency association's application for registration must include a statement of the assets, liabilities and any surplus; (iv) associations of independent MPs are to be able to register and hence issue receipts for the tax credits; and (v) constituency associations must meet various disclosure requirements (see below).

In addition, I would recommend that (i) no candidate's surplus should be permitted to be transferred to other than a properly constituted constituency association. Each party's rules for this purpose should have to be approved by the CEO; and (ii) total payments of a candidate's surplus to the party and/or riding association should be limited to (say) $10,000 (indexed). The excess should be remitted to the Government of Canada.

Trust Funds

In Canada, the practice of setting up trust funds to augment the official income of party leaders (in part to ensure that their family is not called upon to sacrifice an appropriate standard of living) is an old one. Liberal Prime Ministers Wilfrid Laurier, Lester B. Pearson, Louis St. Laurent and Mackenzie King benefitted from trust funds created by anonymous donors.[89] (They also exist at the provincial level.)[90] In 1976 there was some publicity concerning a fund of $300,000 created in 1972 for Claude Wagner designed to induce him to resign his judicial appointment to run as a Tory in Quebec. He was runner-up to Joe Clark in the 1976 Tory leadership convention.[91] During his race for the leadership of the Liberal Party in 1984, the existence of a trust fund to assist John Turner in paying for the education of his children came to light.[92] However, it was soon cancelled and the money returned to donors. It is reported that a fund for Mr. Turner was set up in 1984 out of the surplus from his leadership campaign.[93] Turner raised $2.2 million and Turner's return indicated the campaign cost $1.53 million. Yet the funds made available for Turner's personal use were said to amount to $300,000.[94] In order to ensure that John Turner's job was not put on the line at a leadership review convention, a group of supporters calling themselves "The Friends of John Turner" used a wide variety of standard and questionable political tactics prior to and at the November 1986 Liberal Party convention.[95] Although Turner organizers admit that between $75,000 and $100,000 was spent at the national convention, other sources have stated in the leader's defense that three times that amount was spent.[96]

Secret party trust funds are a political anachronism. In light of the embarrassment they have caused various parties, it is hard to see why they are retained.

Proposals for Reform. Trust funds operated by parties, riding associations, or candidates should be prohibited. However, existing trust funds should be "grandmothered," i.e., existing funds should not be permitted to increase in size through new contributions; they must transfer any interest on their assets to a party riding association or candidate. All transfers of interest or capital from existing funds to a party riding association or candidate must be publicly disclosed. Note that the Royal Commission on Electoral Reform did *not* address the issue of trust funds.

Federally-Receipted Money Used to Elect Provincial Members

Analysis of federally-receipted revenues and the expenditures on federal politics by the NDP revealed that since 1974 several millions of dollars each year raised by the NDP using the federal income tax credit for political contributions is spent on *provincial* political activities. In nominal terms, the amounts ranged from $1.4 million to $2.9 million annually between 1974/75 and 1980; $2.6 million to $4.8 million annually between 1981 and 1984; and $2.3 million to $6.2 million annually between 1985 and 1990. In 1989 dollars, the total "transfer" to the NDP's provincial sections between 1974 and 1989, for the purpose of electing provincial members, exceeded $71 million.[97] The federal government has made no effort to restrict the use of federally-receipted contributions for provincial purposes (i.e., to elect provincial members).

The basic question for policy makers is the following: Is it appropriate to use money for which federal income tax credits are issued to be spent on political activities *other* than those directly or indirectly associated with electing Members of Parliament? In particular, should a party be able to use such money to elect provincial members? I believe the federal tax credit should not be used in this fashion.

Proposals for Reform. The Royal Commission on Electoral Reform (p. 316, V.1) recommends that the *Income Tax Act* be amended to specify that receipts allowing taxpayers to claim the tax credit for political contributions "be issued only for contributions intended to support the activities of a federally registered party, including its registered constituency associations, a candidate during a federal election or a person seeking the nomination as the candidate of a federally registered constituency association or the leadership of a federally

registered party." Thus the NDP will not be able to use the *federal* tax credit to raise money that is spent on provincial (or municipal) politics.

Problems with the Definition of "Election Expenses"

Three issues are central here: the definition of "election expenses" in the

Canada Elections Act; the CEO's interpretation of "election expenses"; and the ability of parties to shift "election expenses" outside the period in which they are limited by law.

One of the central tenets of the 1974 amendments to the *Canada Elections Act* was the imposition of a limit on "election expenses" incurred by candidates and parties. In the 1988 general election, the average limit for candidates was $46,900 while that for parties was $8 million (if it ran a full slate of candidates). "Election expenses" are defined in the Act as including all costs incurred, liabilities assumed, or the commercial value of goods and services donated, other than volunteer labour,[98] for the purpose of directly promoting or opposing a registered political party or a candidate during an election period. The average Canadian might think that the administration of such limits is quite straightforward. It is not. In his 1986 *Statutory Report* the CEO stated that

> the present definition of *election expenses* is so vague and imprecise that its application to various sections of the *Act* has become extremely difficult. Problems relating to pre-writ expenses, the principle of direct promotion of or opposition to a candidate or a political party (third party advertising), the monies paid to agents and campaign workers, fund raising, opinion surveys and the use of capital assets, to name but a few, must be looked at and clarified before the next election.[99]

The controversy surrounding the expenditures of Marcel Masse in 1985 showed that the payment of the expenses of a volunteer need not be included in the candidate's official "election expenses."[100] They must, however, be channelled through the official agent and be labelled "campaign expenses" rather than "election expenses."[101] Moreover, it also revealed there is no provision in the Act with respect to a candidate *asking* a third party to pay the expenses of a volunteer even though such payments by a third party are prohibited. After being cleared by the federal elections commissioner, Mr. Masse was reappointed to the Cabinet as Minister of Communications.

The CEO states in his 1988 *Guidelines* for the interpretation of the legislation that the following items are *not* included in a *candidate's* "election expenses" that are subject to limit under the *Canada Elections Act*:[102] auditor's fees; expenses of a potential candidate for the purpose of obtaining the nomination as a candidate, even if incurred during the writ period; donations by a commercial organization of goods/services it normally uses in its business, but does not normally sell--where the value of each donation is less than $100; the value of volunteer labour;[103] any material (e.g., brochures, signs, etc.) which is not used and remains on hand at the end of a campaign; the cost of printed material used to directly promote the election of a candidate *before* the issue of the writ (the brochures, etc., must be mailed before the writ is issued); payment of the expenses of poll agents or their salary where it is "materially less than the commercial value of their services;" the candidate's "personal expenses,[104] provided they are a "reasonable" amount incurred in respect of such travel, living and other related expenses as the Chief Electoral Officer may designate; the candidate's deposit on nomination ($200); the cost of victory parties held after the close of polls on election day; costs of legal services including a recount; the proportion of rent and other costs of campaign offices before the writ is issued and after election day; interest on loans after polling day; the costs of polls or other types of surveys, because such expenditures do not *directly* promote the election of the candidate; and the costs associated with preparing the various reports required under the *Canada Elections Act*. The list is obviously rather long. Its effect is to exclude a number of items that clearly contribute to the candidate's efforts to get elected.

The CEO does not publish information on candidates' "other expenses," but from his files the author estimated that these totalled $4.7 million for the 1988 election. This amounted to 15% of all candidates' "election expenses." However, these outlays were highly concentrated: of the 277 candidates with largest "other expenses," the average for 155 PC candidates was $14,200; for 69 Liberals the average was $11,400 while for 39 NDP candidates the average was $3700.[105] For a very few candidates, their "other expenses" exceeded their official "election expenses." Obviously, when "unregulated" election-related outlays become a significant fraction of the official, limited "election expenses"--and where they are not publicly reported--serious questions are raised about the integrity of the regulatory policy.

The Chief Electoral Officer specifies in his 1988 *Guidelines* that a number of potentially important election-related outlays are excluded from a *party's* "election expenses." These include:

- polling and research expenses (which could amount to $400,000 to $800,000 during the campaign);
- fund-raising costs (these often amount to one-third of the gross revenue from direct mail);[106]
- costs of developing party policies or election strategy;
- costs of training candidates or election organizers; and
- all the party's internal costs "not incurred as an integral part of endeavours furthering the external exposure of the party."[107]

These exclusions might easily have totalled several million dollars in the case of the Conservative Party in 1988. Surely most of these expenditures are closely related to fighting an election campaign.

If parties are able to *shift* campaign-related outlays to the period prior to the official campaign period (from the day the writ is issued until election day) they will have more money available during the campaign and still not exceed the limit on "election expenses." According to Charlotte Gray, the Liberal and NDP "soft spending" (election expenses not covered by the [Canada Elections] Act) is chicken feed compared to what the Tories spent --and spent legally. The PC victory cost the party at least $18 million. But we will never discover the precise bill. As Harry Near, director of operations for the 1988 campaign, says with a triumphant grin, "That's none of your business, sweetheart."[108]

In calendar 1988 the federal Progressive Conservative Party spent $17.8 million on "operating expenses" plus "election expenses" of $7.92 million. The important point is that in 1987 the Tories' "operating expenses" were $11.5 million and in 1989 they were $10.7 million.[109] If "operating expenses" simply represent the normal activities of the party not directly connected with general elections, why did they rise from 1987 to 1988 and fall so sharply in 1989? Were the Tories able to shift part of their "election expenses"?[110]

The control of campaign-related expenses has been at the heart of Canada's regulatory regime since 1974. Almost 90% of Canadians favour limits on party spending even if disclosure is made.[111] The need to reconsider the level of the limits and--more importantly--to ensure that comprehensive definition of what is being controlled seems obvious.

Proposals for Reform. The Royal Commission on Electoral Reform and Party Financing (pp. 152-164, V.2) made a series of recommendations concerning the definition of "election expenses": (i) the new definition is intended to include virtually all election-related outlays, namely the cost of goods and services whether purchased or contributed to promote or oppose, directly or *indirectly*, the election of a candidate, the policies/program of a party or its leader; (ii) there is to be a list of 10 exclusions from the limit on "election expenses" including the costs of seeking nomination, the candidate's performance guarantee expenses for a fund-raising function (deficits counted as election expenses), expenses exclusively for ongoing administration of the riding or party, post-election parties and thank-you ads, interest on the candidate's loans, expenditures to comply with the Act, personal expenses (as defined under the Act)--all specified exclusions must be *reported*, however; (iii) personal expenses are to be defined as only those reasonable expenditures for child care, travel to and within the constituency, rental of temporary residence, lodging, meals and incidentals when travelling to or within the riding, expenses that result from the candidate's physical disability, and other expenses allowed by the new Canada Elections Commission.

The Royal Commission (pp. 341-348, V.1) recommended that the limit on "election expenses" be increased substantially. For parties it is to be 70 cents per registered voter in constituencies where the party has candidates (as compared to 54 cents if an election were held before April 1, 1992). Thus a party running a candidate in all 295 ridings would have a limit of $12.63 million versus $8 million in 1988. For candidates, the limit is to be computed as the sum of $2.00 per registered voter for the first 20,000; $1.00 for the next 10,000 and 50 cents for each voter over 30,000. This would produce an average limit for candidates of $69,197 if an election were held before 1 April 1992. By comparison, the average limit in 1988 was $46,900. Further, the "bonus" for sparsely populated ridings is to be increased to result in an average limit of $71,280 for those ridings.

Disclosure

Both the observers of and participants in the financing of parties and candidates agree that one of the cornerstones of the regulation of such financing is public disclosure. Disclosure involves not only what is disclosed, but also when it is made public and in what form it is made public. For example, the annual list of donors of over $100 to each party that is filed with the CEO is filed only in the form of a printed list in alphabetical order. In 1990, these lists contained the names of over 218,000 individuals and 13,000 corporations. Any useful analysis of these donors (e.g., the number who gave more than $X, etc.) had to be done by hand because the information is not available in a machine readable form (e.g., computer tape or diskette).

The preparation of this study revealed that the Chief Electoral Officer does not publish any information on candidates' surplus (or to whom it is transferred, i.e., party and/or local association), or candidates' "other expenses," i.e., outlays for which tax credits were issued over and above official "election expenses" and "personal expenses" (some $4.7 million in 1988). The forms on revenues and expenditures which parties must fill out and file annually have not been changed since 1974. Further, they are not very detailed and they are filed six months after the end of the relevant calendar year. Moreover, there is no indication *when* a donation was made during a year, e.g., a corporation may wait until after the election results are in before making a large contribution in the hope that it will improve its relations with the party in power.

Proposals for Reform.   The Royal Commission (pp. 421-432, V.1) recommends that (i) registered parties and constituency associations must file an unaudited report on contributions for first six months of the year and a full audited return for the entire year; (ii) all financial reports (parties, candidates, ridings and leadership candidates) are to be due in three months but one month after a nomination meeting (except if during election period); (iii) these reports must disclose the name, full address and date of contribution for persons/organizations giving over $250 in any year; in the case of numbered corporations the name under which it is registered provincially or name on letterhead or names of directors must be disclosed; (iv) financial statements must be prepared according to generally accepted accounting principles; (v) the information must be available in machine readable form; (vi) the new Canada Elections Commission (see below) is to prepare an analytical summary annually and after each election; (vii) MPs are to be required to disclose any contributions as if they were a candidate; (viii) disclosure must be made for seven categories of contributors for all registered entities; (ix) constituency associations must provide audited returns annually if there is no election and twice during years in which there is an election. The return must include a statement of income and expenses, balance sheet, information on contributors. They can use a short form if *both* income and expenses are under $5000; (x) in the case of candidates, the post-election return is to consist of a balance sheet, all election expenses, including exclusions from the limit, and information on contributions. Election expenses of candidates using the fixed assets of a constituency association are to include depreciation of 10% of assets (excluding real estate and fixtures) and the fair market value of premises equivalent to those owned by the association for real estate and fixtures. Candidates can file a short form if revenues and expenses are both less than $5000 (pp. 172-176, v2).

However, the Commission did *not* propose to require the CEO to publish amounts and disposition of each candidate's *surplus* or the amount of their deficit or to require the CEO to publish amount of any *assignment* of his/her reimbursement and identity of recipient. However, the fact that constituency associations are to be registered and their revenues and expenditures are to be reported will help to identify the disposal of surpluses.

Administration

The CEO has an important, wide-ranging and difficult job, only part of which involves administering the regulations governing the financing of parties and candidates. In theory, because he reports directly to Parliament, the CEO has a high degree of independence in carrying out his responsibilities. In practice, however, the CEO has chosen to rely heavily on the informal Ad Hoc Committee of party representatives. The nature and role of the Committee raises several serious questions about matters of institutional design. First, the Committee has no formal recognition: it was not set up pursuant to any statutory provision. It was created for entirely practical reasons: to assist the CEO in implementing the 1974 legislation but it has continued to function since then. The Committee consists only of representatives of federal parties, primarily the Liberal, Conservative and New Democratic parties. Surely there are other interests--most importantly the public interest--that need to be represented. The obvious danger is that the CEO will find it easier to "go along" with the wishes of the parties on many of the detailed matters that are entailed in any system of regulation. The potential problem is exacerbated when one realizes that the CEO is very unlikely to be criticized in Parliament for decisions/actions that have been approved by the Ad Hoc Committee. The public, however, is unlikely to be well served by a regulatory regime under which the regulatees have unusual opportunities to shape the actions of the regulator.

Third, the minutes of the meetings of the Ad Hoc Committee are secret[112] --unlike, for example, those of Parliamentary committees. While the membership of a Parliamentary committee would necessarily be limited to MPs, it could call witnesses and thus gain advice from whatever source it saw fit. Secret committees smack of the Star Chamber. Surely the CEO would be better able to assert his independence if the means by which he obtained advice were more broadly-based and conducted in a fashion that was accessible to the public.[113]

The CEO presently has the power to, in effect, make regulations concerning the financing provisions of the *Canada Elections Act*. He does so when he issues his *Guidelines* for parties and candidates. They specify the way in which the CEO will interpret the statute in the course of carrying out his responsibilities. The potential problem, however, is that, unlike subordinate legislation, the *Guidelines* have not been submitted to Cabinet and approved by the committee of cabinet which examines new regulations and other forms of subordinate legislation. In the case of an appointed official responsible to Parliament, the idea of requiring their proposed regulations to be approved by the Cabinet may seem anomalous. But surely no official should, in effect, be able to "make law" without the authority of either the Cabinet (Government of the day) or Parliament. Perhaps the problem could be resolved by having the CEO submit proposed regulations (now called *Guidelines*) to an all Parliamentary committee with the clear understanding that Cabinet approval will be automatic once the Committee approves the regulations. This process would have several advantages:

- The status of the *Guidelines* would be clear--they would be enforceable regulations.

- The independence of the CEO would be reinforced as would his role as a servant of Parliament.

- The process of making new laws (in the form of regulations) would be clear and open.

The general objective is to open up the process and to try to overcome the institutional bias in favour of accommodating the interest of the major parties due to the CEO's almost "daily machine-gun-like impact" of continuous contact with the representatives of the parties.

Proposals for Reform. The Royal Commission on Electoral Reform (pp. 217-227, V.2) recommends the creation of a seven-member Canada Elections

Commission (CEC) appointed by a two-thirds vote of the House of Commons for five-year terms (seven for the CEO/chair of the CEC). The powers of the CEC would be to formulate policy and direct the CEO; issue policy statements; review decisions of election officials; conduct public hearings on regulations, policies and guidelines; provide advance rulings or interpretation bulletins; make regulations to be submitted directly to the Speaker of the House of Commons and deemed to have been approved if not referred for debate or to a committee within 15 sitting days; act as broadcast arbitrator; maintain register of parties, constituencies and party foundations; and provide an annual report to Parliament. The CEC is to combine administration, investigation and adjudication of functions. The last two are to be kept separate as the members are to act as a superior court of record (in panels of three) in *civil* law matters. The choice of civil or criminal law will depend upon the gravity of the alleged violation. A Director of Enforcement is to be appointed by the Cabinet and is to be removed only for cause during the five-year term.

Other Recommendations of the Royal Commission on Electoral Reform and Party Financing

The purpose of this section is to outline other recommendations that are related to the financing of federal parties and candidates.

Government Financial Assistance. (1) Reimbursement of Election Expenses: The Commission recommends that each party receive 60 cents for each vote it obtains provided it obtains at least 1% of the popular vote, but the amount is to be limited to 50% of its "election expenses." If the overall percentage of women in Parliament falls below 20% following either of the next two elections, the Commission recommended (i) for the following two elections the reimbursement of each party with at least 20% female MPs be increased by an amount equivalent to the percentage of its female MPs up to a maximum of 150%; (ii) this measure would be automatically eliminated once the overall percentage of female MPs is 40% or more; (iii) this provision to be reviewed following the third general election--if it is still in place). The Commission recommends that each candidate is to receive $1.00 per vote obtained, if he/she receives 1% of the votes cast. (The reimbursement rate is higher in the case of smaller or remote ridings.) Candidates who are disabled persons and who obtain 1% of the vote are to be reimbursed for 75% of their expenses for assistive devices up to a maximum of 30% of their spending limit. The proposed reimbursement rates are to be reviewed after every election.

The recommended formula for reimbursing candidates would have increased the number receiving reimbursement from 739 to 1157 in 1988, largely NDP candidates and those of smaller parties and independents. If an election were held in late 1992, the electorate will be 5% larger and the *total* cost of reimbursement would be $20.02 million ($12.43 million to candidates and $7.59 million to parties) versus $18.69 million in 1988 ($13.73 million to candidates and $4.96 million to parties).

(2) Income Tax Credits: no change (but the use of the credit is to be extended to contributions to nomination campaigns and leadership campaigns, but now excludes contributions intended to support the provincial-level activities of a federally-registered party. This is really only of concern to the NDP.

(3) Tax Deductions should be permitted for expenditures on attendant care for disabled persons seeking a nomination and/or running as a candidate, and child care expenses incurred by the primary caregiver when she/he is seeking the nomination or running as a candidate.

Contributions Through Income Tax Returns. The Royal Commission (pp. 452-455, V.1) recommends that individuals be able to donate up to $100 to a party when filing their income tax return and to claim the tax credit for that fiscal year. Thus, the cost to the treasury is only the credit, not the donation.

Time Periods. The Commission recommends that the campaign period be shortened to be between 40 and 47 days; and that nominations be completed at least 21 days before election day.

Contributions in Kind. The Royal Commission (pp. 159-164, V.2) recommends that a contribution of goods or services includes a contribution by way of donation, advance, deposit, discount or otherwise of any tangible property, except money or services of any description. However, goods and services valued at less than $250, volunteer labour, and free advertising space provided on an equitable basis would be excluded. The recommended definition of volunteer labour is to be based on the person receiving no remuneration or direct material benefit except for (i) the labour of a self-employed person if normally sold by that person, (ii) the labour of a person whose services are made available by an employer. The commercial value of contributions of goods and services is to be based on the lowest price charged for equivalent amount in the market area at the relevant time. The Commission proposes to prevent MPs from mailing "householders" after the writs are issued (they can do so now, but have to include the cost in their "election expenses").

Paid Broadcasting. The Royal Commission on Electoral Reform (pp. 383-397, V.1) recommends that (i) each radio and television broadcaster to provide up to 360 minutes in prime time; (ii) no party can purchase more than 100 minutes from any broadcaster (so the real limit is based on dollars of "election expenses"); (iii) there be no broadcasting from outside Canada (same as at present); (iv) broadcasters to be required to provide time to registered parties at 50% of the most favourable rate at which comparable time is sold to other advertisers (but one-half the paid time would be counted as program time rather than advertising to make it easier to stay under limits on advertising time, i.e., 12 min/hr on TV); (v) the advertising period is to begin 11 days after the writs are issued and end two days *before* voting day; and (vi) only parties be allowed to buy time provided under *Canada Elections Act*.

Free Broadcast Time.   The Royal Commission (pp. 397-411, V.1) recommends that each network operator (two English and one French) and all broadcasters specializing in general news and public affairs (e.g., "Newsworld") be required to provide the Canada Elections Commission with ten 30-minute free time broadcasts in prime time (at least 24 minutes available to parties). French language networks focusing on Quebec and those focusing on French-language majorities outside Quebec are to be required to provide *five* 30-minute broadcasts in prime time (24 minutes to parties). If the Commission's other recommendations concerning the allocation of free time among parties were to be adopted, the allocation of free time would be as follows:

Party	1988 actual (CBC)	Proposed (based on 1988 vote)	
PC	101 min.	63 min.	(15 segments)
Lib	46	49.5	(12 segments)
NDP	35	31.5	(7 segments)
14 others	2-4 min.each	7 each	(2 segments)

Party Foundations.   The Royal Commission (pp. 290-302, V.1) recommends that parties be encouraged to establish party foundations supported in part by government subsidies. Their functions/roles would be to create an institutional base for the development of policy alternatives, to provide a forum for policy debates (seminars/conferences), to educate members through publications, to be a source of policy advice, and to assist the party during the transitions from opposition to government or the reverse. To be eligible for government subsidies, the foundations would have to be a non-profit organization under *Canada Corporations Act*, have a constitution separate from the party, have a representative board of directors, have to ensure that directors/personnel do not prepare election material or participate in campaigns-- except on unpaid leaves, provide full disclosure of revenues and expenditures and publish an annual report, and make no financial transfers from the foundation to the party (except for specific administrative services provided by the party). Annual government funding would consist of 25 cents per number of votes in last election each year (if the party received more than 5% of the popular vote). The formula (based on the 1988 election) would provide $3.04 million to the Conservative Party, $1.57 million to the Liberal Party, and

$590,000 to the NDP. The party foundations could solicit donations using the tax credit for *charitable* contributions. Thus they must meet requirements for being a charitable organization under the *Income Tax Act* (thus they would have to spend 80% of the amount collected in previous year during the current year).

Important Provisions Left Undisturbed. The Royal Commission on Electoral Reform and Party Financing examined but decided to leave unchanged (i) the absence of regulation of leaders' debates on television; (ii) the absence of any limits on the *amount* of contributions; (iii) the absence of restrictions on the *sources* of contributions (except foreign sources); and (iv) the amount of the income tax credit for political contributions.

Notes

1.   Quoted in the [Toronto] *Globe and Mail*, March 14, 1990, p. A9.

2.   Khayyam Z. Paltiel, *Party, Candidate and Election Finance*, Study No. 22 for the Royal Commission on Corporate Concentration (Ottawa: Minister of Supply and Services, 1977), p. 198.

3.   Useful earlier studies include   Khayyam Z. Paltiel "Canadian Election Expense Legislation, 1963-1985: A Critical Appraisal or Was the Effort Worth It?" in R.J. Jackson et al., eds., *Contemporary Canadian Politics* (Scarborough: Prentice-Hall Canada, 1987), pp. 228-247; F. Leslie Seidle and Khayyam Z. Paltiel, "Party Finance, the Election Expenses Act and Campaign Spending in 1979 and 1980" in H.R. Penniman, ed. *Canada at the Polls, 1979 and 1980* (Washington, D.C.: American Enterprise Institute, 1981), pp. 226-279; and W.T. Stanbury, *Business-Government Relations in Canada* (Toronto: Methuen, 1986), Ch. 10.

4.   More generally, see Khayyam Z. Paltiel, *Political Party Financing in Canada* (Toronto: McGraw Hill, 1970); F. Leslie Seidle, "Electoral Law and Its Effects on Election Expenditure and Party Finance in Great Britain and Canada" (Unpublished PhD thesis, Oxford University, 1980); and Paltiel, *Party, Candidate and Election Finance* (1977).

5.   Seidle ("Electoral Law...," 1980, p. 149) indicates that between 20% and 28% of candidates failed to submit the required return in the general elections between 1962 and 1974.

6.   "Round Table: The Party Perspectives on Election Expenses," *Parliamentary Government* 2(2), Winter/Spring, 1981, pp. 7-11.

7.   For more detail, see Seidle ("Electoral Law...," 1980); J. Patrick Boyer, *Money and Message: The Law Governing Election Financing, Advertising, Broadcasting and Campaigning in Canada* (Toronto: Butterworths, 1983); and W.T. Stanbury, *Money in Politics: Financing Federal Parties and Candidates in Canada* (Study for the Royal Commission on Electoral Reform and Party Financing, Toronto: Dundurn Press, 1991).

8.   Certain expenses are not "election expenses". Specifically excluded by statute are (a) a candidate's travelling expenses, (b) the candidate's "personal expenses," (c) the commercial value of certain free network broadcast time provided to registered parties, and (d) the outlays of a registered party to support a candidate's campaign expenses. Such outlays are recorded by the candidate as campaign contributions and, if expended,

must be accounted for in his/her return filed with the Chief Electoral Officer (CEO).

9.   Broadcasters are not required to make time available to individual candidates. However, "once he does sell or contribute time to one candidate, he would be required by virtue of S.3 of the Broadcasting Act to make equitable time available to all other candidates in that riding, except ... where it is actually party time that is being turned over by a party to a particular candidate" (Boyer, *Money and Message...*, 1983, p. 456).

10.   Parties and candidates may not advertise in a periodical publication or on TV or radio prior to the 29th day before polling day. Ads giving notice of a meeting for nominating a candidate or meeting a party leader are not a breach of this rule.

11.   While these lengthy lists are available for public inspection at the office of the CEO and may be obtained on request, only summary data are published in the CEO's report after each general election.

12.   Corporate political contributions are not deductible expenses in computing taxable income under the federal *Income Tax Act*.

13.   The national party often takes a fraction of the contribution, e.g., for the Conservatives it is 25% while for the NDP it is 15%.

14.   The efforts to change the existing regime, including Bill C-79, are discussed in Stanbury (*Money in Politics*, Ch. 2).

15.   See Chief Electoral Officer, *Guidelines Respecting Election Expenses of Registered Parties* (Ottawa: CEO, 1988); Chief Electoral Officer, *Guidelines Respecting Election Expenses of Candidates* (Ottawa: CEO, 1988).

16.   In its brief to the Royal Commission on Electoral Reform, the NDP noted that while the CPI increased by 17.5% between election years 1984 and 1988, its costs increased by 38% for commercial travel, 42% for charter aircraft travel, between 20% and 54% for accommodation (depending on location), upwards of a 20% increase in advertising costs, and a 20% increase in salaries and benefits. See New Democratic Party, "Submission to the Royal Commission on Electoral Reform and Party Financing" (Ottawa: NDP, 1990), p. 6.

17.   It is generally agreed that some of these outlays, e.g., on polling and other forms of research, are election-related, but are not included in official "election expenses."

18.   NDP I = Party data as reported by the Chief Electoral Officer plus certain minor adjustments.

19.   Stanbury, *Money in Politics*, Ch. 3.

20.   Ibid., Table 3-5.

21.   Stanbury, *Money in Politics*, Ch. 6.

22.   *Ibid.*, Table 3-6.

23.   See Seidle and Paltiel ("Party Finance...," 1981); and Khayyam Z. Paltiel, "Campaign Financing in Canada and its Reform," in H. Penniman, ed., *Canada and the Polls: The General Election of 1974* (Washington: American Enterprise Institute, 1975), pp. 190, 192.

24.   Stanbury, *Money in Politics*, Ch. 5.

25.   For example, in 1989 and 1990 the Liberal Party of Canada (LPC) reduced its bank debt by about $2 million, but the members' equity is still negative. As important, beginning in 1989 various sources of funds were divided between LPC headquarters and the provincial or territorial association (PTA). Headquarters now has exclusive use of the Revenue Committee's list of large firms, the Laurier Club

(individuals who contribute over $1000), nation wide direct mail and the leader's dinners. The PTAs and the riding associations retain all the revenues from door-to-door canvassing, solicitation of individuals and small to medium-sized businesses, membership dues, local dinners, social events and direct mail within their own area. See Stanbury, *Money in Politics*, Ch. 5.

26. Stanbury, *Money in Politics*, Ch. 6.

27. That is, contributions from individuals, corporations, unions and other organizations whether raised by direct mail, personal solicitation or dinners.

28. Stanbury, *Money in Politics*, Ch. 6.

29. In 1988, for the first time, the NDP ran a truly national federal election campaign. The party spent over $2 million in Quebec, versus only about $50,000 in the previous election. It spent more than the Liberal Party on "election expenses" in 1988. For the first time, the party had to worry about "hitting the limit," rather than trying to shift outlays into the "election expenses" column so as to benefit from the 22.5% reimbursement. One effect of making such a major effort in Quebec was that "election expenses" in other provinces fell below the 1984 level in real terms. See Stanbury, *Money in Politics*, Ch. 6.

30. In 1984, 730 of 8744 union locals affiliated with the Canadian Labour Congress (CLC) were affiliated with the NDP. However, only 56.1% of all union members are in unions affiliated with the CLC. Overall, 7.3% of union members in 1984 were in locals affiliated with the NDP. See Keith Archer, *Political Choices and Electoral Consequences: A Study of Organized Labour and the New Democratic Party* (Montreal and Kingston: McGill-Queen's Press, 1990), pp. 51, 53.

31. Note that these figures are for federally-receipted contributions only. However, part of these funds are in fact spent on provincial political activities.

32. Stanbury, *Money in Politics*, Ch. 8.

33. In the case of the NDP federally-receipted contributions by individuals was divided by total federally-receipted contributions from all sources plus other income (non-receipted) plus the federal "election expenses" rebate.

34. Stanbury, *Money in Politics*, Figure 8-6.

35. A slight amount is due to the 22.5% rebate on "election expenses," but it is a smaller fraction of PC party revenues than it is of Liberal or NDP revenues.

36. In 1979, 1980 and 1988 contributions from individuals were only 17%, 27% and 27% respectively for several reasons. First, corporate contributions increased relative to individual contributions. Second, the election expense rebate is a source of revenue only available in election years. Third, the party received transfers from candidates of part of the reimbursement of their "election expenses."

37. Defined arbitrarily by the author as $2000 or more. The same threshold was used in 1983 as in 1989. During this period the CPI increased by 29%--hence $2000 in 1989 is equivalent of $1552 in 1983.

38. Paltiel, *Political Party Financing*, 1970, p. 29.

39. Stanbury, *Money in Politics*, Table 8-13.

40. *Ibid.*, Table 8-14.

41. *Ibid.*, Table 8-6.

42. *Ibid.*, Table 8-7.

43. *Ibid.*, Table 8-4.

44. *Ibid.*, Table 8-6.

45.   *Ibid.*, Table 8-11.

46.   *Ibid.*, Table 11-1.

47.   Between 1980 and 1988 the fraction of corporations making a contribution to a federal party and/or candidate ranged from 2.4% (1987) to 9.1% (1984, an election year)-- see Stanbury, *Money in Politics*, Table 11-7.

48.   Stanbury, *Money in Politics*, Table 11-4.

49.   After the 1974 election Prime Minister Trudeau imposed a limit of $25,000 annually on contributions to the Liberal Party from any corporation and twice that in an election year.   Party fund raisers were not pleased.

50.   A large contribution is arbitrarily defined by the author as one of $10,000 or more in nominal terms.   Between 1983 and 1989, the CPI increased by 28.9%, which means that a contribution of $10,000 in 1983 is equivalent in real terms to a contribution of $12,890 in 1989.

51.   Stanbury, *Money in Politics*, Table 11-6.

52.   Stanbury, *Money in Politics*, Table 11-6.

53.   *Ibid.*, Table 11-6.

54.   *Ibid.*, Ch. 11.

55.   *Ibid.*, Table 11-17.

56.   The Chief Electoral Officer uses the term contributions to refer to <u>all</u> forms of revenue received by candidates.   Candidates often receive <u>transfers</u> from their riding association and provincial and territorial associations as well as from party headquarters in Ottawa.   We use the term total revenues to refer to all sources of revenues.

57.   Stanbury, *Money in Politics*, Table 12-9.

58.   Pursuant to Bill C-169 in 1983 the requirement that the candidate's "personal expenses" exceeding $2000 be included in "election expenses" for the purpose of calculating the limit was eliminated.

59.   Note that candidates have to obtain at least 15% of the votes cast and the reimbursement is subject to two minor variations.

60.   This term is the author's.   It is not the same as "surplus" as defined by the CEO which is computed taking into account "other expenses."

61.   Stanbury, *Money in Politics*, Ch. 12.

62.   Pascale Michaud and Pierre Laferriere, "Economic Analysis of the Funding of Political Parties in Canada" in F. Leslie Seidle (ed.) *Issues in Party and Election Finances* Vol. 5 of the Research Studies for the Royal Commission on Electoral Reform and Party Financing (Toronto: Dundurn Press, 1991).

63.   Stanbury, *Money in Politics*, Table 12-30.

64.   Michaud and Laferriere, 1991.

65.   Andre Blais and Elisabeth Gidengill, "Attitudes About Electoral Institutions in Canada" (Study for the Royal Commission on Electoral Reform and Party Financing, March 1991, mimeo).

66.   *Ibid.*

67.   F. Leslie Seidle, "The Election Expenses Act: The House of Commons and the Parties" in J.C. Courtney (ed.) *The Canadian House of Commons: Essays in Honour of Norman Ward* (Calgary: University of Calgary Press), p. 125.

68.   House of Commons, *Debates*, October 25, 1983, p. 28299.

69. *National Citizens' Coalition Inc. v. Attorney General of Canada* (1985) 11 *Dominion Law Reports* (4th) 481. Note that a case under the *Quebec Elections Act*, Bernier J. of the Quebec Provincial Court ruled that the legislation limits "not the right of free speech but the right to spend money to express oneself." *Boucher* v. *Centrale de l'Enseignement du Quebec*, Unreported decision, Quebec Provincial Court, February 10, 1982 (per Paltiel, "Canadian Election Expense...," 1987, p. 236).

70. (1985) 11 *Dominion Law Reports* (4th) 481 at p. 496.

71. Janet Hiebert, "Interest Groups and Canadian Federal Elections" (Study for the Royal Commission on Electoral Reform and Party Financing, April, 1991). The figure excludes voluntary labour, internal organizational or administrative costs. The largest expenditures were by the Alliance for Trade and Job Opportunities ($2.31 million), the Pro Canada Network ($752,247) and the Province of Alberta ($727,000).

72. Hiebert, "Interest Groups...," 1991, p. 25.

73. Note that the Alliance for Trade and Job Opportunities, funded by large business firms, "had no intention of becoming financially involved during the 1988 campaign but intervened following the leaders' debate [October 24, 25] as 'an attempt to save the Agreement'" (Hiebert, "Interest Groups...," 1991, p. 28). Note that support for the Liberal Party rose very sharply after the debates and "as late as the second to last weekend of the campaign, the numbers were too close to call." Hiebert ("Interest Groups...," 1991, p. 26) continues, "During the final week of the campaign, something happened. A significant shift in support occurred in which the Conservatives recovered."

74. Hiebert, "Interest Groups...," 1991, p. 27.

75. Royal Commission on Electoral Reform and Party Financing, *Final Report: Reforming Electoral Democracy*, Vol. 1 and 2 (Ottawa: Minister of Supply and Services, 1991). The recommendations are summarized in Vol. 2, pp. 267-336. To reduce the number of citations, the relevant page numbers and volume number have been inserted in the text.

76. Stanbury, *Money in Politics*, Ch. 3.

77. Joseph Wearing, "The High Cost of High Tech: Financing the Modern Leadership Campaign" in George Perlin, ed., *Party Democracy in Canada: The Politics of National Party Conventions* (Scarborough, Ont.: Prentice-Hall Canada, 1988), p. 72.

78. A Tory official interviewed by the author contends that leadership races and the nomination process are the true fulcrums in the political process. It is here that individuals/groups can obtain the greatest leverage for their efforts (money, organization/campaign work, etc.) on behalf of a candidate. Note that the motives of the backers may be benign (helping a friend to gain a position of power with no desire for reward other than being appreciated), or they may be questionable (e.g., access/information to be used in one's business or profession).

79. In the Liberal Party's 1990 leadership campaign, the Party issued tax receipts for $1.89 million of the approximately $6 million raised by the six candidates ([Toronto] *Globe and Mail*, November 8, 1990, pp. A1, A4).

80. [Toronto] *Globe and Mail*, January 19, 1990, p. A6.

81. Wearing, "The High Cost...," p. 82. In July 1986, Ontario became the first jurisdiction in Canada to publicly regulate the financing of leadership campaigns. Candidates must register with the Commission on Election Finances, file an audited statement of their revenue and expenses and disclose the names and amounts of all contributions over $100. However, there are no limits on either contributions or on

expenditures (as there are on total contributions to parties and/or candidates and on expenditures by candidates). Further, constituency associations are prohibited from contributing or transferring funds to a leadership contestant. Note also that contributions to a leadership contestant are not eligible for Ontario's individual or corporate tax credits. See *Election Finances Act, 1986* S.O., 1986 Chapter 33 as amended by 1987, Ch. 5 and 1988, Ch. 16. Sections 15, 30(2), 43(4).

82.   Charlotte Gray, "Purchasing Power," *Saturday Night*, March, 1989, p. 18.

83.   Robert Mason Lee, *One Hundred Monkeys: The Triumph of Popular Wisdom in Canadian Politics* (Toronto: MacFarlane Walter & Ross, 1989).

84.   Robert Sheppard, "Broadview Liberal has $130,000 head start on opponents," *Globe and Mail*, October 6, 1988: A10.

85.   R.K. Carty and Lynda Erickson, "Candidate Nomination in Canada's National Political Parties" (Study for the Royal Commission on Electoral Reform and Party Financing, April, 1991).

86.   Stanbury, *Money in Politics*, Table 12-25.

87.   Carty and Erickson, "Candidate Nomination...," Table 1.5.

88.   While Bill C-79 in 1987 would have permitted an association to register itself through the party, it did not require a local association to publicly report all funds received and what use is made of those funds, although most of this money was provided out of public funds (Stanbury, *Money in Politics*, Ch. 2).

89.   Reginald Whitaker, *The Government Party: Organizing and Financing the Liberal Party of Canada, 1930-1958* (Toronto: University of Toronto Press, 1977).

90.   Stanbury, *Money in Politics*, Ch. 13.

91.   See *Maclean's*, February 23, 1976, pp. 14-15.

92.   Greg Weston, *Reign of Error* (Toronto: McGraw-Hill, Ryerson), pp. 39-40.

93.   In the U.S. surpluses from election campaigns have been used for purely personal purposes although federal law requires disclosure of how any surplus is spent. The 1979 legislation allows members of Congress to give unused campaign money to a charity, the member's political party, or to return it to contributors. Members elected before 1980, however, can keep surplus campaign funds for personal use upon their retirement (see *Time*, July 4, 1988, p. 2; *Newsweek*, June 6, 1988, p. 41).

94.   Bruce Wallace and Ross Laver, "Private Funds and the Parties," *Maclean's*, September 12, 1988, pp. 10-12.

95.   Weston, *Reign of Error*.

96.   Wallace and Laver, "Private Funds..."

97.   Stanbury, *Money in Politics*, Ch. 6.

98.   Volunteer labour is a contribution by a person made on his/her own time. Self-employed volunteers cannot perform services for which they would otherwise be paid. If a "volunteer" is paid, the value of his work is deemed to be an election expense.

99.   Chief Electoral Officer, *1986 Satutory Report of the Chief Electoral Officer of Canada* (Ottawa: CEO, 1986), p. 10.

100. Hugh Winsor, "Flawed Expenses Law Real Culrpit," [Toronto] *Globe and Mail*, February 15, 1988, p. A2.

101. Lavalin Inc. (Masse's former employer) and two campaign workers pleaded guilty to three charges of making illegal contributions to Mr. Masse's campaign by paying the expenses of some volunteers working on the campaign. Such expenses must be paid by the candidate's official agent. Lavalin was fined $800 plus costs for a total

of $2400 ([Toronto] *Globe and Mail,* February 18, 1986, p.A3).

102. CEO, *Guidelines Respecting Election Expenses of Candidates,* 1988.

103. Volunteer labour means "any service provided free of charge by a person outside that person's working hours, but does *not* include service provided by a person who is self-employed if the service is one that is normally sold or otherwise charged for by that person" (CEO, *Guidelines,* p. 19). Volunteer labour includes unemployed or retired persons working any time, employees on unpaid leaves of absence and self-employed persons working any time if the service they are providing is one for which they do not normally charge.

104. The outlays may be made from the candidate's personal resources or out of funds advanced by his official agent.

105. Stanbury, *Money in Politics,* Table 12-25.

106. Stanbury, *Money in Politics,* Ch. 9.

107. CEO, *Guidelines Respecting Election Expenses of Registered Parties,* 1988, p. 41.

108. Gray, "Purchasing Power," p. 15

109. A similar pattern occurred for the 1984 election for both the PC and Liberal parties. See Stanbury, *Money in Politics,* Ch. 13.

110. Officials of the Conservative Party told the author in October 1990 that the Party "does not use any techniques to 'front end load' election expenses. It is our policy and indeed our practice to recognize expenses in the period they are consumed, rather than in the period they are incurred. That is, materials which are purchased in the period before a general election is called, but which are used during a general election and qualify as an election expense based on our interpretation of the statute, are recorded as election expenses in the Party's return."

111. Blais and Gidengill, "Attitudes...," 1991.

112. The author was denied copies of the minutes.

113. An obvious exception occurs where the CEO (or one of his subordinates) is receiving legal advice in respect to possible violations of the law.

PART THREE

Political Finance in Western Europe

5

Great Britain:
Twentieth Century Parties
Operating Under
Nineteenth Century Regulations

R. J. Johnston and C. J. Pattie

The income and spending of political parties in Great Britain has been a subject of political debate for over 150 years. While the salience of that debate has waxed and waned repeatedly over the years, it has never entirely subsided. In part, argument has concentrated on the difficulties of applying legislation designed for the late nineteenth and early twentieth centuries to elections held in the late twentieth century. In part, it has been conditioned by concerns that providers of funds might gain possible undue influence over the elected government. In part, also, controversy has been driven by the extent to which governments of each major party have tried to influence legislation so as to disadvantage its opponents.

In this chapter, we look first at the historical background to the present situation in Great Britain. (Although the legislation relates to the whole of the United Kingdom, to our knowledge nothing has been written specifically about the situation in Northern Ireland--where the party system differs from that in Great Britain--and so our entire discussion relates to the British rather than the UK context.) We turn then to a survey of trends in party income and expenditure. The final sections deal with the impact of party spending on recent election results and on current issues relating to the possible reform of the law as it relates to party finance.

British Party Finance and the Law

Charting the changing nature of party finance and the development of legislative controls to the present involves a recapitulation of some key moments in British political history. Britain's movement towards a mass democracy during the nineteenth and early twentieth centuries was marked by increasing legal regulation of the income and expenditure of British political parties. We discuss some of the most important developments; for more detailed accounts, see Ewing[1] and Pinto-Duschinsky.[2]

The Development of Legislative Control

In his major text on the subject, Pinto-Duschinsky[3] describes three main historical "eras" of British party finance since the early nineteenth century:

(1) The Aristocratic Era (up till 1883);
(2) The Plutocratic Era (1883 to c. 1922); and
(3) The Modern Era (c. 1922 to the present).

Each era is marked by a distinctive "regime" of party income and expenditure and legislation. This should not be taken to indicate a series of "clean breaks" with the past, however. Each era contains, to a greater or lesser extent, remnants of the previous one. The questions of interest to us here are: (i) how did each regime operate? (ii) how and why did governments try to legislate on party finance, and how effective were they? and (iii) how did the political parties respond to the changing regimes?

For much of the nineteenth century, party income and expenditure were marked by high costs and, by modern standards, corrupt practices. Both main parties, the Liberals and Conservatives, relied for a large proportion of their income upon gifts and donations from the landed aristocracy. Despite the two Reform Acts of 1832 and 1867, which began the process of extending the franchise to ever-larger proportions of the British population and which attempted to remove the worst excesses of the "Old Corruption," elections were won or lost in each constituency effectively by the size of the candidates' "war-chests" of campaign funds. Bribery was rife in electoral competitions. In 1832, 850 of the 1000 voters of Stamford were bribed. In the twenty-five years following the Reform Act of 1832, 443 petitions were presented to invalidate parliamentary elections on the grounds of various electoral malpractices.[4] Even after the passage of the 1867 Reform Act, Pinto-Duschinsky estimates, corrupt practices remained common in at least half of the English borough (i.e., urban) constituencies.

Aristocratic era campaigning was very much a rich man's game. No limit was placed upon candidates' abilities to spend, beyond their ability to raise sufficient income. Party organizations at both local and national levels contributed very little to the costs of constituency campaigns, relative to the amounts expected from individual candidates (one estimate for the period 1874-1880 has Conservative central office spending almost nothing on campaigns, while candidates were spending around £500,000 at 1880 prices).[5] As a result, only the most wealthy could afford to fight an election; many seats were uncontested as few potential candidates could raise the funds necessary to mount an effective campaign. In effect, the aristocracy not only bankrolled the routine income of the main parties, but also provided many of their candidates. Entering Parliament brought its own benefits in the shape of power and access to patronage, so, despite the difficulties imposed by the sheer cost of fighting a seat, there was rarely any real difficulty in finding someone willing to pay the cost.

A number of factors in the second half of the nineteenth century combined to bring the Aristocratic era to an end, however. The extension of the franchise from around 440,000 after the passage of the 1832 Reform Act to 2,230,000 after the 1867 Act made election campaigns under the existing conditions increasingly expensive: quite simply, there were many more voters to bribe. The 1872 Ballot Act carried this process further by introducing the compulsory secret ballot for general elections, thereby cutting the clear link between bribe and vote that had existed under public voting. Also, the latter half of the century saw the emergence of stronger party loyalties and the effective "nationalisation" of party politics, as both Liberals and Conservatives began to contest more seats, hence cutting the proportion of MPs who were returned unopposed. Another consequence of this development was that the patronage powers of individual MPs declined as they increasingly became the creatures of their parliamentary parties.

Even so, candidates' election expenses remained very high into the 1870s and 1880s. What finally ended parties' reliance on the landed aristocracy for funds were two events in the 1880s. First, a serious economic recession hit British farming, weakening severely the economic position of the landed aristocracy. Second, a general sense of revulsion over the effects of the costs of and methods employed in election campaigns led to the passage of the Corrupt and Illegal Practices (Prevention) Act of 1883. Much of current British legislation controlling election expenses has its origins in this Act. Reflecting concern over wealthy candidates' ability to buy votes, the Act introduced strict limits on the amount of money allowed to be spent on an electoral campaign in a constituency, placed tight controls on which sorts of expenditure were permitted and which were banned (removing almost all scope for the grosser bribes), and applied strict rules of accountancy and accountability for local campaign spending, making the candidate and the candidate's agent responsible for every item of spending on the campaign.

The 1883 Act had mixed effects on the major parties. Limitation of the amount of campaign spending allowed in each constituency meant that the costs of campaigning remained relatively steady, despite a growing electorate. However, the loss of wealthy candidates, able and willing to pay for their own election, and the growth of a true two-party system, with electoral competition in almost all constituencies, meant that increasing demands were being placed on central party organisations to fund local constituency campaigns.

At the turn of the century, therefore, the Liberals and the Conservatives were both faced with the need to find new sources of income to fund their activities and campaigns. The Liberals, and later the Conservatives, increasingly turned from the declining old order of the aristocracy to the new plutocracy of successful businessmen and industrialists. Not only was there a shift in the main backers of the two major parties, however, but there was also a change in the financing of campaigns.[6] Unlike the aristocracy, few of the new business class had a direct interest in seeking elected office. They did desire the prestige that went with aristocratic titles, however; the parties were able to exploit this wish by offering to use their influence over the honours system, when in government, to gain preferment and titles for their backers, so that "[b]y the beginning of the twentieth century, titles were being marketed by the party managers like merchandise."[7] Both the Liberals and the Conservatives were able to build up considerable reserves of money in their central party funds from this trade to pay for local campaigns in the early years of the present century.

The "beginning of the end" for the plutocratic system of party finance came at its zenith. The First World War caused the suspension of normal party politics and hence removed the drain on party reserves caused by election expenditure. This notwithstanding, the Liberals and the Conservatives continued in their trade of titles for cash and thereby massively increased their reserves during the war years to levels which almost took them beyond the need to raise further funds.

In 1916, with Conservative support, the leading Liberal politician, David Lloyd George, ousted Asquith, the Liberal Prime Minister. In the process, Lloyd George split the Liberal party and cut himself off from the considerable reserves built up by the Asquithian Liberal party headquarters.[8] It was only to be expected, therefore, that he too should use his newly-won discretionary powers as Prime Minister and turn to the sale of honours to build up his own "war-chest" of campaign funds. The National Liberal-Conservative coalition put together by Lloyd George in 1916 to fight the remainder of the war easily won the first election of the peace in 1918, beating the "official" Asquithian Liberals and the newly emergent Labour Party, and Lloyd George was able to continue the sale of honours into the 1920s. Economic problems in the first years of the new decade quickly tarnished his government's appeal, however, and in 1922 his Conservative coalition partners withdrew their support, bringing down his government. The sale of honours contributed to his downfall.[9] The June 1922 honours list, seen by Lloyd George as a "last chance" to meet his commitments to his backers before an impending, and possibly unwinnable, election, contained some conspicuously questionable names, and became a cause celebre.

Ultimately, the furore raised by the Lloyd George "honours scandal" brought the plutocratic system of party finance to an ignoble end: in 1925 the Honours (Prevention of Abuses) Act was passed, making it a criminal offence to accept "any gift, money, or valuable consideration as an inducement for procuring ... the grant of a dignity or title of honour," thus effectively closing the door to the sale of titles for party funds.

The seeds of the contemporary "era" of party finance had already been sown, however. In the era of mass democracy ushered in by the 1884 Reform Act, the great disadvantage of the aristocratic system of party finance, and to an extent of the plutocratic system too, was that members of the working class, now the largest section of the electorate, found it almost impossible to enter parliament. The Labour Representation Committee (the precursor of the modern Labour Party) was set up in 1900 by a number of trade unions and several socialist societies to help remedy this situation.

Election candidates for the new party had their expenses paid by the trade unions and by the socialist societies. This marked a considerable departure in party finance, in that the soon-to-be Labour Party was reliant for its funds not on individual but on institutional sources. The institutions (unions and socialist societies) in their turn raised their donations to the party from subscriptions among their memberships.

In the early years of the century, Labour's income from the trades unions could not rival that of the Liberals and Conservatives from plutocratic sources. However, for its size, the party had a large and reliable source of funds. Even so, that income base was open to challenge.[10] In 1908, the Liberal secretary of a branch of the railworkers' union took legal action to declare his union's political levy of funds for the Labour Party illegal under the terms of the Acts passed between 1871 and 1876 which legalised trade unions.

This was a major threat to the future of the new party, but two factors helped alleviate the problems for Labour. First, in 1911 the Liberal government enacted legislation which, for the first time, made MPs' salaries a charge on public expenditure. This removed a major financial burden from the parties, which had previously met MPs' costs from their own funds. Second, during the period prior to the First World War Labour worked alongside the Liberals in a loose electoral pact: in return for the Liberals giving Labour candidates an unopposed run in selected constituencies, Labour MPs helped support the Liberal party in parliament. As a result, the Liberals were unwilling to see their partner go under, and, in 1913, introduced a Trade Union Act which overturned the 1908 ruling against political levies. Under the new Act, the unions had to ballot their members on whether to have a political levy. Only if a majority of the membership voting supported a levy could the union proceed with one.

However, a vote on a levy was a once-and-for-all event, and was binding on future generations of union members. Individual members' rights were to be protected by arrangements for "contracting out" of the levy if they did not agree with it. This, critics of the legislation argued, allowed the unions to rely on the apathy of their members to keep up the volume of their contributions to Labour, since many members would oppose a levy, but would be unwilling or insufficiently concerned to contract out.

This concern notwithstanding, the 1913 Act assured Labour's financial future. The party was able to build up a sizeable war-chest from union levies during the War, ready for the 1918 peace-time election, when it began its rapid ascent to major-party status, eclipsing the Liberals as the second party in British politics by the mid-1920s.

The other parties, increasingly faced from 1925 onwards with a problem of finding funds due to the effective removal of plutocratic sources, responded to the new environment in different ways.[11] The Conservatives were the more flexible, becoming less reliant upon donations from individual businessmen, and drawing increasingly upon contributions from corporations. In essence, they have continued this practice to the present (see below). The Liberals, on the other hand, already weakened by splits and by the 1922 "honours scandal", were less quick to adapt. Years of financial "good times" for the party had atrophied its organisation, especially at the local level, and the Liberals found it difficult to regain momentum and to find new funding sources. By the first few post-World War Two elections, Liberal central funds were so depleted that the party could no longer afford to run candidates in every constituency, and the Liberals ceased, for some thirty years, to be a truly national political party.

In the first decade after the First World War, successive governments took further steps to control party finances. Two Acts were of particular importance. The first, the 1918 Representation of the People Act, had broadly the same impact on all parties. It continued the spirit of the 1911 Act concerning MPs' salaries, in that it further increased those areas of political spending which were effectively subsidised by the state.[12] The 1918 Act extended state funding to several aspects of constituency election campaigns: (i) it covered the costs of voter registration, previously met by the candidates in each constituency; (ii) it made provision for a postal subsidy, paying for one free electoral communication from each candidate in a constituency to each elector; (iii) it met the basic costs of hiring meeting places during the campaign; and (iv) it paid the returning officer's (the local election official) fee in each constituency. All of these changes released substantial amounts of money for other campaigning activities by the candidates.

Other legislation was more partisan in its intention and execution. As mentioned above, the 1913 Trade Union Act legalising political levies had been the subject of some criticism, especially over its provisions for contracting out. This controversy has resurfaced at various times ever since. One of the earliest occasions was in the aftermath of the unsuccessful 1926 General Strike. A Conservative government, fearing the possibility of a Communist take-over, and looking for some means of punishing the unions for their part in the strike, introduced legislation in 1927 which replaced the "contracting out" clause in the 1913 Act. In its stead, they introduced a "contracting in" clause, whereby individual union members had positively to opt to contribute to the political fund: ministers sought to use their own "apathetic union member" argument to their own advantage.

Clearly, this presented a problem to the Labour Party, newly established as the second force in British politics. Economic recession was already cutting away at the party's financial base, as unions lost members, and hence contributions to the political levy, through unemployment. Those union members remaining were less likely to contribute themselves to the party's funds: the percentage of unionists paying the levy fell from 75 in 1925 to 48 in 1938.[13] Not surprisingly, when Labour won a landslide majority at the first post-World War Two election in 1945, one of their first actions was to repeal the 1927 legislation and return to the 1913 Trade Union Act and the "contracting out" clause. Even so, it is arguable that the 1927 legislation had only a limited effect on the party's finances, since unions raised the levy on those contracting in to cover the shortfall.[14]

The Contemporary Legal Framework

With some alterations to take account of price inflation, the major legal structures controlling party finance in the post-war period were instituted in the later years of the nineteenth century and in the first half of this. Most of them have been discussed above. In this section, we draw attention to: (1) some anomalies in the contemporary legal framework; (2) current controls on party campaign spending; and (3) recent political controversies over party finance. The contemporary legal framework is discussed in more detail by Ewing [15] and Rawlings. [16]

Anomalies in the Legal Framework

Two anomalies deserve particular attention here. First, there is a disjuncture between national and local campaigns. Second, the incomes of the two major parties, Labour and Conservative, differ in legal status.

As argued above, much of the legislation controlling campaign spending emerged either late last or early this century. It is hardly surprising to find, therefore, that legislation does not reflect some of the realities of a changed world.

When the major legislation was first enacted, between 1883 (the Corrupt Practices Act) and 1918 (the Representation of the People Act), general elections were genuinely local affairs. The contest decided the composition of the national parliament, but was fought by local candidates in each constituency. The main way of reaching the electorate was via constituency mass meetings, canvasses and mail drops. The bulk of party election spending was thus incurred by candidates in the constituencies, and the main thrust of legislation was to control spending at that scale.

Since then, however, major advances in communications technology, beginning with national newspapers, extending with the introduction of radio and cinema, and culminating in television, have lessened the parties' reliance on a series of strong local campaigns. Increasingly, campaigns are fought at a national scale, and the bulk of party spending goes on that national campaign: buying advertising space in the national press, paying for marketing consultants, and so on. Indeed, access to the electronic mass media of television and radio is, to all intents and purposes, free once the party has paid for the production of its broadcast: the costs of transmission are met by the broadcasting companies, and access is decided solely on the criterion of each party's share of the vote at the previous general election.[17]

Legislation has not kept pace with this reality, however, and the burgeoning cost of the national campaign is subject to very few constraints. Local campaigns, on the other hand, although of apparently decreasing importance in all but a few key marginal seats, are still subject to stringent controls. Parties are therefore able to sidestep the spirit of much of the legislation by concentrating their efforts on the national campaign. However, the existence of this national/local anomaly means that parties have to be careful in the treatment of their main spokespersons: these people have to be identified in the party's national campaign not as candidates for particular seats (in which case part of the cost of the national campaign could be charged to their--legally limited--local campaign expenses) but as national spokespersons.

The other anomaly concerns the different legal status of the incomes of the Labour and Conservative parties. As we saw above, and as we will see again, both parties at present are, and for much of the century have been, heavily reliant on institutional sources of finance. However, trade union donations to the Labour Party are much more tightly regulated by law than are company donations to the Conservatives. While unions have been obliged to hold a ballot among their members before opening a political fund, and also must allow individual members to opt out of the fund, there has been no comparable arrangement in company law.[18] As we will argue below, this situation became even more pronounced in the 1980s.

Current Controls on Party Campaign Spending

The current situation is anomalous in that it controls the level of spending in local (i.e., constituency) campaigns but applies very few constraints to national-level campaigning. Those controls derive in large part from the 1883 and 1918 Acts. The most recent legislation on campaign spending is contained in the 1983, 1985 and 1989 Representation of the People Acts. The 1983 Act consolidates previous legislation, and the later Acts remove anomalies and update the rules to take account of inflation. The 1985 Act gives the Secretary of State for the Home Office the power to alter the cash limits specified in the 1983 Act whenever he feels this is justified by inflation, subject to parliamentary approval, but without the need to bring in a new Act.

Under current law, parties are limited in their constituency campaign spending. The maximum permissible expenditure depends on the size and situation of the constituency. As of 1989, candidates in the (largely rural and small town) county constituencies can spend up to £3,648 plus 4.1p for every elector on the electoral register whereas candidates in the (urban) borough constituencies can spend up to £3,648 plus 3.1p for every person on the register (the Representation of the People [Variation of Limits of Candidates' Election Expenses] Order, 1989: Statutory Instruments 1989 no 634). Only spending which is directly sanctioned by either the candidate or his/her designated election agent is permissible under the law, however, and every candidate must submit a full account of expenditure to the returning officer for the constituency: all expenditure on items costing over £20 must be "vouched for by bill and receipt" (Representation of the People Act, 1985, s.14[1]: the limit was raised from £2 in the 1983 Act). Persons other than either the candidate or agent can add to campaign spending only where expenditure on an item is less than £5 (Representation of the People Act, 1985 s.14[3]).

The 1983 and subsequent Representation of the People Acts continued another "traditional" spending control on constituency candidates' spending, in the form of the deposit, which must be submitted to the returning officer for a constituency by all candidates in order to make their nominations valid. Deposits are returnable as long as candidates win more than a specified share of the constituency vote. The intention behind the deposit system is to remove "non-serious" candidates from the poll. Under the conditions of the 1983 Act, every candidate had to deposit £150, returnable if they won more than 12.5 percent of the vote. Inflation had reduced the "deterrent effect" of the deposit, however, and many key seats in the 1983 general election were contested by "joke" candidates seeking media attention. In response to this, the government raised the deposit to £500 in the 1985 Act. As a quid pro quo, however, it lowered the threshold necessary to retain the deposit to 5 percent of the vote (Representation of the People Act, 1985 s.13). This change was questioned at the time as an attack on democracy, making it more difficult for citizens to stand for election. At by-elections since the change, and at the 1987 general election, however, there was little appreciable difference in the participation of non-mainstream candidates from that previously encountered.

Recent Political Controversies over Party Finance

After the revocation of the 1927 Trade Union Act by the 1945 Labour government, the basis of funding for the Labour Party remained the same for almost forty years: it depended heavily on unions' political levies, which were backed up in their turn by the "contracting out" clause. Many Conservatives, in particular, remained strongly opposed to this. Until the 1980s, however, no government was willing to tackle the issue, but the election of a new Conservative government under Margaret Thatcher in 1979 heralded a change. From early in its period of office, the Thatcher government showed itself more willing than its predecessors to confront the unions.

In 1984, early in the Thatcher government's second term, Tory concerns over union power and a covert desire to damage Labour party finances came together in a new Trade Union Act, the main feature of which was its attempt to remove unions' political funds. The 1913 Trade Union Act had enforced a ballot of union members before a political fund could be established, but had no clauses allowing for a fresh membership ballot on the continuation of a fund once it had been started. Many trade unions, therefore, were raising a political levy on the basis of ballots held before most of their current members had joined the union. The 1984 Act sought to remedy this by enforcing a mandatory ten-year cycle on political fund ballots: unions now have to hold a fresh, and secret, ballot every decade to sanction continuing with a political fund.

There can be little doubt that, together with the professed aim of democratising unions' internal affairs, the 1984 Act had a more direct political motive. Senior Conservatives were well aware that many trade union members had not voted for the Labour Party at the 1983 general election.[19] They hoped that this would result in substantial majorities against the continuation of union political funds, with the clear implications this would have for Labour.

Not surprisingly, the 1984 Trade Union Act proved highly controversial. Labour MPs pointed out the double standards which forced unions to consult their members over contributions to political parties but did not similarly involve controls forcing companies to consult their shareholders. This undoubtedly added to the perception of the legislation as partisan. Many Conservative MPs were equally critical, but on the grounds that they felt the Act did not go far enough. Many, indeed, had hoped for the return of the "contracting in" rules contained in the 1927 legislation. Instead the 1984 Act retained "contracting out," but forced unions to inform members of their individual right to opt out of the political levy, whatever the outcome of the ballot.

The results of the ballots were rather different from that expected, however.[20] Under the Act, every union which had not held a ballot of its members on a political levy in the nine years preceding the 31st of March 1985 had to do so by the 31st of March 1986. Thirty-seven unions found themselves in this position and, after some initial protests, went ahead with ballots. Much to the relief of the union leaders and the Labour Party, and to the discomfiture of the Conservative government, every union which held a ballot in this period opted to retain its political fund. Even worse for the government, some unions which had not previously had a political fund used the legislation to begin one (for instance, the Inland Revenue Staff Federation and the National Union of Knitwear and Hosiery Workers), and some unions have broadened the range of their political activity using those funds.[21]

General Trends in Party Income and Expenditure

Because British party finance legislation has focused exclusively on expenditure by candidates during individual constituency campaigns only, there are no comparable data showing long-term trends in the total financing of political parties. Furthermore, even at the constituency level it is just the spending during the relatively brief official campaign which is subject to the legal constraints, so local party finance is under scrutiny for only about five weeks in every 200 (assuming a general election every four years and an official campaign period of five weeks). Thus for most of our information on British party finance we are dependent on what either the parties themselves or those who fund them are prepared to divulge. Such information has been compiled for the period 1830-1980 by Pinto-Duschinsky,[22] and updated by him for the period since.[23] This section, which concentrates on the "Modern Era", relies substantially on his material, plus that obtained for the Committee on Financial Aid to Political Parties (1976--the "Houghton Committee") and which Pinto-Duschinsky[24] has used in his standard text on the subject. Each party is considered in turn.

The Conservative Party

Figure 5.1 shows the general trends in income for the Conservative Party centrally. It shows that over the period the volume increased more than fourteenfold in general election years (i.e., 1950 to 1987-88) and some sixteenfold in non-election years (i.e., 1952 to 1986-87). Broadly, the party's income in election years was approximately double that in adjacent non-election years throughout the period, with the increases being obtained largely from donations. (During the period, inflation was very substantial of course: from 1922 to 1987 the retail price index increased about eleven-fold.)

Most of the Conservative Party's income from donations comes from both individuals and corporate bodies who see a Tory victory as highly desirable for their particular interests. The party itself does not declare this income publicly, but work by the Labour Research Department (which is funded by the trades

FIGURE 5.1 Conservative Party Central Income Since 1950

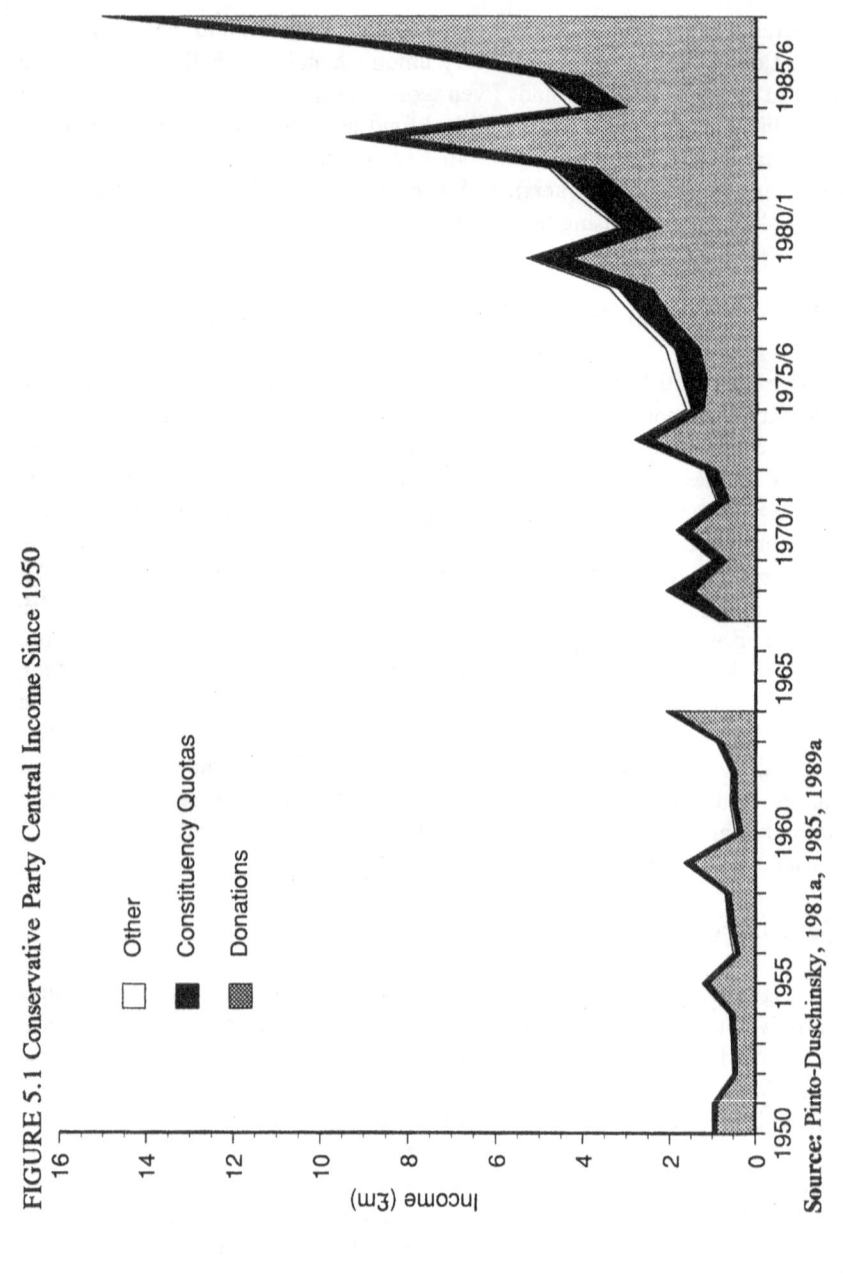

Source: Pinto-Duschinsky, 1981a, 1985, 1989a

unions and not by the Labour Party) using published company accounts has identified many of the major sources. In 1989, the Department reported (in Labour Research, Volume 78, Number 10) that in the 1987-88 election year there were 397 separate political donations to the Conservative Party by companies totalling £5,250,238 compared to only 246 (to a value of £2,930,624) in the following year. In each year these donations comprised the majority of all political donations identified in company accounts by the researchers. The totals were 495 (£5,771,278) and 296 (£3,212,134) respectively: the implication is that the other donations went either to other political parties or to campaigning groups. Thus in the election year the Conservative Party received 80 percent of all company political donations and 91 percent of all the money donated: in the succeeding non-election year its percentages were 83 and 91 respectively.

Many of the donations which did not go to the Conservative Party directly nevertheless went to bodies which supported the Conservative cause, such as British United Industrialists (on which see the article in Labour Research, Volume 77, Number 7, 1988), the Economic League, and the Centre for Policy Studies; some of the contributors to these organisations also gave directly to the party. In its election year survey for 1987 (Labour Research, Volume 77, Number 12, 1988), the Labour Research Department identified only 26 donations (totalling £115,248) to other political parties: 11 to the Social Democratic Party, 2 to the Liberal Party, 12 to the Alliance of the two parties, and one to the Labour Party. The largest donation to the Conservative Party in that year was £167,000 by an investment trust: eight other companies donated £100,000 or more.[25]

Many Conservative MPs, including ex-Ministers, have close connections with some of these donor firms. Additionally, many of the private sector industrialists involved have received peerages or other honours from the Conservative governments of 1979 onwards. Walker lists eleven industrialists who obtained peerages between 1979 and 1985, all of whom were directors of companies which made substantial donations to the party during that period: in addition, 64 industrialists were knighted, of whom 44 directed companies which were donors in those years.[26] Comparing the Thatcher government to that led by Heath a decade earlier, Walker concludes that the former was much more likely to honour her party's financial sponsors than was her predecessor. Such a trend caused a leading political journalist, Adam Raphael, to write in *The Observer* (23 December 1990) that "No Prime Minister this century, with the exception of Lloyd George, has been more ruthless or calculating in the use of patronage than Mrs Thatcher." He reminded his readers that Lloyd George's blatant selling of honours (at £100,000 for a peerage, £40,000 for a knighthood and £10,000 for a baronetcy[27]) led to the passing of the Honours (Prevention of Abuses) Act.[28] Raphael then continues:

> Of course, the award of honours is now conducted with slightly more discretion. But the correlation between those who give large sums of money and those who receive high political honours remains disturbingly close...
> During Mrs Thatcher's period as Prime Minister, 17 private sector industrialists have been made peers. Between them their companies contributed more than £5 million to the Conservative Party or one of its front organisations.

That works out, he notes, at about £300,000 per peerage (and other data suggest to him a "price" of £150,000 per knighthood).

With regard to expenditure, the amount spent by the party centrally on elections grew from only £135,000 in 1950 to £8,700,000 in 1987-8, or 63-fold (Figure 5.2) : even allowing for inflation, this is a massive increase which reflects the growing sophistication of campaigning and its associated costs.[29] Perhaps as a consequence of this, and especially the costs of computerisation and computer use in the campaign plus aspects of party presentation to the media, the 1987 election saw the end of what Pinto-Duschinsky[30] represented as a virtual standstill in the real costs of the campaigns centrally. At 1984 prices, the 1983 election cost the party less than that in 1929 (Figure 5.3), and he wrote that:

> ... national level spending by the Conservatives had reached its modern levels, in real terms, by 1929. The national campaigns in 1979 and 1983 have been more expensive for the two main parties than those of 1966-1974 but cheaper than those of 1959 and 1964 and, for the Conservatives, far cheaper than those of 1929 and 1935.

Four years later, his data for 1987 showed a doubling in the cost of the central campaign over the 1983 figure, in real terms[31]--though of course we cannot generalise about a "new trend" from one observation!

In the constituencies, most of the money spent by the Conservatives is raised locally, either by the constituency party itself or by its affiliated ward parties--which may be given fund-raising quotas. Individual party subscriptions (annual dues) and separate donations generally account for no more than one-quarter of all the income raised, and most is obtained through separate fund-raising efforts, which represents a major development in the party's local operations according to Pinto-Duschinsky.[32] The main feature of Conservative finance since 1945 has been the party's relative success in harnessing the enthusiasm of local party members for fund-raising purposes. In recent decades, small-scale social events have yielded as much money for the Conservative party as company contributions.

This success has allowed the local parties to employ their own agents, and to be relatively independent of the central organization, which has received and used the bulk of the corporate donations.

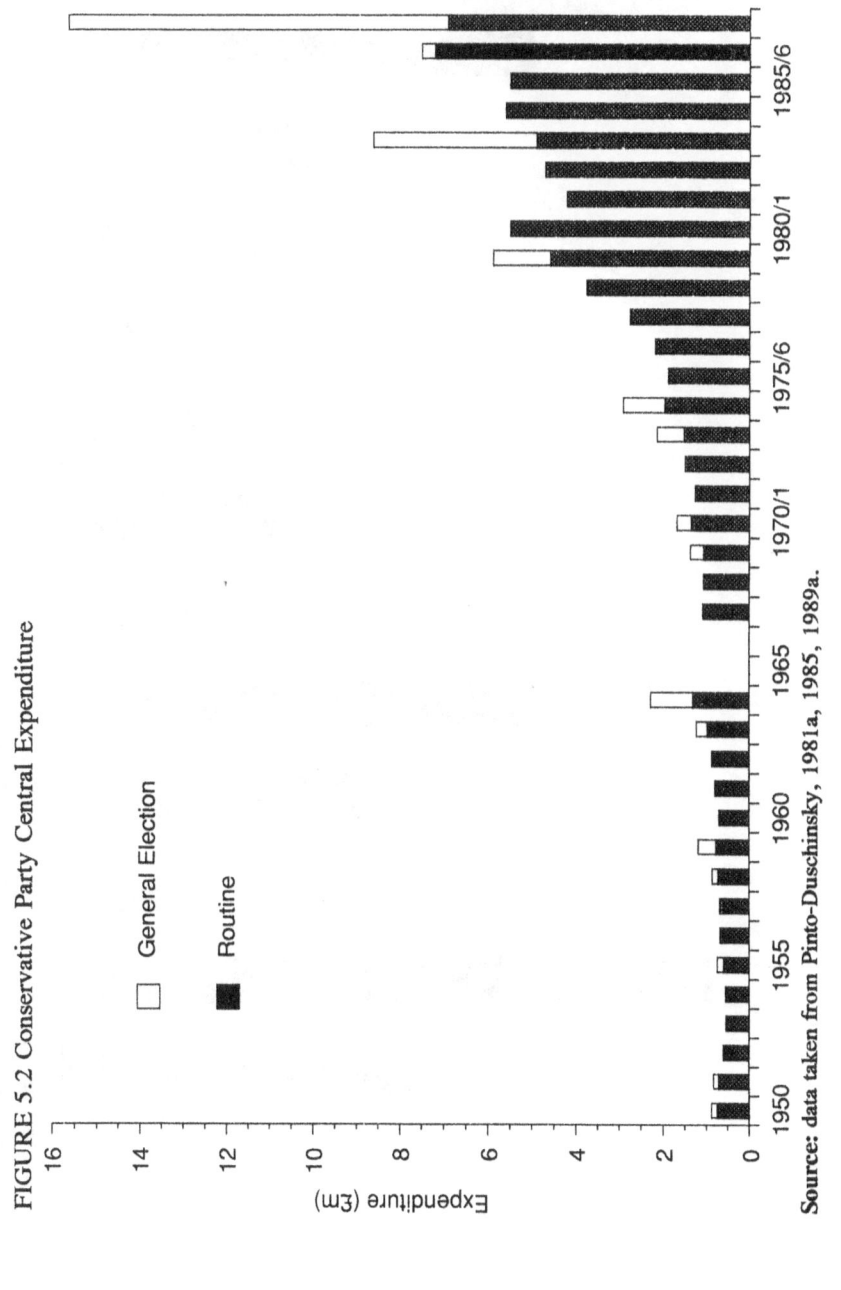

FIGURE 5.2 Conservative Party Central Expenditure

Source: data taken from Pinto-Duschinsky, 1981a, 1985, 1989a.

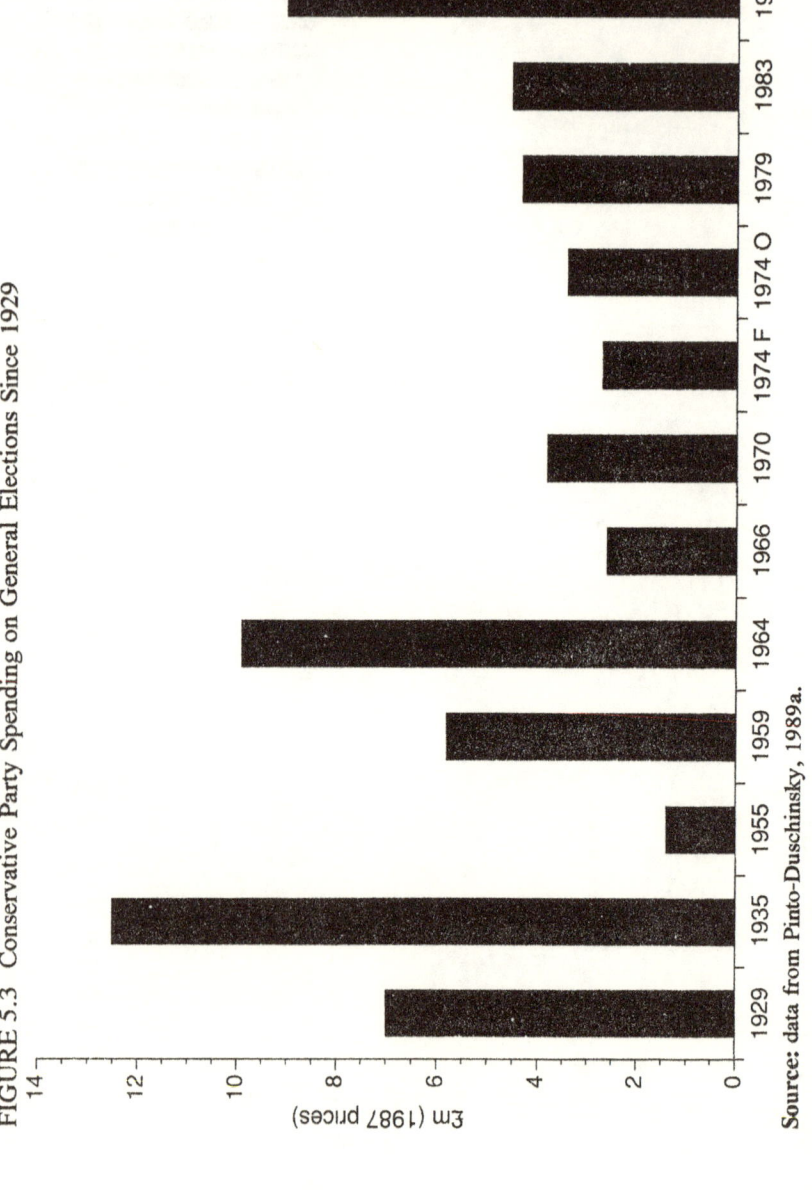

FIGURE 5.3 Conservative Party Spending on General Elections Since 1929

Source: data from Pinto-Duschinsky, 1989a.

In non-general election years most of the income obtained by constituency parties, according to the "Houghton Report" data for the mid-1970s, was spent on two items--salaries and office expenses: local elections, which are held in most years, used up on average only 8 percent of the available funds. In general election years, the costs of the constituency campaign also have to be met.However, this represents only a small sum relative to the routine expenditure, because of the constraints on constituency campaign spending: Pinto-Duschinsky[33] estimates that during the four years between the 1966 and the 1970 general elections, and including the latter but not the former, Conservative constituency associations spent nearly £10,000,000, of which the 1970 general election campaign accounted for only 6 percent. Most money is spent in the constituencies on the day-to-day party activities, and very little on mobilizing the electorate in the few weeks of the general election campaigns. By comparison, he shows that during the same period total expenditure centrally was about £5,000,000, of which about 13 percent was spent on the 1970 general election campaign.

Of the money which is spent during the official general election campaign period, the great majority--because of the constraints imposed by the Representation of the People Act--goes on advertising. Printing and stationery costs have consumed about 80 percent of the moneys in recent years (for all parties, not just the Conservative); most of it is spent on leaflets distributed to voters, and on posters; purchasing of advertising time on radio or TV is precluded.

The Labour Party

Comparable data to those in Figure 5.1 are given in Figure 5.4 for the Labour Party centrally and indicate the importance of income from the trade unions. In most years, union affiliation fees accounted for the bulk of the income: these are based not on the numbers of members in the affiliated unions but on the numbers that the unions choose to declare--which may actually exceed their membership. (One reason for declaring and paying the fees for more members than are actually affiliated is to increase the size of a union's block vote at the Labour Party Conference.) In recent years, constituency affiliation fees, representing the number of individual party members, have increased as a percentage of the central party's total income. In general election years, these affiliation fees account for much smaller proportions of the total income, however, because of the additional donations obtained towards campaign costs, most of them from the unions.

Since 1950, the Labour Party's income centrally increased from £292,000 in a general election year (1950) and £202,000 in a non-election year (1952) to £10,000,000 in an election year (1987) and £6,100,000 in the preceding non-election year: the growth rates were 33- and 29-fold respectively. These are about twice the rates reported above for the Conservative Party. They indicate substantial "catching-up" by Labour, which nevertheless had an income only about two-thirds that of the Conservative Party in the 1987 election year (compared to less than 30 percent in 1950). Labour's central general election expenditure increased between those dates from £78,000 to £4,4000,000--or 55-fold, which was less than the Conservative figure. In 1987 Labour spent little more than half of that reported by the Conservative Party on its attempt to win the general election.

For the Labour Party, as with the Conservative, the costs of the 1987 election centrally were substantially larger than those for 1983--£4,700,000 compared to £2,800,000 in 1987 prices (Figure 5.5). It was not the first time in recent decades that Labour expenditure had increased substantially: there was at least a doubling in real terms between 1955 and 1959, almost a doubling between 1959 and 1964, and more than a doubling between 1966 and 1970--though between 1964 and 1966 expenditure dropped by some 67 per cent (see Figure 5.6). In 1981, Pinto-Duschinsky concluded that Labour's "election spending has grown in real terms since the postwar years":[34] it apparently stabilised between 1979 and 1983 (perhaps reflecting the party's internal difficulties at that time plus the associated formation of the break-away Social Democratic Party). In 1987 "the campaign was, in real terms, a record equalled only by the cost of its effort before the 1964 election."[35]

Just as donations from private sector companies to the Conservative Party have drawn considerable critical comment, so the reliance of Labour on the trades unions for electoral finance has been the subject of attention: Pinto-Duschinsky reports that the trades unions contributed 93 percent of Labour's Head Office election income in 1987, when the eight largest union contributors provided £3,019,363 in affiliation fees plus a further £3,008,820 in special donations to the party's general election fund.[36] In addition, as he points out, the unions also contributed to "front organisations" such as Trade Unions for Labour, which spent £202,000 on posters and leaflets between April and June 1987, and "Individual unions also produced anti-Conservative literature during the campaign."[37] This flow of income led Bogdanor to conclude not only that there is virtually no corruption in British political party finance but also that the current arrangements "seemed, until recently, to be operating effectively in sustaining a working two-party system in which the financial gap between the major parties, although real, was not such as to impose an insuperable handicap upon the financially weaker party--Labour."[38]

Local Labour parties draw income from both subscriptions paid by individual members and trade union affiliation fees, but they have increasingly relied, like their Conservative counterparts, on local fund-raising initiatives. The data collected for the "Houghton Report," and used by Pinto-Duschinsky,[39] suggest that gambling schemes run by the parties provide their major source of income. The sums raised are not especially large, however, and few of the local

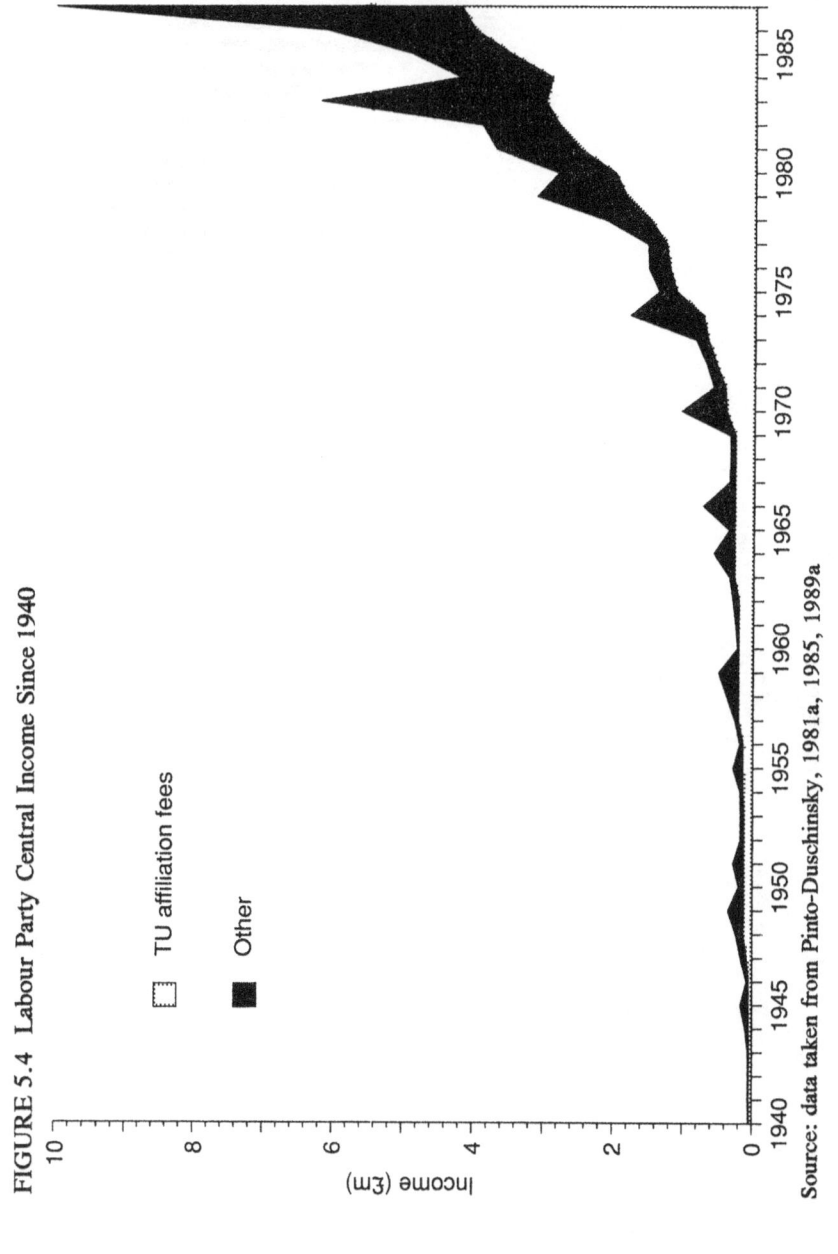

FIGURE 5.4 Labour Party Central Income Since 1940

Source: data taken from Pinto-Duschinsky, 1981a, 1985, 1989a

FIGURE 5.5 Labour Party Central Expenditure Since 1940

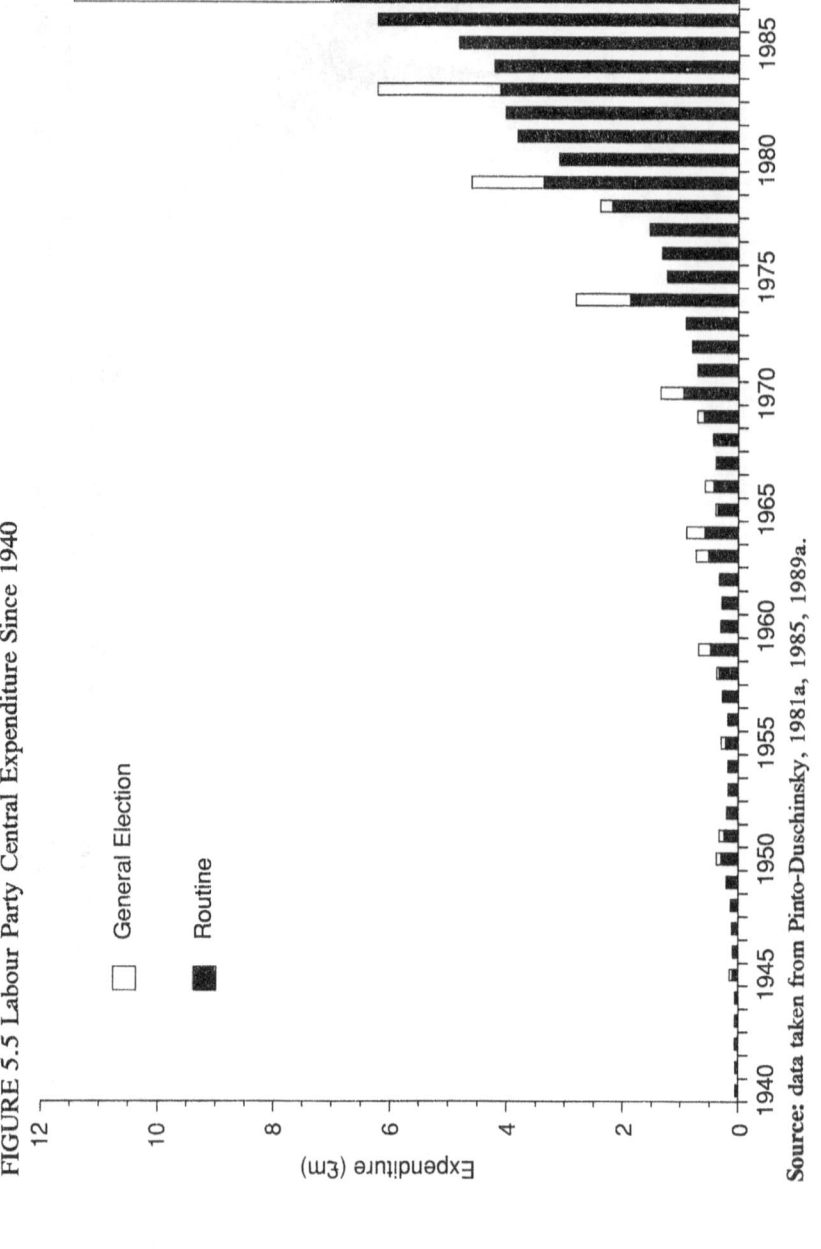

Source: data taken from Pinto-Duschinsky, 1981a, 1985, 1989a.

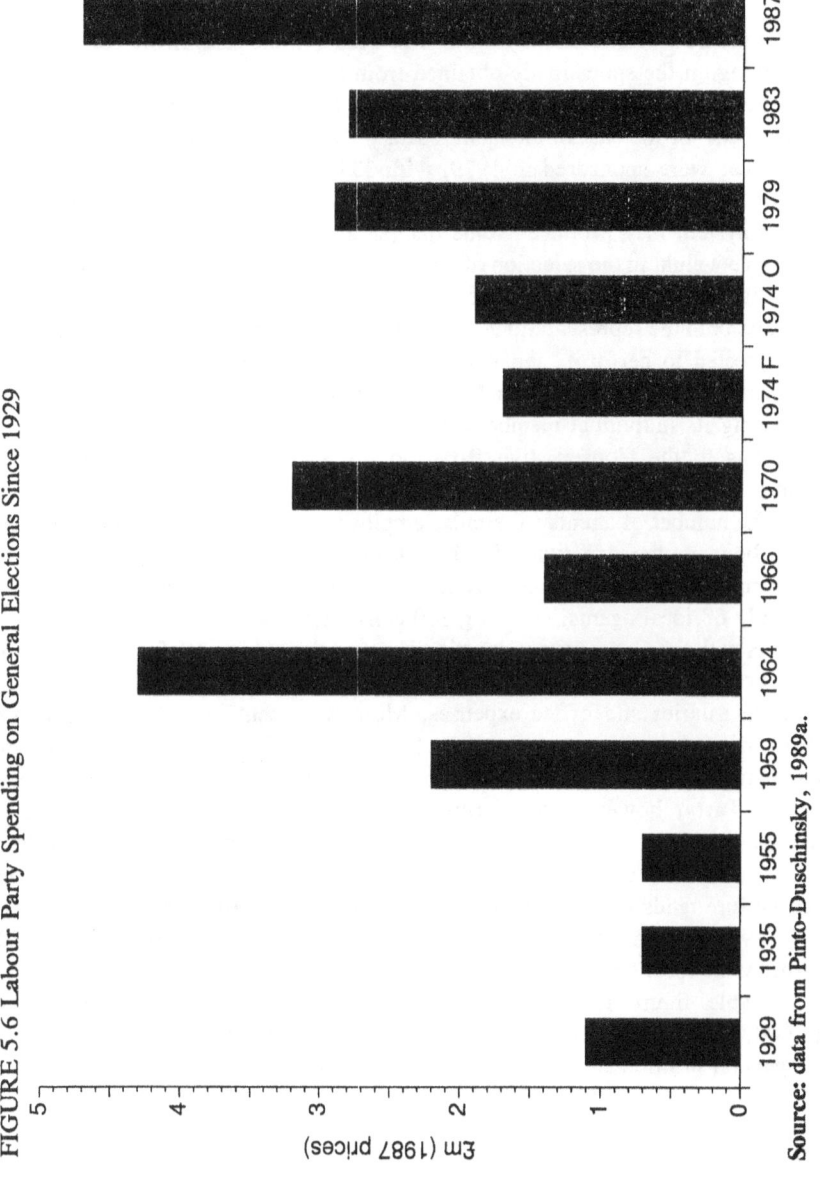

FIGURE 5.6 Labour Party Spending on General Elections Since 1929

Source: data from Pinto-Duschinsky, 1989a.

parties are now able to employ a full-time agent. In the past, many could do so by relying on the sponsorship obtained from trades unions--such sponsorship involved paying up to 80 per cent of the candidate's expenses and 70 per cent of the cost of an agent's salary. Bogdanor reports that 165 Labour candidates were sponsored in 1979, with 134 of them elected--almost exactly half of the total Labour Parliamentary delegation: this led him to conclude that such a system may produce "some danger that the trade unions are given an excessive weight in the selection of parliamentary candidates as opposed to other interests equally deserving of representation."[40] He further suggests that this "distorts both the representational and the policy-making functions which parties are expected to perform; and it may serve to inhibit popular participation in politics by allowing the Labour Party to maintain its financial viability without increasing its individual membership." (In contrast, he argues that "company donations to the Conservative Party do not yield voting privileges for the donors, nor any other form of *direct* political power" [our italics].)

The number of agents (or similar employees with different titles) employed by Labour in the constituencies has declined substantially in recent years. Between 1951 and 1970 it fell from 296 to 141.[41] Two decades later, Labour had only 68 local agents, covering 100 constituencies.[42]

As with the Conservative constituency associations, most of the expenditure by constituency Labour parties in non-general election years in the mid-1970s went on salaries and office expenses. More was spent by Labour in relative terms on local elections. Because the average Conservative constituency association spent 2.5 times more per annum than the average constituency Labour Party, however, the former spent more in absolute terms on local election expenses (£384 compared with £331). Local Labour parties spend less in "normal years" than their Conservative counterparts, so their general election expenditure tends to be relatively higher. Pinto-Duschinsky's estimates for the 1970-1974 Parliamentary election cycle suggest that of the nearly £4,000,000 spent by the local Labour parties 18 per cent went on campaign expenditure: the comparable figure for the Party nationally was 10 percent (of just over £3,000,000).[43] Centrally, therefore, the Labour Party spent relatively less on the general election campaigns than did the Conservative Party.

The Liberal Party (Liberal Democrat from 1988 Plus the Social Democratic Party, 1981-1987)

The Liberal Party has a fragmented central organization and full details of the income and expenditure of its various parts are not known.[44] In general terms, the party is much poorer than either Conservative or Labour, because, as Pinto-Duschinsky describes it:

> The central Liberal party has not been bereft of support from some companies
> and from individual subscribers. However, these sources have been erratic.
> ... The party has benefited from bursts of generosity by individuals and
> companies...but it has not been able to make longterm financial commitments
> in anticipation of obtaining such donations.[45]

Its partner in the Alliance for the general elections of 1983 and 1987--the Social
Democratic Party (SDP)--similarly lacked secure income from either companies
or trades unions. It relied heavily on one corporate backer (a member of the
Sainsbury family) plus relatively large membership fees paid by individuals.

Liberal Party central income and expenditure is more difficult to enumerate
than that for Conservative and Labour, but Pinto-Duschinsky's data suggest that
it has traditionally been small: even in 1987, for example, it was reportedly
obtaining and spending less than £750,000.[46] The SDP rapidly achieved a
central income in excess of £1,500,000 per annum, though this fell away after
1983 to less than £1,000,000 in 1986-87: according to Pinto-Duschinsky, "The
resounding political success of the Liberal-Social Democrat Alliance in the
election of June 1983 was not matched by the new grouping's fund-raising
success in 1983-7."[47]

Locally, the Liberal Party has traditionally relied on individual donations
and fund-raising activities to sustain constituency organisations, though "Poor
Liberal organization has gone hand in hand with rudimentary record
keeping."[48] The local parties were much poorer than their Conservative and
Labour counterparts, and "have frequently been unprepared to foot the bill of
a parliamentary campaign without assistance from central party funds or from
the candidates themselves. Where money has been unavailable from these
sources, many Liberal associations have simply declined to put forward a
candidate."[49] Central grants to local party organizations are much more
common with the Liberals, therefore (as they were also with the SDP in 1983
and 1987, especially for the seats it identified as "winnable" and also those being
defended by SDP members). Thus locally, over the 1970-1974 parliamentary
cycle 20 percent of Liberal Party expenditure was on the 1974 general election
campaign, as was 12 percent of the Party's central expenditure.

The Impact of Party Spending

Very little work has sought to evaluate the impact of party spending in the
United Kingdom, especially at the national level. In large part this is because of
the great difficulties involved in establishing a baseline: it is almost impossible
to identify the counterfactual situation--the relative electoral position that the
parties would occupy if either there were no spending at all or all parties spent
the same amount.[50] Some attempts have been made, especially by those

concerned with reforming the law of party finance,[51] to establish whether one party benefits more than another from the current situation; as detailed below, however, no firm steps have been taken on the basis of the cases presented.

Each of the last three general elections has been followed by a major conference on the campaign and its impact, with selections of the papers then published.[52] These have focused almost exclusively on the national campaign; though extremely informative, these volumes have contained little in the way of detailed evaluation of the campaign's impact.[53] Pinto-Duschinsky's conclusion for 1987 was simply that "its advertising, although not decisive, was useful to the Conservative campaign. ... If this assessment is correct, the election result was probably influenced by the financial superiority of Conservative Central Office."[54]

Compared to the paucity of information and the difficulty of evaluating campaign activity nationally, there is a plethora of data available on the campaign in the constituencies, because of the necessity to report spending under the Representation of the People Act. Both Gordon and Whiteley[55] and Rawlings[56] have pointed to likely "inaccuracies" in the reported data. These have been recognised by their analysts--e.g. Johnston[57] and Johnston, Pattie and Johnston[58]--who nevertheless point out that the relative pattern of spending is consistent with rational models of party behaviour. In the absence of anything better, these data allow some evaluation of the impact of party spending during the campaign period, if not of that during the interim years, which could be just as important in terms of mobilising the electorate. (Though it could be argued that strong local parties throughout the parliamentary cycle are likely to be those best able to raise money for local campaigns at general elections.) Somewhat surprisingly, therefore, political scientists and other electoral analysts have almost entirely ignored the potential of these data.

The one set of major studies of the impact of constituency campaign spending has been based on models developed in the United States. These have been summarised for the period up to and including 1983 by Johnston,[59] and updated for the 1987 general election in Johnston, Pattie and Johnston.[60] With regard to differences between constituencies in the level of spending (recalling that under the relevant Act the amount that can be spent is constrained), several hypotheses were presented[61]:

(1) a party's ability to raise funds for the campaign in a constituency is much greater if it holds the seat than if it does not;

(2) a party's ability to raise funds for the campaign in a constituency is greater if its candidate was also the candidate at the previous election than it is if a new candidate is being fielded; and

(3) a party's level of spending in a constituency reflects the constituency's marginality at the last election.

With regard to the impact of the money expended, it was hypothesised that

(4) a party's share of the vote at any election in a constituency is a function of the amount that it spends on the campaign.

These hypotheses were tested for all general elections from 1951 on where the data allowed (which required comparable constituencies at adjacent contests).

With regard to the first three hypotheses, the analyses produced substantial evidence to support the first and third, but little in favour of the second. Incumbent parties were better able to raise money and more was spent in marginal seats, but incumbent individuals had little effect on their party's fund-raising outcome. In other words, parties spent most on defending that which they held, especially where their hold was relatively tenuous, and on challenging for that which they had some hope of winning (the marginal seats held by their opponents). In general terms, the less money spent by a party overall the greater the concentration of its spending on the seats it already held and in the more marginal contests.

The first and third hypotheses assume rationality in the fundraising activities of constituency parties: they will work harder where they have something to defend (especially if their hold on it is under threat) and where they have a chance of electoral gain. But does this rational behaviour bring rewards, as suggested by the fourth hypothesis? The models tested allow for continuity in voting behaviour over time and have the general form:

$$OT2 = f (OT1, OS, TS)$$

where

OT1 and OT2 are the ratios between the number of votes gained by parties O and T at elections 1 and 2 respectively;
OS is spending by party O at election 2; and
TS is spending by party T at election 2.

In a regression format, the coefficient for OT1 should be positive and highly significant: that for OS should also be positive and significant (indicating that the more that a party spent the greater its proportion of the two-party vote total, ceteris paribus) whereas that for OT should be negative and significant (indicating that the more that a party's opponent spent the larger would be the opponent's share of the two-party vote total, ceteris paribus).

Overall, the weight of results of the tests of this fourth hypothesis clearly favours the argument that money spent by parties on advertising brings electoral benefits. In general, expenditure by challengers has more impact than that spent by incumbents (there being greater variation in the former), and money spent by the Conservative Party defending a seat is more likely to bring rewards than that spent by the Labour Party. Among challengers, the amount spent by the Liberal

Party had most impact overall and that spent by the Conservative Party had least. Over time, it seems that the impact of spending increased, even though in real terms--because of the limits imposed by the Act--less was being spent.

A paper on the impact of spending in Canadian elections asked, "Can you spend your way into the House of Commons?"[62] The answer was a qualified "yes". It is the same with the British House of Commons. Simulations have suggested that at certain elections different patterns of spending could have resulted in a substantial number of seats changing hands (notably in 1979, when Labour could have lost up to 40 percent of those which it won).[63]

The model employed in this work is a simple one. The majority of the money spent in local campaigns goes on advertising--or providing information about--the parties and their candidates.[64] According to the model the greater the advertising expenditure, the greater the market share: according to the tests, the model works. Local campaign spending in Great Britain has an electoral impact.

Reforming Party Finances

The legal framework covering British party finances is the product of over a century of legislation; much of it is obsolete and marked by major anomalies. As Johnston notes, however, "(a)t the present time, discussion of political finance is somewhat dwarfed by debates over reform of other aspects of the electoral system--notably the case for proportional representation."[65]

There have been some attempts at reform, however: the Conservative government's 1980s legislation on trade union political funds is a clear example. Over the last twenty years, concern over the funding of political parties has also stimulated the production of two major reports, one from the government-sponsored Houghton Committee (1976) and the other from the non-governmental Hansard Commission (1981). Both expressed concern over the main parties' falling incomes during the 1970s, an outcome, they argued, of rising inflation and declining party memberships.[66] This, it was felt, reduced the parties' effectiveness precisely at a time when the increasing complexity of politics and the growing responsibilities of government placed more demands on party expenditure in terms of campaigning, of organization, and of research and policy formulation. Furthermore, both reports pointed to the possibility of adverse consequences resulting from the two main parties (Conservative and Labour) relying upon strong institutional sources for most of their income (Labour on the trade unions, and the Conservatives on business; however, in July 1991 several businesses, including recently-privatised companies, indicated that as a reaction to the recession--and the assumed government responsibility for its depth and length--they were cutting their political donations to the Conservative Party.

Both committees recommended extensions to the current system of state aid for political parties, beyond the various subsidies-in-kind discussed above, to allow for direct grants to parties which could at least partially equalise their available financial resources. The Houghton Committee (1976, p.64), for example, recommended that:

> (i) annual grants ... be paid from Exchequer to the central organisations of the parties for their general purposes, the amounts being determined according to the extent of each party's electoral support; and (ii) at local level, a limited reimbursement of the election expenses of Parliamentary and local government candidates.

In their evidence to the Committee, both the Labour and the Liberal Party (though not the Scottish Liberal Party, which is a partly-separate organization from the English Liberal Party) favoured increased state aid to political parties. For the Liberals, in particular, a major attraction was that "state subsidies would ... reduce the dependence of the two main parties ... on corporate finance." This was of particular concern to the Liberals, because their party is "at a disadvantage compared with the Conservative and Labour parties in not having institutional support. Such a situation has a harmful effect on democracy in Britain" (Houghton Committee Report, 1976, p.9). Not surprisingly, the Liberal-Social Democrat Alliance of the early and mid-1980s and, since 1988, the Liberal Democrat Party have shared a belief and a financial interest in state funds for political parties. Labour, too, continues to support the principle, though less overtly.

Support for reform is not universal among parties, however, for the Conservative Party opposed state grants to political parties in its evidence to Houghton, and continues to. It argues that aid would decrease parties' freedom to criticise the state: parties are not the only victims of inflation and should not receive preferential treatment, it claimed, and argued that if parties are not sufficiently popular to rely on their own fund-raising then state aid would "only lead to further alienation" (Houghton Committee Report, 1976, p.7). Similarly, some trades unions and the right wing pressure group Aims of Industry were sceptical in their evidence to the committee, and four of the committee's members entered a dissenting report opposing the extension of state aid. (The academic community was divided on the issue, too.[67])

The Houghton Committee's recommendations were not acted on and were quietly forgotten by the minority Labour government of the time. The Conservative governments of the 1980s saw no advantage in reopening the issue, and no legislation has been proposed. Both main opposition parties (Labour and Liberal Democrat) remain in favour of some aid, however, leading Ewing to conclude that "the question is not whether, but when public subsidies for the parties will be introduced."[68]

Although state subsidies for political parties have received most attention, they are not the only potential reform which could be made to the legislation governing British party finance. As noted earlier, there is no general compulsion on political parties to disclose their annual accounts fully, so that evidence of sources of income and of patterns of expenditure is necessarily incomplete. Over the years, a number of commentators have argued that party accounts should be published in order to allow voters to see who "bankrolls" the parties and to what extent. In general, they have claimed that this would clarify whether backers have "bought" undue influence over parties' actions, especially when they are in government. An early contribution to that debate appeared in the Hansard Society's journal *Parliamentary Affairs* in 1948, when it published the opinions of each of the three then main parties. Labour and Liberal were broadly in favour of the publication of accounts (although the extent to which they produced complete accounts was open to question).[69] The Conservatives were opposed.[70] The matter was raised in a Private Member's Bill in 1949, but once again the Conservatives opposed reform, arguing that naming sources of funds would breach the individual's right to confidentiality and would limit the secrecy of the ballot. The Bill was not enacted.[71]

Whereas both Labour and Liberal (now Liberal Democrat) parties have published regular, if sometimes partial, accounts, the Conservative Party has been more reticent. Evidence of contributions from industry to the Conservatives relies upon research into company accounts, for instance. For a period in the early 1980s, the party refused to publish its own accounts and only pressure from the constituency parties forced the central office to resume such publication in 1985. Reform in this sphere, while not currently a strong concern, would seek to make it compulsory for all parties to account for their income and expenditure.

Similarly, there is some pressure, especially from the Labour Party's backbench MPs, to equalise the constraints on union and company donations to political parties. As we have shown, the Conservatives placed stringent controls on union political funds in the 1980s, but no equivalent controls pertain to company donations. There is no automatic right for shareholders to opt out of political donations if they do not agree with them, for example, nor do company directors have to consult their shareholders before making a donation. Some attempts have been made to regulate company donations, notably by Labour MPs Doug Hoyle (in his 1978 Companies [Regulation of Political Funds] Bill) and Ian Mikardo (in an amendment to the 1974-1979 Labour government's Companies Bill, which was lost at the dissolution of Parliament in 1979); they proposed that companies should only be allowed to make political donations if shareholders agreed.[72] Since 1979, the Conservative government has introduced no legislation in this area: a future Labour government may act.

Potential reform of party finances is not limited to income sources. As discussed above, one of the largest of the current anomalies is that although legislation limits campaign expenditure in constituencies there are no curbs on the national campaign. This, it could be argued, is to the advantage of parties with large incomes, and helps the Conservatives in particular. Some have contended, therefore, that there is a strong case for imposing a national maximum limit on campaign expenditure, which would equalise the parties' abilities to reach the electorate. There is a number of counters to this argument, However. As Pinto-Duschinsky points out, the main vehicle for the national campaign is television and the parties get free access to this via their quota of election broadcasts and by regular news coverage of their campaigns.[73] Furthermore, attempts to curb spending on press and billboard advertising (TV and radio advertising are not allowed) would have to deal with political advertising by non-party organizations. Two recent examples of this are the 1983 campaign against government spending cuts by the local government employees' union (NALGO) and the 1974 campaign against the nationalization of industry by Aims of Industry. Neither campaign directly encouraged the electorate to vote for a particular party, but each carried a clear anti-party message. Recent legislation has sought to limit trades unions' abilities to conduct such campaigns, but there is no comparable control on industry. What is more, legislation curbing national campaign spending would have to deal with the well-documented pro-Conservative bias in the British press, especially the mass-market sector.[74]

Overall, the probability of substantial changes to the law on party and campaign finance in Britain in the next few years seems low. The country may well enter the twenty-first century with legislation largely drawn up to cope with the situation in the nineteenth.

Notes

1. K. Ewing, *The Funding of Political Parties in Britain* (Cambridge: Cambridge University Press, 1987).

2. M. Pinto-Duschinsky, *British Political Finance 1830-1980* (Washington: American Enterprise Institute, 1981).

3. Ibid. p. 15.

4. Ibid.

5. Ibid., p. 24.

6. Ibid., p. 31ff.

7. Ibid., p. 32.

8. K. Morgan, *Consensus and Disunity: the Lloyd George Coalition Government 1918-1922* (Oxford: The Clarendon Press, 1979).

9. Ibid. and Pinto-Duschinsky, *British Political Finance*, p. 87.

152

10. Ewing, *The Funding of Political Parties, p. 49.*

11. Pinto-Duschinsky, *British Political Finance, p. 31ff.*

12. Ewing, *The Funding of Political Parties in Britain*, pp. 104-108.

13. Ibid., p. 51.

14. Pinto-Duschinsky, *British Political Finance*, p. 76.

15. Ewing, *The Funding of Political Parties.*

16. H. F. Rawlings, *Law and the Electoral Process* (London: Sweet and Maxwell, 1988).

17. Ibid., p. 155.

18. Ewing. *The Funding of Political Parties, p. 49.*

19. R. Rose and I. McAllister, *Voters Begin to Choose* (London: Sage Publications, 1988), p. 58.

20. D. Grant, "Mrs Thatcher's Own Goal: Unions and the Political Funds Ballots," in *Parliamentary Affairs*, Vol. 40, pp. 57-72.

21. J. Fisher, "Trade Union Political Funds and the Labour Party," Paper presented to the annual conference of the Elections, Parties and Public Opinion in Britain Specialist Group of the Political Studies Association, Worcester College Oxford, 28 September 1991.

22. Pinto-Duschinsky, *British Political Finance.*

23. M. Pinto-Duschinsky, "Financing the British General Election of 1989," in H.R. Penniman, ed., *Britain at the Polls* (Washington D.C.: American Enterprise Institute, 1981) pp. 210-240; M. Pinto-Duschinsky, "Trends in British Political Funding 1979-1983," in *Parliamentary Affairs*, Vol. 42, pp. 197-212; M. Pinto- Duschinsky, "Funding the General Election of 1987," in I. Crewe and M. Harrop, eds., *Political Communications: The General Election of 1987* (Cambridge: Cambridge University Press, 1989) pp. 15-28.

24. Pinto-Duschinsky, *British Political Finance.*

25. Pinto-Duschinsky, "Financing the British General Election."

26. J. Walker, *The Queen Has Been Pleased* (London: Secker and Warburg, 1986).

27. Morgan, *Consensus and Disunity.*

28. Ibid., p. 207; gives full wording of the 1925 Act.

29. K. Swaddle, "Ancient and Modern: Innovations in Electioneering at the Constituency Level," in Crewe and Harrop, eds., *Political Communications*, pp. 29-40.

30. Pinto-Duschinsky, "Trends in British Political Spending," pp. 340-341.

31. Pinto-Duschinsky, "Funding the General Elections of 1987," p. 206.

32. Pinto-Duschinsky, *British Political Finance*, p. 152.

33. Ibid., p. 148.

34. Ibid., p. 166.

35. Ibid., p. 24; Labour won in 1964 for the first time since 1950.

36. Pinto-Duschinsky, "Funding the General Election of 1987," p. 201.

37. Pinto-Duschinsky, " Trends in British Party Spending," p. 23.

38. V. Bogdanor, "Reflections on British Political Finance," in *Parliamentary Affairs*, Vol. 35, 1982, p. 150.

39. Pinto-Duschinsky, *British Political Finance.*

40. Bogdanor, "Reflections," p. 369.

41. D. Butler and M. Pinto-Duschinsky, *The British General Election of 1970* (London: Macmillan, 1971), pp. 269-271; The Conservative Party had 399 at the latter date, p. 281.

42. D. Butler and D. Kavanagh, *The British General Election of 1987* (London: Macmillan, 1988), p. 228.

43. Pinto-Duschinsky, *British Political Finance*, p. 174.

44. Ibid., p. 183.

45. Ibid., p. 209.

46. Pinto-Duschinsky, "Trends in British Political Funding,"; Pinto-Duschinsky, "Financing the British General Election."

47. Ibid., p. 202.

48. Ibid., p. 204.

49. Ibid., p. 206.

50. As Pinto-Duschinsky has said, "Judgements must necessarily be unscientific."; Pinto-Duschinsky, "Trends in British Party Spending," p. 27.

51. E.g., Ewing, *The Funding of Political Parties*, p. 125ff.

52. M. Harrop and R. M. Worcester., eds., *Political Communications: The General Election of 1979* (London: Allen and Unwin, 1982); I. Crewe and M. Harrop., eds., *Political Communications: The General Election of 1983* (Cambridge, Cambridge University Press, 1986,1989).

53. Though see, alternatively, W. L. Miller *et al.*, *How Voters Change.* (Oxford: The Clarendon Press, 1990).

54. Pinto-Duschinsky, "Trends in British Party Spending," p. 28.

55. I. Gordon and P. Whiteley, "Comment: Johnston on Campaign Expenditure and the Efficacy of Advertising," in *Political Studies*, Vol. 28, 1980, pp. 283-284.

56. Rawlings, *Law and the Electoral Process.*

57. R. J. Johnston, *Money and Votes: Constituency Campaign Spending and Election Results* (London: Croom Helm, 1987).

58. C. J. Pattie and Johnston, "The Impact of Constituency Spending on the Results of the 1987 British General Election," in *Electoral Studies*, Vol. 8, 1989, pp. 143-155.

59. Johnston, *Money and Votes.*

60. Johnston, Pattie, and Johnston, "The Impact of Constituency Spending."

61. R. J. Johnston, *Money and Votes*, p. 48.

62. S. Isenberg, "Can You Spend Your Way into the House of Commons?" in *Optimum*, Vol. 1, 1980, pp. 28-39.

63. Johnston, *Money and Votes*, p. 193.

64. R. J. Johnston, "Political Advertising and the Geography of Voting in England at the 1983 General Election," in *International Journal of Advertising*, Vol. 4, pp. 1-10.

65. Johnston, *Money and Votes*, p. 205.

66. Although see Pinto-Duschinsky, *British Political Finance*, chapter 10.

67. Pinto-Duschinsky, *British Political Finance*, chapter 10, has argued strongly against state aid, while, R. Rose, *The Problem of Party and Government* (Harmondsworth: Penguin Books, 1976), was in favour.

68. Ewing, *The Funding of Political Parties*, p. 130.

69. A. Greenwood, "The Labour View," in *Parliamentary Affairs* Vol. 1, 1948, pp. 47-49; P. Fothergill, "The Labour View," in *Parliamentary Affairs*, Vol. 1, 1948, pp. 50-53.

70. S. Pierssene, "The Conservative View," in *Parliamentary Affairs*, Vol. 1, 1948, pp. 49-50.

71. Ewing, *The Funding of Political Parties*, p. 11.

72. Ibid., p. 47.

73. Pinto-Duschinsky, *British Political Finance*, pp. 264-267.

74. Crewe and Harrop, *Political Communications: The General Election of 1983*; Crewe and Harrop, *Political Communications: The General Election of 1987*; Ewing, *The Funding of Political Parties in Britain*, pp. 187-188; Butler and Kavanagh, *The British General Election of 1987*, pp. 163-190; Miller *et al.*, *How Voters Change*, p. 277.

6

The New French System of
Political Finance

Thomas Drysch

Introduction

Because of the professionalization of politics in the past few decades, it became apparent in some Western democracies that in election campaign and party finance the traditional forms of fund-raising through membership dues and donations were no longer sufficient. Therefore, the parties in these countries sought to tap public sources. The situation of the political parties in France was especially serious. While the candidates were reimbursed relatively early for certain campaign costs, the parties were ignored financially and legally by the state. Not until 1988 were election campaign and party financing subjected to sweeping reforms and the overall role of the parties in France strengthened. In this chapter we shall discuss the previous and present legal regulations concerning election campaign and party finance in France, followed by an analysis of the effect on the political culture in France of these new regulations that were the result of far reaching legislation in 1988 and 1990.

In our review of the history of election campaign and party finance in France, it is necessary to differentiate between two distinct time periods. First, there is the dark chapter of party financing which ran like a red thread through the Fifth Republic until 1988. This phase was characterized by the weak position of the parties that were not even allowed to accept donations. There were no direct subsidies from the treasury. The parties often raised funds through illegal sources. Discussion of campaign and party financing in this period was in negative terms, because party funding was studded with scandals and corruption affairs. Party fund-raising was a complete mystery to the public. Transparency in campaign or party funding was not even an issue. It was impossible to receive even somewhat reliable figures concerning revenues and expenditures of the French parties,[1] since they were not required to account for their revenues and expenditures. Thus, it is of no surprise that one of the few books dealing with party financing bears the title *L'argent secret*, or secret money.[2] One of the most recent publications on this subject came to the conclusion that one could only guess how the French parties were financed.[3] As soon as one went looking for reliable information, one was confronted with difficulties.[4] Only the Communist Party published reports about its finances; however, the accuracy of this information is very questionable.[5]

The unsatisfactory situation regarding party finance finally led to a series of reform suggestions which did not bear fruit until 1988. As early as the beginning of the 1970s, the French National Assembly was presented with proposals for the reform of party funding that included restrictions with regard to campaign expenditures.[6] Furthermore, the introduction of public subventions to the parties in the form of subsidies for party organizations or reimbursement of campaign costs were considered. This took place at a time when other Western democracies, e.g., the Federal Republic of Germany, Austria, Italy or Sweden, had just had their initial experiences with public party funding. In the countries mentioned above, the parties had recognized that they were no longer in a position to finance themselves solely from membership dues and donations, while this still seemed possible for the parties in certain other countries like Great Britain and Switzerland.

In France the problem appears to have been even more serious at this point in time, since parties were not permitted to accept donations, and regulations limited the amounts charged for membership dues. The fact that the reform proposals during this time were not successful may be a reason for the many corruption affairs which had a negative impact on the political culture of France. One of the last unsuccessful reform proposals was the bill introduced in 1979 by former Prime Minister Raymond Barre. Its failure was attributed to the strong resistance of the Communist Party against public party funding.[7] The Communist Party was not plagued by any financial worries, because of their adequate legal and illegal financial sources, and they threatened to use all of the means of propaganda at their disposal to brand public party funding a self-service of the parties at the tax payers' expense.

The Socialist Party, whose candidate had to rely on the votes of the Communist Party in order to win the presidential elections, agreed to follow the position of the communists regarding political funding and rejected the proposal of Prime Minister Barre. The right-of-center coalition parties then felt they could not pursue their legislative proposals against the will of the opposition in light of the coming election. Thus it was not until 1988 that a public party finance law could be passed in the Assemblée Nationale, in which 29 proposals and a legal initiative had failed on previous occasions.[8] The reason finally for legislative success was the affair concerning the illegal arms sales to Iran. Due to this affair President François Mitterrand[9] pressured then Prime Minister, Jacques Chirac, to introduce legislation on election campaign and party finance prior to the presidential elections in April 1988.[10]

With the organic law "loi organique" no 88-226 of 11 March 1988 in respect to the transparency of finances in political life, and the law no 88-227 of the same day, light was to be brought into the murky waters of election campaign and party funding.[11] Since then direct public funding of parties as well as additional indirect public funding in the form of public reimbursement of candidates for election campaign costs exist in France. In the process parliament has tied together limitations of expenditures for election campaigns and accountability for parties and candidates. However, since not all the loopholes in the legislation could be closed through the laws of 1988, and given the fact that in the meantime new scandals in conjunction with party funding were made public, parliament saw the need once again to take action in this matter. The result is law no. 90-55 of 15 January 1990 concerning the limits on election expenditures and a clarification of the funding of political activities; and law no 90-393 of 10 May 1990 concerning the funding of campaigns of candidates in presidential elections and in elections for the Assemblée Nationale.[12] These laws complete the reform legislation and should now bring more transparency into the funding of election campaigns and political parties.

Aims of the Public Election Campaign and Party Funding

The funding of election campaigns and political parties through the private efforts of the party members and party supporters was previously the regular method of financing. Today there are only a few Western democracies in which the parties are without any form of public support. The introduction of public campaign and party finance in France raises the questions of the goals which are to be pursued by public funding and whether they have been achieved.

In part the introduction of public financing for election campaigns and political parties may be justified on the grounds of equal opportunity.[13] The public funds must contribute to the removal of the differing opportunities enjoyed by candidates and parties. This principle is disregarded, for example, if smaller parties are excluded from public funding.[14]

Furthermore, public funding of political parties should be designed to reduce or even to prevent the influence of lobbies upon the candidates and parties. A dependency of the political actors upon strong financial backers should be avoided. Nevertheless, at the same time public funding should not be allowed to create a dependency of the candidates and the parties upon the state.

Another goal is the avoidance or, if already present, abolition of corruption. Corruption encourages political cynicism and contributes to undermining the trust of the citizens in the legal order. Many examples of these dangers can be found in various Western democracies.[15]

Moreover, it is often hoped that in conjunction with public financing campaign costs can be subjected to certain expenditure limitations, thus assisting in the goal of achieving equal opportunity. If public funds are granted, however, it is necessary also to make the candidates and parties accountable for the use of the public funds.[16] Furthermore, controls are necessary for the realization of the goals of expenditure limits and the use of public funds. Once determined that legal regulations have been offended, the offender should then be penalized according to electoral law or even criminal law.

If these aims are achieved by the introduction of public party funding, one could place the expenses incurred under the heading, "costs of the democracy." On the other hand, if the goals are not achieved, it is then a question of the parties' dipping into the pockets of the taxpayers.[17]

Historical Review

From the very beginning of the Fifth Republic in 1958, French political parties occupied a weak position, even though they were guaranteed constitutional recognition in Article 4 of the Gaullist-inspired constitution which confirmed their role in electoral participation. General de Gaulle, however, disliked the parties and saw in them the cause of constant political unrest; he made them responsible for the division of the nation and accused them of an insincere willingness to compromise and of selfish behaviour.[18] In the politics of the Fifth Republic, General de Gaulle degraded the parties to a virtual state of meaninglessness and reduced their position to that of mere electoral associations. He limited the political influence of the parties and strengthened instead the role of the president who was elected directly by the public, with the aim of ending the domination of the parties.[19] Of course General de Gaulle revived the Gaullist Party at the beginning of the Fifth Republic after having disbanded it earlier; however, the purpose of this revival was to provide political support for himself as the president of the republic. The Gaullist Party was no longer a party in the real sense of the word. It had been reduced to an electoral alliance.[20]

De Gaulle's attitude towards the parties discouraged the founding fathers in 1958 from including a modern, more closely defined party provision in the Fifth Republic constitution. As a result parties were subjected to the law of 1 July 1901 relating to associations and all of that law's restrictions.[21] Article 6 of the law stipulates that membership dues may not exceed 100 Francs (about $ 20). However, the law did not make clear whether the 100 Francs were to be paid monthly or yearly. In any case this regulation hindered the collection of sizeable amounts of membership dues.[22] According to the law relating to associations, parties were also prohibited from accepting donations and gifts. Thus the possibility of receiving donations from legal and natural persons as member dues was prohibited. However, since the parties did not receive any direct payments from the treasury, the parties often obtained the funds by illegal means in order to finance election campaigns and their organization.

These historic barriers have contributed to the relative weakness of the French party system as compared with the strongly developed parties in most other Western democracies. While on the left side of the party spectrum there are two parties, the Parti Communiste Français (PCF) and the Parti Socialiste (PS), there are three parties on the right.[23] They are the neo-Gaullist party Rassemblement pour la République (RPR), the liberal Union pour la Démocratie Français (UDF) and the right extremist Front National (FN). In fact, however, the UDF is not a party, but rather an electoral alliance of three parties: Parti Radical-Socialiste, Centre des Démocrates Sociaux and Parti Républicain.

The electoral law supported the weak position of the parties. The single-member district or majority electoral law which had been in use up until the 1986 election of the Assemblée Nationale strengthened the position of the candidates as opposed to the parties. Thus an election proposal for the presidential election and the election to the Assemblée Nationale can be raised only by the candidates and not by the parties.

Election Campaign and Party Finance Prior to 1988

Election Campaign Funding

The foremost goal of the French election campaign legislation was to ensure equal opportunity among the individual candidates rather than to support the parties.[24] Thus it is of no surprise that until 1988 the subventions granted in France had been directed at the candidates. For election campaign funding, it is necessary to differentiate between presidential elections and the election to the Assemblée Nationale.

Presidential Elections. One of the few financial subsidies granted by the treasury up until 1988 was received by those presidential candidates who received more than 5 percent of the votes on the first ballot. Qualifying candidates were entitled to a flat rate for campaign costs in the amount of 250,000 Francs.[25]

During the presidential elections, the costs of certain campaign materials were also covered by the state. These included the costs for paper, printing and forwarding of ballots and the election programs of the candidates as well as the costs of approximately 154,000 election posters.[26] This entitlement to reimbursement was provided during presidential elections even if the candidate received less than 5 percent of the votes. In addition each candidate on the first ballot had the right to approximately two hours of television air-time at no charge.[27] The candidates on the second ballot each received an additional two hours of television air-time.

Furthermore, the candidates who received more than 5 percent of the votes were reimbursed for their deposits of 10,000 Francs[28] which they had to put up prior to the first ballot. If the candidate did not reach the 5 percent minimum, the deposit was forfeited.

Elections to the Assemblée Nationale. For the elections to the Assemblée Nationale, certain campaign expenditures of the candidates were also refunded by the state. Each candidate who received more than 5 percent of the district votes on the first ballot was reimbursed for the costs of a campaign letter sent to the voters in the constituency, for election flyers, and for campaign posters.[29] The decree of 17 August 1945 and the law of 6 October 1946 granted each candidate who ran for a seat in the Assemblée Nationale two posters of a specified format for the notification of the campaign program and two posters half as large with the announcement of the campaign events.[30]

In order to avoid uncontrolled placarding, these posters were permitted to be hung only in official poster areas designated by the municipalities. The number of poster boards authorized was determined according to the size of the municipality.[31]

All candidates who received more than 5 percent of the votes in their constituency were reimbursed for the aforementioned campaign costs. Depending on the size of the constituency, the costs per candidate may have amounted to over 10,000 Francs.[32] If the candidate received more than 5 percent of the votes, the deposit of 1,000 Francs put up prior to the election was also refunded.

Questions could be raised about the 5 percent clause which is still in effect today. On the other hand one must consider carefully the purpose of discouraging frivolous candidacies. Nonetheless, the seriousness of a candidate also becomes apparent at less than 5 percent. Although the 5 percent hurdle for the reimbursement of the deposit and the reimbursement of certain election campaign costs can be regarded as very high, the Conseil Constitutionnel has decided that the reimbursement of the deposit and certain campaign subsidies can be made dependent on attaining a 5 percent minimum vote share.[33] One might add somewhat cynically that the 5 percent clause helps keep national expenditures for political purposes within limits.[34]

Party Funding

Until 1988 there was no direct public funding of political parties. Only the reimbursement of certain campaign costs for the candidates contributed indirectly to the financing of party activities.[35] The parties also received the following individual support:

Television Air-Time. Every month 20 minutes of free time was made available to the parties represented in the Assemblée Nationale.[36] During election campaigns, the parties which were already represented in parliament received additional air-time at no charge.[37] This amounted to three hours prior to the first ballot and was distributed in equal shares among the governing and the opposition parties.

In 1986, after long and heated disputes between the communists and the socialists, the air-time was distributed as follows:[38]

Governing parties:		Opposition parties:	
Parti Socialiste	65 minutes	UDF	45 minutes
Parti Communiste	25 minutes	RPR	45 minutes

Prior to the second ballot, one-and-a-half hours of air-time were made available.

The parties that were not represented in the Assemblée Nationale, but had nominated at least 75 candidates for the first ballot each received seven minutes of free television time for the first ballot and five minutes for the second ballot.[39]

Basically, the amount of air time was based on the agreement by the participants themselves. Where there was disagreement, a mediation committee was summoned. Not only was the air-time for the parties free; production costs for the spots were also covered by the state. Otherwise, there were no other benefits for the parties provided by the state.[40]

Membership Dues and Party Assessments. While most parties stated that they financed themselves almost solely from membership dues, it was clear from the experiencies of other Western democracies that no party, no matter how many members it has, is capable of financing itself solely on the basis of membership dues. Only the Communist Party, which had many members, received a sizeable income from membership dues, and this was the result in large part of the discipline shown by their members in paying their dues.

One further source of party income was and still is today the party group or caucus assessment.[41] This is a sum of money members of the Assemblée Nationale have to pay their parties above and beyond their normal membership dues. As a general rule the more left-wing the party is, the higher the party assessment is. The highest assessments are those of the Communist Party, whose members of the Assemblée Nationale are required to transfer their entire salaries of 28,273 Francs[42] per month directly to an account of the party. In return they receive from the party the equivalent of wages of a skilled worker. This amounts to little more than 8,000 Francs. In the other parties a direct transfer of the parliamentary allowances has been rejected. Nonetheless, it is common practice for the members of the Assemblée Nationale to pay a certain amount to their party. Next to the communists, the socialist member of the Assemblée

Nationale must pay the highest assessment, i.e., 8,000 Francs per month. The assessments of the other parties are much lower.[43]

Illegal Ways of Funding. Since donations were prohibited, and direct public party funding was not available, the French parties raised the necessary funds increasingly through illegal means of financing. It is of no surprise, therefore, that the history of the French parties has also become a history of financial scandals.[44]

Thus Article 6 of the law relating to associations which prohibits the acceptance of donations has been circumvented in various ways.[45] There was often a resort to cash donations which was tolerated by government officials. For example, campaign costs which arose through opinion polls or printing costs were often paid by firms associated with the parties. Many companies signed fictitious contracts with the parties. A respected Senator, A. Diligent, even admitted in the newspaper *Le Monde* of 30 August 1986 that the government parties had received bribes for awarding foreign contracts.[46] Thus, Iraq is once supposed to have financially supported the Gaullist Party in return for French investment in Iraq.[47] And in the scandal surrounding the illegal arms deals with Iran, funds are said to have found their way into the coffers of the Socialist Party.[48]

One of the most important indirect funding methods may be seen in the "secret funds" which were made available to the government every year. These could be used to finance plans which were not to be made public on the grounds of raison d'état.[49] The government was not required to account publicly for the use of these funds,[50] which led constantly to speculations in regard to party funding. For many observers it was apparent that the governing party received direct allocations from these funds.[51] Thus the satirical weekly newspaper, Le *Canard Enchaîné*, reported that the government distributed approximately 12 million Francs to the candidates of its own party in 1978.[52]

Even at the municipal level, politicians were bribed who, for example, were responsible for the building permits for shopping centers. Thus in 1990 investigations were conducted concerning 35 politicians and individuals in Marseille. With forged invoices and several million Francs, the industrialists had influenced the decision-making process by several mayors and their parties about the building permits and sites of new super-markets.[53]

The parties or the candidates are said to have received further illegal benefits from the municipal administrations. The party work of at least 60 staff members of the Socialist Party was directly funded through the municipal budgets in Lille and Marseille which were governed in the mid-1980s by socialist mayors. According to common opinion, there is no doubt that the proven practices of direct or indirect allocations of municipal offices to the parties is only the tip of the iceberg.[54]

In addition the Communist Party is believed to have received substantial financial support for years from its sister-parties in the eastern European countries.[55] Due to the recent political changes in Eastern Europe, there can be little doubt that this source in the meantime is no longer available.

Election Campaign Funding Since 1988

Since the laws no 88-226 and no 88-227 of 11 March 1988 went into effect, a comprehensive system of public election campaign and party funding has been in the existence. Law no 88-226 governs the funding of the election campaigns of the presidential candidates and of the candidates of the Assemblée Nationale. This "loi organique" (organic law) was passed with 320 votes of the RPR, the UDF and the ultra-rightwing Front National against 36 votes of the Communist Party. The deputies of the Socialist Party did not take part in the vote.[56]

Parallel to this law, the law no 88-227 was passed. This law established for the first time public party funding and guaranteed the tax deductibility of donations to candidates. The bill was passed with 287 votes of the RPR and the UDF against the votes of the Communist Party and the Front National. This time the Socialist Party also abstained from voting.

Public Election Campaign Funding

Prior to the enactment of the election campaign and party funding laws of 1988, the state was required to provide partial reimbursement to candidates for certain campaign costs such as the printing of ballots, campaign letters to the voters as well as the costs for campaign posters. Even after the promulgation of the new laws, the old regulations remained in effect with regard to reimbursement of certain campaign costs for the candidates.[57] This pertains to the presidential elections as well as to the elections to the Assemblée Nationale.

Presidential Elections. The provisions of law no 88-226 of 11 March 1988 on the transparency of the finances in political life are suggested by the title of the law. Therefore, Article 1 requires that the presidential candidates disclose their financial circumstances prior to the election. The required statement is to be given to the Conseil Constitutionnel by all presidential candidates prior to the election. The statement of the elected president is printed shortly after the election in the *Journal Officiel* of the French Republic.[58] Before the end of the term of office or in the case of resignation, the president is required to present a new statement which is also published in the *Journal Officiel*.

Article 2 of this law governs the public financing of election campaigns of the presidential candidates. Above and beyond the previous reimbursement of expenses, the candidates of the presidential election now receive a set sum as a flat rate reimbursement for campaign costs.[59] Candidates who win less than 5 percent of the votes receive six million Francs. The candidates who have cleared the 5 percent hurdle are entitled to public subventions amounting to 30 million Francs. The two candidates on the second ballot receive an additional five million Francs, or a total of 35 million Francs. For the next election in 1995 the presidential candidates on the second ballot will receive a flat-rate campaign cost refund amounting to 40 million Francs. The payment of the flat rate for campaign costs is based on the condition that the respective candidate actually incurred so many expenses during the campaign.[60]

For the 1988 presidential election, President François Mitterrand and his challenger, Jacques Chirac, who lost on the second ballot, each received the campaign cost refund amounting to 35 million Francs. Three candidates who obtained between 6.8 percent and 16.5 percent of the votes on the first ballot each received 30 million Francs, while the four candidates who received less than 5 percent of the votes (with the exeption of Pierre Boussel who only spent four million Francs and was therefore only entitled to a reimbursement of campaign costs in the amount of his expenses) each received six million Francs. Consequently, the costs to the state for the direct election campaign refund amounted to a total of 182 million Francs for the 1988 presidential election.

Elections to the Assemblée Nationale. Like the presidential candidates, the members of the Assemblée Nationale must prepare a statement about their wealth.[61] This statement must be submitted to the bureau of the Assemblée Nationale two weeks after taking office. A second statement is required at the end of the term of office.

Candidates for a seat in the Assemblée Nationale are also entitled to a flat rate campaign cost refund.[62] Those candidates who obtain more than 5 percent of the votes in their constituency receive public support amounting to 50,000 Francs. The remaining candidates receive nothing.

Decision of the Conseil Constitutionnel. The French constitutional court, the Conseil Constitutionnel,[63] explained in a review of the "loi organique" no 88-226 of 11 March 1988, which concerns the candidates' election cost refund, that the election campaign cost reimbursement must be distributed according to objective criteria in favour of the candidates.[64] The Court referred especially to the principle of equality, and in addition it stressed that the election campaign cost reimbursement may not lead to the candidates' becoming dependent on the state or on financially strong donors.

Private Election Campaign Funding

In addition to public subsidies, candidates today finance their election campaign through private donations. However, donations to the candidates are limited. Thus a natural person may donate yearly a maximum of 30,000 Francs and a legal person a maximum of 50,000 Francs to a candidate.[65] Donations of more than 1,000 Francs must be paid by check.[66] In addition, the donations may cover only 20 percent of the campaign expenditures.

In order to encourage donations from private individuals and companies, contributions to candidates carry tax privileges. The donations to a candidate may be deducted from taxes up to 1.25 percent of the income of a natural person and to 2 pro mille of the turnover of a company.[67] In these cases the state's tax losses are to be regarded as public subventions.

A further source of income for the candidates includes the allocations guaranteed by the party.[68] For these allocations, the aforementioned limitations in the regulation of donations do not apply. Especially during presidential elections, candidates sometimes receive large funds from their own party.

For the 1988 presidential election, the candidates received the following allocations from their parties:

Candidate	Party	Contribution in Millions of Francs
Jacques Chirac	RPR	40.3
François Mitterrand	PS	37.3
André Lajoinie	PCF	17.8
Raymond Barre	UDF	13.9
Arlette Laguiller	Trotskyste	6.5
Jean-Marie Le Pen	FN	6.3

Source: *Journal Officiel* of 16 July 1988, p. 9199-9207

Limitation of Election Campaign Costs

The legislation for campaign and party funding was passed also with the aim of limiting campaign expenditures. In order to qualify for public funds, the presidential candidates as well as the candidates for the Assemblée Nationale are required to keep within the prescribed limits of expenditures for the campaign.

Presidential Elections. The costs of the presidential election campaign were limited by parliament as follows. In the last six months prior to the election, a presidential candidate may spend a maximum of 120 million Francs on the election campaign for the first ballot and 140 million Francs as a candidate on the second ballot.[69] In the 1988 presidential election, this limit on expenditures was not exceeded by any candidate. The candidates on the second ballot, François Mitterrand and Jacques Chirac, had totals for both ballots of 99.9 million and 96.0 million Francs, respectively, the highest expenditures recorded among all candidates.[70] For the next presidential election, the expense limit for the candidates who reach the second ballot has been increased to 160 million Francs.[71]

Elections to the Assemblée Nationale. The expenditures for the election to the Assemblée Nationale are also limited by law. Thus each candidate for a seat in the Assemblée Nationale may spend 500,000 Francs in his or her election district in the last three months prior to the election. The upper limit for election expenses has been lowered to 400,000 Francs in those constituencies with less than 80,000 residents.[72]

These limitations of expenditures contribute to a reduction in campaign expenditures, at least as long as the possibilities of circumvention are excluded. In addition, they discourage an escalation of campaign costs in the final days prior to the election. The limitations of expenditures are accompanied by a prohibition and a limitation of specific advertising measures.[73]

Accountability

Candidates receiving public financing are not only bound by expenditure limitations but also by legislation that requires candidates to account for the campaign costs incurred.

Presidential Elections. The presidential candidates are required within 60 days after the election to present to the Conseil Constitutionnel a statement of accounts which documents their campaign costs. The candidates are required to present the corresponding receipts for the income and expenditures. The statements of accounts concerning the candidates' campaign costs are published in the *Journal Officiel* of the French Republic within ten days of the election.

The statements of accounts of the presidential candidates were first published on 16 July 1988 in the Journal Officiel for the presidential elections (first ballot: 24 April 1988; second ballot: 8 May 1988). According to these statements of accounts, the expenditures of the nine candidates amounted to 353.9 million Francs (see Table 6.1).

Elections to the Assemblée Nationale. The candidates for election to the Assemblée Nationale are also required to account for their campaign costs. Within 60 days after the election, the candidates must disclose personally or through a representative their total income and expenditures for the three months prior to the election. The statements of accounts must be presented to the president of the Assemblée Nationale, who is obligated to make the statement available to the Conseil Constitutionnel or the judicial offices upon request.

Appointment of an "Authorized Financial Agent." According to law no 90-55, a candidate may collect his or her sources of financing only by creating a "society for the funding of the election" or appointing a natural person as an "authorized financial agent."[74] After having made his decision between these two options, the candidate may include the costs incurred throughout the campaign-- with the exception of the desposit--with the agent appointed by himself. The exceptions, however, are practically those expenditures which are covered by the party or the political grouping. The "society for the funding of the election" or the "authorized financial agent" is required to open a bank or postal account for the candidate through which all financial transactions of the candidate are to be settled.

If the candidate has chosen a "society," it will be legally dissolved three months following the termination of the campaign account of the candidate. The functions of the authorized financial agent also end three months following the termination of the campaign account. If a positive balance appears in the campaign account, then the candidate can transfer the "profit" either to a society for the funding of the election, to a society for the funding of a political party, or to a non-profit organization.

It is questionable whether the intervention of a "society for the funding of the election" or an "authorized financial agent" will achieve the desired result, namely, to exclude possibilities of evasion, since they are appointed by the candidate and as a result are also dependent upon the candidate.

Sanctions

The law authorizes severe punishments for offenses against the new legal provisions.[75] Thus a member of the Assemblée Nationale who does not present a statement of accounts is considered ineligible for election for the period of one year and therefore forfeits the office to which he has just been elected.

A candidate will also be punished if he secured funds in order to finance the campaign while violating the regulations or exceeding the maximum sum for election expenditures. The penalties range from either a fine between 360 and 15,000 Francs or imprisonment from one month to one year.[76]

TABLE 6.1 Revenues, Expenditures, and Public Campaign Cost Refund for the Candidates of the 1988 Presidential Election (in millions of Francs)

Candidate	Party	Election Result First Ballot	Election Result Second Ballot	Income[a]	Expenditures	Public Campaign Cost Refund
Francois Mitterrand	PS	34.1%	54.0%	64.9	99.9	35.0
Jacques Chirac[b]	RPR	19.9	46.0	61.6	96.0	35.0
Raymond Barre	UDF	16.5	—	64.1	64.1	30.0
Jean-Marie Le Pen	FN	14.4	—	37.9	36.0	30.0
Andre Lajoinie	PCF	6.8	—	33.3	33.3	30.0
Antoine Waechter	Ecologist	3.8	—	6.9	6.9	6.0
Pierre Juquin	PCF-Dissident	2.1	—	7.8	6.8	6.0
Arlette Laguiller	Trotzkyte	2.0	—	6.9	6.9	6.0
Pierre Boussel	Independent	0.4	—	4.0	4.0	4.0

[a]Private revenues (without any campaign cost refund).
[b]The revenues for *Jacques Chirac* amounted to 96.0 million Francs according to his statement of accounts. However, the 35 million Franc campaign cost refund is shown separately in the table.

Source: *Journal Officiel* of 16 July 1988, p. 9199-9207.

Party Funding Since 1988

Public Party Funding

Until the promulgation of law no 88-227 of 11 March 1988, the parties were subjected to the provisions of the law of 1901 relating to associations with all of its restrictions. According to Article 7 of the new law no 88-227, every political party is now a regular corporate body, even if it is not registered as an association.[77]

At the same time, this law introduced direct party funding. From 1989 until 1991 a particular sum of money for this purpose has been set aside in the budget[78] and distributed among the parties represented in parliament.[79] Under this provision the parties in France received a total of 105.6 million Francs in 1989.[80] In 1990 this amount increased to 260.3 million Francs,[81] and for 1991 the parties will receive 262 million Francs.[82] This amount is granted in proportion to the number of deputies in the Assemblée Nationale and the Sénat. This means that until 1991 only those parties which are represented in either chamber of parliament receive public support.[83] Until Article 10 of law no 90-55 comes into force after the next election to the Assemblée Nationale in 1992, parties which are not represented in parliament do not qualify for any public funds.[84]

Article 10 of law no 90-55 of 15 January 1990 provides for the division of the amount budgeted for public party funding into two equal parts. The first part is allocated for the funding of parties and political associations and is dependent upon the result of the election to the Assemblée Nationale in 1992. This part is set aside for the parties and political groups that ran candidates in at least 75 constituencies. The distribution is carried out in relation to the number of votes on the first ballot. According to the original legislation, only those parties and political associations that receive more than 5 percent of the votes should benefit from the first part of the subventions. The second part of the public subventions is allocated to those parties and associations represented in parliament. These subventions are granted in proportion to the number of deputies in parliament.

In the meantime the Conseil Constitutionnel has declared the 5 percent clause with regard to use of the first part of the party funding to be inconsistent with the constitution,[85] on the grounds that it fails to recognize the need for the pluralism of ideas and opinions that forms an indispensible foundation of democracy. The 5 percent hurdle for public funding could lead to preventing or at least impeding the emergence of new parties. This would lead in turn to a strengthening of the current party system. The consequences of the decision of the Conseil Constitutionnel are that parties and political associations that have no representatives in parliament or have received less than 5 percent of the votes also should receive public financial support.

It should been noted that the Communist Party, which voted against public party funding from the very beginning, refused any public support in 1989.[86] Having noticed the obvious disadvantage attached to such behavioural purity, the PCF accepted its share of public funds in 1990.

As noted above, the parties may only accept public financial support through an authorized agent, either a "society for the funding of a political party" or a natural person. The authorization of a "society for the funding of a political party" takes place via a commission and is published in the *Journal Officiel*. The statutes of the society are required to include the location of the constituency in which it is active and the intention to open a single bank or postal account in which all donations are deposited. The same rules apply if the party appoints a natural person as the authorized financial agent.

An indirect public subvention for the parties can be seen in the state's tax expenditures through the tax deductibility of the party donations. This issue will be dealt with more closely in the next section.

Private Party Funding

Before 1988 the parties were prohibited from accepting donations of any kind. Now the parties may receive private donations. However, these may not exceed 50,000 Francs per year from a natural person. A legal person may donate up to 500,000 Francs to a party. Any donation of more than 1,000 Francs must be paid by check.

Donations to the parties have been tax deductible since 1990 in the amount of 1.25 percent of the income of a natural person and 2 promille of the sales of a legal person. Tax deductibility for party donations is unknown in most Western democracies; however, even more generous tax benefits than in France are found in the Federal Republic of Germany.[87]

Accountability

While the parties were not required until 1988 to provide any kind of information concerning their income and expenditures, the introduction of public party funding led to the requirement that the parties must now present a financial statement.[88] The parties must submit a statement to the National Commission for Election Campaign Accounts and Political Funding by the end of the first month of the new year. This statement contains the income and expenditures of the past year. It must be certified by two accountants and published in the *Journal Officiel* of the French Republic. However, the law stipulates that the parties and political associations will not be investigated by the Board of Auditors. If the law is violated, especially through failure to hand in the statement of accounts, the party loses its right to lay claim to public privileges in the following year.

TABLE 6.2 Public Party Funding for 1991

| Party/Political Association | *Number of Representatives* | | | *Public Party* |
	Assemblée Nationale	*Sénat*	*Total*	*Funding in Francs*
Parti Socialiste (PS)	258	60	318	93,946,488
Rassemblement pour la République (RPR)	128	89	217	64,108,138
Parti Républicain	51	38	89	26,293,200
Union Centriste		61	61	18,021,182
Centre des Démocrates Sociaux (CDS)	42	3	45	13,294,314
Parti Communiste Francais(PCF)	25	15	40	11,817,168
Association de gestion des adhérents directs de l'Union pour la democratie francaise (UDF)	20	7	27	7,976,589
Mouvement des Radicaux de Gauche (MRG)	8	6	14	4,136,009
Clubs Perspectives et Réalités	10	3	13	3,840,580
Parti Radical	3	7	10	2,954,292
Front National (FN)	1	-	1	295,429
Others:	24	28	52	15,362,308
Total:	570	317	887	262,045,708

Source: Décret no 91-174, 18 February 1991 (*Journal Officiel,* 19 February 1991), p. 2491.

Summary and Evaluation

The new laws of 1988 and 1990 concerning election campaign and party finance were long overdue. These laws are supposed to ameliorate or remove the various problems in existence in the election campaign and party funding system since previous practices were fully unsatisfactory and at times even scandalous.

Before 1988 the parties officially were financed from membership dues. The acceptance of any donations was prohibited; there was no direct public funding. The result was that the parties often raised funds through illegal sources. Despite various reform initiatives taken especially during the 1970s, no legal basis was created for the regulation of election campaign and party funding until 1988.

While politicians were interested in improving the situation, they lacked the strength and courage to realize their reform initiatives. Above all the Communist Party, whose own financial needs were covered through high membership dues and party group/caucus assessments, tried to prevent all reform efforts. The Communists were afraid of losing their strong, financially superior position to other parties as a result of the introduction of public party funding.

The campaign and party funding reform finally carried out at the beginning of 1988 led to a pronounced system of public funding of candidates and parties that was first implemented during the electoral period 1986 to 1988. This is the only electoral period since the beginning of the Fifth Republic in 1959 in which the election to the Assemblée Nationale was carried out according to a modified proportional electoral law.[89] This is of particular interest, since the electoral law and the impact of the law on the position of the parties was bound to have an effect on party finances. In countries with a candidate-oriented simple majority vote, such as the United States and Great Britain, the influence of the parties is relatively weak (at least in the U.S.) and public party and candidate funding exist only on a limited basis. On the other hand in countries where proportional representation is found, the parties play a leading role. The result is a well developed system of public party funding in the Federal Republic of Germany, Austria, Sweden and Italy. It should be noted, however, that elections to the Assemblée Nationale in June 1988 were carried out according to the traditional two-ballot majority system.

There has been little time to formulate generalizations based on practical experiences under the 1988 and 1990 laws for election campaign and party funding. On balance the legislation should be judged positively, in particular due to the provisions regarding the accountability of the candidates and parties as well as the limitations on expenditures for candidates.

Some observers argue that there has already been a first setback in political finance reform through the amnesty granted in conjunction with the law no 90-55 of 15 January 1990 concerning party funding. This law benefited the politicians who had used funds for political purposes under questionable circumstances.[90] The amnesty applied to all criminal acts committed prior to 15 June 1989 in conjunction with the direct or indirect funding of election campaigns or parties and political groups.[91] Only cases of personal enrichment were expressly exempted from the amnesty. Thus with a single stroke of pen, the sins of the past were eradicated. The results of this amnesty became apparent for the first time at the beginning of April 1990, when the proceedings against the former socialist minister for development aid, Nucci, were dropped.[92] Nucci was accused of embezzling public funds amounting to almost 20 million Francs and directing tax revenues into the coffers of the Socialist Party.[93]

With respect to the laws of 1988, one can argue that the regulations regarding the creation of equal opportunities for the parties and candidates remain deficient. This is a result of the 5 percent clause in particular. This clause has the effect of providing dramatically different flat rates for campaign cost reimbursements of candidates in presidential elections. A candidate who obtains 4.9 percent of the votes receives 6 million Francs as opposed to a candidate who obtains 5.1 percent of the votes and receives five times as much, or 30 million Francs.

Reservations arise also from the 5 percent clause which applies to the elections to the Assemblée Nationale. Only candidates who have cleared this hurdle receive public support in the form of a flat rate for election campaign costs, a reimbursement for certain electoral materials as well as a refund of the required deposit. While this restriction certainly discourages non-serious candidacies, it can be argued that serious candidates may receive something less than 5 percent of the votes. The 5 percent barrier should also be lowered on the grounds of equal opportunity. The Conseil Constitutionnel nevertheless has found the coupling of the desposit refund and the reimbursement of certain election materials to a 5 percent share of votes to be constitutional.[94] In contrast to the above, the Conseil Constitutionnel has found the exclusion from public support for those parties that received less than 5 percent of the votes in the elections to the Assemblée Nationale to be unconstitutional.

One may criticize the method of distribution of the public funds not only for being tied to the proportion of the votes received but also because of the focus on the number of representatives in parliament. This has served to stabilize the established party system, since it benefits the large parties. Party system stability has been strengthened further by the French two-ballot system of majority voting.

It is also questionable whether the new regulations for election campaign and party funding are capable of reducing the influence of private lobbies upon candidates and parties. That a lobby may donate 50,000 Francs to a candidate or 500,000 Francs to a party could lead to some dependency on the donor. Had the maximums for the donations been set at a lower rate, this could have been avoided. On the other hand there can be little concern at this point that candidates and parties will become dependent on the state. However, it should be noted that this is just the beginning of public funding, and financial subsidies could be raised in the future.

The limitations of expenditures for the candidates are signs of a positive development. They should contribute to a reduction in election campaign costs unless ways are found to circumvent them.[95] To counter this possibility, the parliament has taken several precautionary steps. On the one hand the candidates must account for the revenues and expenditures, and on the other hand an authorized financial agent must be appointed. However, the fact that donations of more than 1,000 Francs must be paid by check probably contributes little to excluding circumvention.

Through the new legislation, a greater financial transparency of candidate and party funding may be achieved. In the words of Yves Meny, one could even speak of "Glasnost à la française."[96] The accountibility of the candidates and the parties, the appointment of an "authorized financial agent" for the acceptance of private donations, and the acceptance of donations only by checks for amounts exceeding 1,000 Francs can be seen as contributing to this end. Finally, the threat of sanctions which may be imposed for noncompliance should contribute to greater transparency.

An overall assessment of the legal regulations of 1988 and 1990 leads to the conclusion that the French have taken important steps toward campaign and party finance reform. However, it remains to be seen whether political practice may not yet undermine the new laws.[97] One cannot discount the possibility that large donors will discover clever and possibly illegal means of circumventing the laws, for example, through cash payments in the settlement of financial transactions through foreign accounts.[98] In any case, students of French politics will be better able to follow future developments in political finance than they were in the past.

Notes

1.   Udo Kempf, "Die bürgerlichen Parteien Frankreichs: Das Rassemblement Pour la République (R.P.R.), die Partie Republicain (P.R.), und das Centre des Démocrats Sociaux (C.D.S.)," in Hans-Joachim Veen, ed., *Christlich-demokratische und konservative Parteien in Westeuropa*, (Paderborn: Schoening, 1983), pp. 226-228.

2.   André Campana, *L'argent secret: les financement des partis politiques et des campagne électorales* (Paris: Arthaud, 1976).

3.   Michael Pulch, *Parteienfinanzierung in Frankreich und Großbritannien*, Ph. D. Thesis, University of Bonn, 1987, p. 87.

4.   Christine Landfried, *Money and Politics in France*, unpublished report from the workshop "Money and politics" of the European Consortium of Political Research, Paris, April 1989, p. 1.

5.   Jean Montaldo, *Les Finances du P.C.F.* (Paris: Albin Michel, 1977), p. 31 ff.

6.   Yves Marie Doublet, *Le financement de la vie politique* (Paris: Presses Universitaires de France, 1990), p. 61.

7.   Pulch, *Parteienfinanzierung in Frankreich und Großbritannien*, p. 106.

8.   Yves Marie Doublet, "La législation française sur le financement de la vie politique," in *Pouvoirs*, Vol. 56, 1991, p. 163.

9.   Hans-Hagen Bremer, "Regierung contra Mitterrand. Präsident verlangt Gesetz über die Parteienfinanzierung," in *Frankfurter Rundschau*, 19 November 1987, p. 2.

10. One reason for the introduction of public election campaign and party funding may be seen in the fact that the greatest opponent of public funding, the Communist Party, has been increasingly losing importance in the past years. See Adolf Kimmel, "Das französische Parteiensystem. Von der Bipolarisierung zum Konsens?" in *Aus Politik und Zeitgeschichte*, B 39/1989, 22 September 1989, pp. 21-22; Udo Kempf, "Frankreichs Parteiensystem im Wandel. Formationen, programmatische Ausrichtungen, Strukturen, Anhängerschaft," in *Der Bürger im Staat*, Vol. 39, No. 2, 1989, p. 105.

11. Loi organique no 88-226 and loi ordinaire no 88-227 11 March 1988 (*Journal*

Officiel, 12 March 1988, p. 3288.

12. Loi ordinare no 90-55, 15 January 1990 (*Journal Officiel,* 16 January 1990, p. 639) and loi organique no 90-383, 10 May 1990 (*Journal Officiel,* 11 May 1990), p. 5615.

13. Karl-Heinz Naßmacher, "Öffentliche Parteifinanzierung in westlichen Demokratien," in *Journal für Sozialforschung,* Vol. 21, No. 4, 1981, pp. 351, 354.

14. See Hans Herbert von Arnim, *Die Partei, der Abgeordnete und das Geld* (Mainz: v. Hase & Koehler, 1991), pp. 234, 237 ff.

15. Christine Landfried, *Parteifinanzen und politische Macht. Eine vergleichende Studie zur Bundesrepublik Deutschland, zu Italien und den USA* (Baden-Baden: Nomos, 1990), p. 173 ff.

16. See Doublet, *Le financement de la vie politique,* p. 5.

17. Karl-Heinz Naßmacher, "Parteienfinanzierung als verfassungspolitisches Problem," in *Aus Politik und Zeitgeschichte,* B 11/ 1989, 10 March 1989, pp. 27, 33.

18. Kurt Weigelt, *Staatliche Parteienfinanzierung. Zu den Möglichkeiten einer staatlichen Parteienfinanzierung in der Schweiz unter vergleichender Berücksichtigung der Gesetzgebung in Frankreich, der Bundesrepublik Deutschland und den Vereinigten Staaten von Amerika* (Gruesch: Ruegger, 1988), p. 17.

19. Jürgen Hartmann, *Frankreichs Parteien* (Köln: Wissenschaft und Politik, 1985), p. 10.

20. Michel Fromont, "Die Institution der politischen Partei in Frankreich," in Dimitris Th. Tsatsos/ Dian Schefold/ Hans-Peter Schneider, ed., *Parteienrecht im europäischen Vergleich* (Baden-Baden. Nomos, 1990), p. 224.

21. See Michèle Berthod, "Le financement des partis politiques en France," in *Parlaments et Francophonie* 1990, p. 69.

22. Pulch, *Parteienfinanzierung in Frankreich und Großbritannien,* p. 65.

23. Fromont, "Die Institution der politischen Partei in Frankreich," pp. 255-256.

24. Weigelt, *Staatliche Parteienfinanzierung,* p. 116.

25. Décret no 64-231, 14 March 1964 in the version of the Décret no 80-212, 11 March 1980.

26. Weigelt, *Staatliche Parteienfinanzierung,* p. 118.

27. Art. 12 of the Décret no 64-231, 14 March 1964.

28. Doublet, *Le financement de la vie politique,* p. 60.

29. See Ibid., p. 59.

30. Rainer Kraehe, *Le financement des partis politiques* (Paris: Presses Universitaires de France, 1972), p. 49.

31. Weigelt, *Staatliche Parteienfinanzierung,* p. 117.

32. Ibid., p. 118.

33. See Kraehe, *Le financement des partis politiques,* p. 75, footnote 5.

34. Weigelt, *Staatliche Parteienfinanzierung,* p. 119.

35. Doublet, *Le financement de la vie politique,* p. 57.

36. Kraehe, *Le financement des partis politiques,* p. 31.

37. See Doublet, *Le financement de la vie politique,* p. 58 f.

38. Fromont, *Die Institution der politischen Partei in Frankreich,* p. 250.

39. Doublet, *Le financement de la vie politique,* p. 59.

40. Pulch, *Parteienfinanzierung in Frankreich und Großbritannien,* p. 77.

41. Comparisons of the problems associated with party group assessments can be

176

found in: von Arnim, *Die Partei, der Abgeordnete und das Geld*, p. 205-211.

42. State of the compensation of representatives according to Décret no 90-322, 5 April 1990.

43. See *Le Monde*, 15 Juin 1986.

44. Pulch, *Parteienfinanzierung in Frankreich und Großbritannien*, p. 87.

45. Ibid., p. 66f.

46. Quoted from: Fromont, "Die Institution der politischen Partei in Frankreich," p. 254.

47. Roger de Weck, "Kungeln und kassieren. Krumme Wege bei der Parteienfinanzierung sind üblich," in *Die Zeit*, 14 March 1986, p. 34.

48. Hans-Hagen Bremer, "Finanzskandale sollten die Parteikasse füllen. Kurz vor den Präsidentschaftswahlen ist in Frankreich die Arbeit der Schatzmeister das Thema," in *Frankfurter Rundschau*, 13 November 1987, p. 16.

49. Pulch, *Parteienfinanzierung in Frankreich und Großbritannien*, p. 64.

50. Fromont, "Die Institution der politischen Partei in Frankreich," p. 254.

51. Kempf, "Die bürgerlichen Parteien Frankreichs," p. 226.

52. Quoted from: Kempf, "Die bürgerlichen Parteien Frankreichs," p. 226.

53. Joachim Fritz-Vannahme, "Die Narren der Republik, Frankreichs Richter kuschen vor den Politikern," in *Die Zeit*, 20 April 1990, p. 11.

54. Pulch, *Parteienfinanzierung in Frankreich und Großbritannien*, p. 91.

55. Ibid., p. 89.

56. Thierry Bréhier, "L'adoption des projets de loi sur le financement de la vie politique. Les députés socialistes se réfugient dans l'abstention," in *Le Monde*, 6 February 1988, p. 7.

57. Fromont, *Die Institution der politischen Partei in Frankreich*, p. 249.

58. The statement of President François Mitterrand, elected in 1988, is printed in the *Journal Officiel*, 12 May 1988, p. 7044.

59. Art. 3, V, Law no 62-1292, 6 Juin 1962 in the version of law no 88-226, 11 March 1988.

60. See Yves Meny, *La "transparence financiére de la vie politiques": Glasnost à la française*, unpublished paper, Paris 1988, p. 6.

61. Art.L.O. 135-1 Code électoral in the version of law no 88-226, 11 March 1988.

62. Art.L.O. 163-2 Code életoral in the version of the law no 88-226, 11 March 1988.

63. In France, the Conseil Constitutionnel investigates the constitutionality of a law prior to its passage. After acceptance of the law by the President of the Republic, the Conseil Constitutionnel can no longer be consulted. See Axel Spies, "Verfassungsgerichtliche Normenkontrolle in Frankreich: der Conseil constitutionnel," in *Neue Zeitschrift für Verwaltungsrecht 1990*, pp. 1040-1041.

64. Decision of the Conseil Constitutionnel no 88/242 DC,10 March 1988 (*Journal Officiel*, 12 March 1988, p. 3350).

65. Art. L. 52-8 of law no 90-55, 15 January 1990.

66. Doublet, *Le financement de la vie politique*, p. 73f.

67. Art. 238 a of the Code General des Impots.

68. See the section about party finance.

69. Art. L.O. 163-2 Code électoral in the version of law no 88-226, 11 March 1988.

70. *Journal Officiel*, 16 July 1988, p. 9199-9207.

71. L.O. no 90-393, 10 May 1990 (*Journal Officiel* 11 May 1990), p. 5615.

72. Art. L.O. 52-11 of law no 90-55, 15 January 1990 (*Journal Officiel*, 16 January 1990), p. 639; See Guy Drouot, "Le financement des campagne électorales et des activités politiques: les nouvelles régles du jeu. La loi du 15 janv. 1990 et la loi organique du 11. Mai 1990," in *Actualité Législative Dalloz*, Vol. 8, No. 14, 1990, pp. 125f., 131.

73. See Doublet, *Le financement de la vie politique*, p. 69.

74. Art. L. 52-4 to 52-7 of law no 90-55, 15 January 1990.

75. L 113-1 of Code électoral in the version of law no 90-55, 15 January 1990.

76. Doublet, *Le financement de la vie politique*, p. 72.

77. Fromont, "Die Institution der politischen Partei in Frankreich," pp. 229f.

78. Art. 8 of law no 88-227, 11 March 1988 (Journal Officiel 12 March 1988), p. 3288.

79. Art.9 of law no 88-227, 11 March 1988.

80. Décret no 89-75, 7 February 1989 (*Journal Officiel*, 8 February 1989, p. 1793).

81. Décret no 90-210, 9 March 1990 (*Journal Officiel* 10 March 1990, p. 2971).

82. Décret no 91-174, 18 February 1991 (*Journal Officiel*, 19 February 1991, p. 2491).

83. Fromont, "Die Institution der politischen Partei in Frankreich," p. 248.

84. Art. 23 of law no 90-55, 15 January 1990.

85. Decision of the Conseil Constitutionnel no 89/271 DC, 11 January 1990 (*Journal Officiel*, 13 January 1990, p. 573).

86. Berthod, *"Le financement,"* p. 72.

87. See von Arnim, *Die Partei, der Abgeordnete und das Geld*, pp. 28-46.

88. Doublet, *Le financement de la vie politique*, p. 63.

89. Kimmel, "Das französische Parteiensystem," p. 16.

90. See Axel Spies, *Amnestiemaßnahmen und deren Verfassungsmäßigkeit in Frankreich und Deutschland* (Frankfurt am Main/Bern/New York/Paris: Peter Lang, 1991), pp. 219-233, p. 221; Thankman von Münchkkausen, "Zweierlei Recht. Das Gesetz über die Parteienfinanzierung in Frankreich und Ärger mit einer Amnestie," in *Frankfurter Allgemeine Zeitung*, 9 May 1990, p. 16.

91. Article 19 of law no 90-55, 15 January 1990, (*Journal Officiel*, 16 January 1990, p. 639).

92. Axel Spies, *Amnestiemaßnahmen und deren Verfassungsmäßigkeit in Frankreich und Deutschland*, p. 222.

93. See Joachim Fritz-Vannahme, "Die Narren der Republik, Frankreichs Richter kuschen vor den Politikern," in *Die Zeit*, 20.

94. See Kraehe, *Le financement des partis politiques*, p. 75, footnote 5.

95. Doublet, *Le financement de la vie politique*, p. 124.

96. Meny, *"La transparence,"* p. 1

97. See Doublet,*Le financement de la vie politique*, pp. 124-125.

98. See Doublet, *"La legislation,"* p. 174.

7

Financing Parties and Elections in Small European Democracies: Austria and Sweden

Gudrun Klee

The Austrian and Swedish representative democracies are usually characterized as systems of party government.[1]   In both countries the proportional electoral system is based on party choice rather than candidate choice. Consequently, it is not an exaggeration to say that parties have complete control over the nomination of candidates in the federal republic of Austria as well as in the unitarian constitutional monarchy of Sweden. In both countries political parties have built up strong organizations at the national, regional and local level. Hence, public subsidies are given to permanent party organizations in Sweden and Austria and not to specific candidates.

Until the rise of Ecological Parties in the mid 1980s, the party systems in both countries were extraordinarily stable. The results of the national elections are shown in Tables 7.1 and 7.2.

Today an extensive system of state subsidies to political parties exists in Sweden and Austria, and these subsidies have become the predominant source of party income. Both countries can look back on a long tradition of public party financing. Nevertheless, state subsidies for political parties have not been accepted publicly in Austria to the same degree as in Sweden. In contrast to Sweden, broad popular acceptance of party financing in Austria is still missing.[2] In Austria complaints persist about the lack of transparency concerning party financing, about "self-serving" politicians, about the parties' growing expenses, and about the process of estrangement on the part of party members and electors.[3]   The ideal of a self-financing mass party is raised continuously in discussions about the pros and cons of public funding.

TABLE 7.1 Austrian National Election Results, 1970-1990 (percentage of votes and number of seats won)

	1970	1971	1975	1979	1983	1986	1990
Conservatives(ÖVP)	44.7%	43.1%	42.9%	41.9%	43.2%	41.3%	32.1%
	(78)	(80)	(80)	(77)	(81)	(77)	(60)
Socialist Party (SPÖ)	48.4	50.0	51.0	51.0	47.6	43.1	43.0
	(81)	(93)	(95)	(95)	(90)	(80)	(81)
Liberals (FPÖ)	5.5	5.4	5.4	6.1	5.0	9.7	16.6
	(6)	(10)	(10)	(11)	(12)	(18)	(33)
Green Alternatives	----	----	----	----	3.3	4.8	4.5
	----	----	----	----	----	(8)	(9)
Others	1.4	1.4	1.2	1.0	0.9	1.0	3.8

TABLE 7.2 Swedish National Election Results, 1970-1988 (percentage of votes and number of seats won)

	1970	1973	1976	1979	1982	1985	1988
Social Democrats (SAP)	45.3%	43.6%	42.7%	43.2%	45.6%	44.7%	43.2%
	(163)	(156)	(152)	(154)	(166)	(159)	(156)
Communists (Vp)	4.8	5.3	4.8	5.6	5.6	5.4	5.9
	(17)	(19)	(17)	(20)	(20)	(19)	(21)
Conservatives (M)	11.5	14.3	15.6	20.3	23.6	21.3	18.3
	(41)	(51)	(55)	(73)	(86)	(76)	(66)
Liberals (Fp)	16.2	9.4	11.1	10.6	5.9	14.2	12.2
	(58)	(34)	(39)	(38)	(21)	(51)	(44)
Centre (C)	19.9	25.1	24.1	18.1	15.5	12.4	11.3
	(71)	(90)	(86)	(64)	(56)	(44)	(42)
Green Party (Mp)	----	----	----	----	1.6	1.5	5.5
	----	----	----	----	----	----	(20)
Christian Democratic	1.8	1.4	1.4	1.9	2.5	3.0	
Community Party (KdS)	----	----	----	----	----	(1)	*

* Electoral Alliance between Centre Party and Christian Democratic Community Party (KdS).

Against this background it is helpful to take a look at empirical data about the real extent of public party financing and the development of party income and expenditure. Therefore the aim of this chapter is to present an overall view of the various methods of party financing in Sweden and Austria, their development over time, and the distribution of funds. Moreover, with the help of the comparative approach both the contrasts and similarities of party financing in these countries will be illuminated.

In both countries the financial resources of political parties are well documented at the national level. In Austria a Party Act and in Sweden a voluntary agreement requires the national party organizations to publish their income and expenditures. However, at the regional and local levels information about the budgets of parties is significantly less extensive, because at these levels parties are not required to report their income and expenditure data. The only exception is the state *(Land)* of Salzburg in Austria. Here party financing is subject to a specific Party Act which requires the party organizations in Salzburg to make their income and expenditure figures public.[4] Consequently, the financial data for political parties in Austria and Sweden are limited to the national level in this chapter.

The Development of Public Funding for Political Parties

Sweden

Until the introduction of direct public subsidies in Sweden in 1965, party financing was not subject to any regulations, and the parties were more or less exclusively financed by private sources. Even during the election campaign in 1948 the question of public subsidies became a focus of attention, and the government created a commission of inquiry to study the issue. But in its report the Party Finance Commission spoke out strictly against the legal regulation of party finance in Sweden.[5] About ten years later the idea of public party funding was taken up again, but this time in connection with discussions about a direct press subsidy. The Swedish press, which was owned up to 83 percent by political parties and affiliated organizations, had run up high deficits and demanded more and more subsidies from their respective party organizations. Therefore the Social Democrats came up with the idea of a direct press subsidy; however, in their own ranks as well as in the opposition this plan was met with disapproval.[6] So the Social Democratic government decided to meet the need for press subsidies indirectly by providing funds for political parties, which could use this money to finance their newspapers or for other purposes.[7]

Against the strong opposition of the Conservatives and Liberals, but with the support of the Centre Party and the Communists (both parties had financial difficulties at the time), the Social Democratic Party introduced in 1965 a bill granting national subsidies to political parties. All members of parliament agreed that political parties fulfill an important function in maintaining democracy and that therefore society has a responsibility to secure the existence of political parties.[8] But they differed on the means and extent to which parties should be subsidized.[9] Four years later, however, the differences between the parties about the general principle of state subsidies had been resolved. When the Riksdag (the national parliament) authorized county councils and municipalities in 1969 to finance political parties at the regional and local levels in addition to financing at the national level, all parties agreed on the means to which local and provincial party organizations should be subsidized.[10]

Austria

In Austria a system of direct party financing was not introduced on the national level until 1975. Nevertheless, Austria has a long tradition of public party financing at the regional level. In 1960 the state of Vorarlberg granted political parties two Austrian Schilling (AS) for each vote. The other states soon followed and in addition introduced further measures to grant money to political parties[11] (such as subsidies for educational activities). But even on the national level an indirect public subsidy system existed for the national party organizations prior to the Party Act of 1975. In 1963 public funding for the financing of caucusses, or party groups, in the Nationalrat (the national parliament) was introduced, and since 1972 even political academies (institutes of the national parties) have received public money.[12]

Considering the historical roots of public subsidies on the national and regional levels in Austria, it is not surprising that there was no general debate on the principle of public funding for political parties in 1975. The primary motivation for all parties to establish a system of general direct public subsidies by means of the Party Act of 1975 was concern about the growing costs of party activities.[13] It was not until 1984 as a result of several party scandals that a general debate about the legitimacy of public funding was held in Austria's Nationalrat.[14]

Direct Party Financing Schemes

General Subsidies

Sweden. In both countries public party financing is concentrated on general direct subsidies for party organizations. The Swedish law on national subsidies for political parties provides payments of 239,000 Swedish Kroner (SEK)[15] per annum and per seat gained in elections to the Riksdag. Parties have to overcome a 4 percent national minimum vote threshold or must have gained at least 12

TABLE 7.3 National Subsidies in Sweden 1980-1989 (in millions SEK)

	M^a	C	Fp	SAP	Vp	Mp	KdS	Total
1980	11.8	15.4	8.7	27.1	5.5	-	-	69
1981	12.7	14.3	8.7	27.2	5.7	-	-	69
1982	16.0	15.3	9.9	31.6	6.7	-	-	79
1983	17.0	14.6	9.3	31.4	6.7	-	-	79
1984	17.9	14.1	8.4	32.1	6.7	-	-	79
1985	22.4	16.3	8.9	39.4	8.0	-	-	95
1986	22.2	15.5	9.8	39.5	8.0	-	-	95
1987	21.6	14.6	11.8	39.1	8.0	-	-	95
1988	*	*	*	*	*	*	*	110
1989	23.0	15.2	16.9	43.9	9.0	5.2	0.4	113

* Not available

^{a} = See Table 7.2 for party names

Source: Riksgäldskontoret ed., *Verksamhetsberättelser 1979-1989*

percent in one of the 28 multi-member constituencies to be eligible for representation in parliament and to receive the full amount of the direct public payments. Therefore, the subsidy scheme was designed to assist only parties with considerable support. Nevertheless, in 1972 the Social Democratic government introduced a reduction of the threshold for eligibility for public funding to help the Communist Party, the votes for which had fluctuated around the 4 percent mark for many years[16] and which more than once secured majorities in parliament for Social Democratic minority governments. Since 1972 parties without representation in the Riksdag that pass a 2.5 percent national threshold in one of the last two elections receive a reduced subsidy.[17] The amounts received by the five or six parties in the Riksdag since 1979, and the diminished subsidy for the Christian Democratic Community Party (KdS) which gained 3 percent of the national vote in 1988, are given in Table 7.3.

Austria. The principle of distributing public subsidies per seat is also used in Austria but in a modified form. Here, general direct public funding is composed of a fixed amount (base amount) of currently 3 million Austrian Schillings (AS)[18] per party and an additional sum of 529,612 AS per seat in the Nationalrat.[19] In Austria as in Sweden parties have to pass a minimum threshold to be eligible for full direct public funding. Nevertheless, parties which are not represented in the Nationalrat, but have gained at least 1 percent of the total vote in the national election are entitled to claim a reduced amount of public funding in election years only. By using the above described mixed scheme of a base and a supplementary amount, it is possible to favor small parties. For example, if the base amount is relatively high, the small party share of the total sum of direct public funding increased in inverse proportion, at least until 1987. But then the Austrian Party Act was changed. The new Grand Coalition of SPÖ and ÖVP decreased the base amount from 14 to 3 million AS,[20] after the first-time election of Green Party members to the Austrian Nationalrat and the electoral success of the FPÖ. Furthermore, since 1987 the general subsidies to Austrian party organizations have been brought automatically into line with the consumer price index. The amount of public subventions paid to each party since 1976 is shown in Table 7.4.

In 1989 the Grand Coalition created a new, additional form of public funding: the per elector subsidy. This subsidy is payable in national election years only. In 1990 the four parties in the Austrian Nationalrat received about 100 million AS (20 AS for each eligible voter) from this source, which is distributed according to the number of seats in the Nationalrat.[21]

In Austria as well as Sweden, general national party subsidies are paralleled at regional and local levels. In Sweden the law providing for a general party subsidy on the regional and local levels allowed but did not require each province and local authority to introduce party subsidies. The only requirements made in this law were that the subsidies had to be distributed proportionally and by an equal amount per seat. There were no further governmental controls or conditions regarding the use or the amount of party subventions. Since 1980 all of the 284 Swedish municipalities and 24 provinces (län) have taken advantage of the Community Party Subsidy Act of 1969 to pay subsidies of varying amounts to the local and provincial party organizations. The amount per seat ranges from 1,500 SEK in small municipalities up to 13,800 SEK per seat in large cities like Stockholm.[22] In 1990 the total sum paid by the municipalities was 200 million SEK, which was in addition to 121 million SEK from the provinces.[23]

The total amount of general direct public party funding provided by the national government in Sweden decreased continuously in relation to the GNP since 1978. The payments made by provincial governments, however, grew in line with the GNP, and the payments made by local governments far exceeded the growth of the GNP. Hence, payments made by the provincial governments and especially those made by local governments are becoming more and more important to the Swedish parties since the end of the 1970s (See Figure 7.1).

As in Sweden, extensive public subsidies are also paid at the regional and local[24] levels in Austria. Because of the fact that Austria is a federal republic, it is up to each state to determine whether to finance political parties or not. Today, with the exception of the state of Oberösterreich, all Austrian states provide general direct public subsidies in varying amounts to party organizations.[25] Altogether, Austrian political parties received about 464 million AS in 1988 in public subsidies from the state governments[26] in

TABLE 7.4 Public Subsidies to National Party Organizations in Austria (in millions of AS)

Year	SPÖ[a] B[b]	S[c]	ÖVP B	S	FPÖ B	S	Green Party B	S	Total
1976	4	26.344	4	15.956	4	2.660	-	-	57
1977	4	24.911	4	14.913	4	2.715	-	-	54
1978	4	24.911	4	14.913	4	2.271	-	-	54
1979	4	25.032	4	14.772	4	2.750	-	-	54
1980	5	28.350	5	16.210	5	3.023	-	-	62
1981	5	28.350	5	16.210	5	3.368	-	-	63
1982	5	31.412	5	19.644	5	4.720	-	-	71
1983	6	28.897	6	17.507	6	3.043	-	-	67
1984	6	32.261	6	29.265	6	5.553	-	-	85
1985	14	40.214	14	24.656	14	3.994	-	-	111
1986	14	39.209	14	24.316	14	4.309	-	-	110
1987	3	37.001	3	35.514	3	8.351	3	4.139	97
1988	3	37.592	3	36.004	3	8.485	3	4.205	98
1989	3	38.437	3	36.813	3	8.675	3	4.299	100

[a] = See Table 7.1 for party names
[b] = Base Amount
[c] = Supplementary Amount

Source: Österreichische Bundesrechnungsabschlüsse 1976-1989

comparison to 98 million AS from the federal government.[27] Unfortunately, the data concerning the amount of public party financing at the local level in Austria is not extensive enough to make any reliable statements about the total amount of public funding provided to political parties. Only for the state of Salzburg is data available on the amount of public funding by local governments.[28] Using this data as a base, one can make the projection that all local governments taken together pay a total amount of at least 25 million AS in subsidies to political parties. Hence, in Austria the lion's share of direct public funding comes from the state governments.

Whether caucus or party group subsidies have to be seen as direct subventions to political parties or as indirect public funding is a controversial question. But considering the fact that especially the public relations work of caucusses is an advantage to their respective party organizations, caucus subsidies will be dealt with as direct subsidies to political parties in the following analysis.

FIGURE 7.1 Development of Public Party Financing at all Level in Sweden

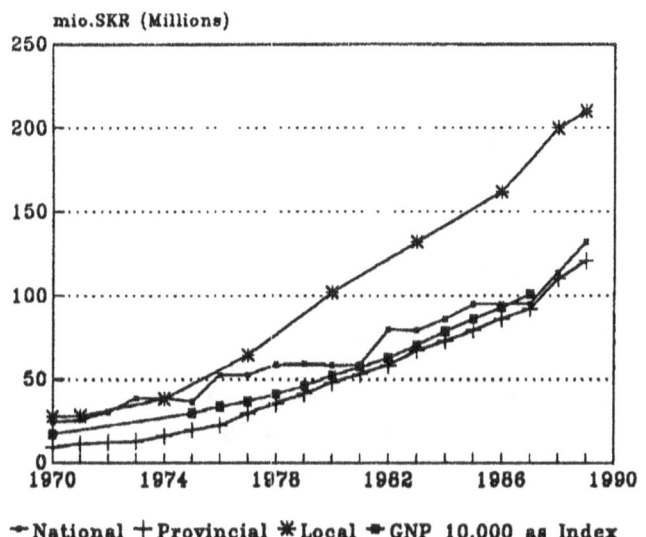

mio.SKR (Millions)

-- National + Provincial ✳ Local ◆ GNP 10.000 as Index

Source: *Statistik Arsbok for Landstinget 1970-1990*, Svenska Kommunförbundet ed., Kommunalt förtroendevalda och deras arvoden 1989, Stockholm 1990, p. 39 and Riksgäldskontoret Verksamhetsberättelser 1970-1989.

Besides the subsidies to party organizations, parliamentary caucusses in Austria and Sweden receive public fundings for their offices and their public relations activities. Considering the fact that a clear distinction between the activities of the caucus and the respective party organization is difficult to make, Swedish legislation provides that subsidies for the caucusses can be paid either directly to the parliamentary party groups or on request to the national party organization which then administers the money. The latter possibility is used by all political parties with the exception of the Social Democrats.[29]

Contrary to the general public subsidies to political parties, the principle for distribution to the caucusses favors small parties in the Swedish Riksdag. Allparties represented in the national parliament receive a base subsidy of 4,174,000 SEK. In addition they get a supplementary subsidy which is higher for opposition parties than for parties in government. A party represented in government receives 11,650 SEK per seat and year, parties in opposition 17,540 SEK.[30] Furthermore, in 1974 a special guarantee for established parties was introduced. A party which was represented in the Riksdag but failed the 4 percent limit in the next election still receives a diminished subsidy for the following three years.

In Austria the distribution scheme for party organizations (base amount and supplementary payment based on seats) is also used for financial support of caucusses. Contrary to the reduction in the base amount for party organizations in 1987, the base sum for caucusses in the Nationalrat is still relatively high and consequently favors small parties. In 1989, for example, the FPÖ received a caucus subsidy of 44,440 AS per seat, the SPÖ 20,000 AS and the ÖVP 20,779[31] AS. The payments to caucusses increase automatically, since they are linked to the salaries of certain civil service categories. They amounted to 68 million AS in 1989. There is also a certain contribution to caucusses in the parliaments of all Austrian states.[32] In Sweden, however, subventions for caucusses at regional and local levels are unusual.

In summary, one can say that public payments to political parties are distributed equally by seat in Sweden, whereas in Austria the distribution scheme generally favors small, established parties. Nevertheless, in both countries the respective subsidy scheme operates to the advantage of established parties. In spite of this feature, however, new parties--especially the Green Parties -- were able to gain a number of seats in the national, regional and local parliaments in Sweden and Austria.

Selective Subsidies

Grants for Party Education Programs

Political parties gain financial advantages from public grants to political academies. In Sweden political party academies are unkown, and therefore no public subventions for this purpose are provided. In Austria, however, the financial burden of political parties is eased considerably by public subsidies to party academies, because the main task of the Austrian party academies is to provide services to the respective party members.[33]

As in the case of the description of the distribution scheme of general public party subsidies to party organizations in Austria, political academies receive a base and a supplementary amount proportional to the representation of their respective political party in the Nationalrat. Since 1984 the public subventions to political academies have increased automatically in tandem with the salaries of certain civil servants. In 1990 public subsidies in the amount of 82 million AS were provided for the four party academies existing in Austria.[34]

Press Subsidies

Public contributions to the press represent a further possibility to ease the financial burden of political parties. Since 1972 special public funds have been provided for the Swedish press. Most of this subsidy is given to the political parties, because most Swedish newspapers are owned by the parties. In 1988, 440 million SEK were provided for press subsidies in Sweden.[35]

In Austria press subsidies are less important for political parties than in Sweden, because the market share of party owned newspapers amounts to only 18 percent.[36] In spite of this small market share, Austrian party newspapers benefit considerably from the press subsidy. Since the grants are divided into a base amount and a supplementary sum, party newspapers receive a proportionally higher amount vis-a-vis their market share than other, independent newspapers. In 1989 a total of 67.2 million AS in "general press subsidies" was distributed to the Austrian press. Furthermore, party newspapers profit from the additional "special press subsidy" introduced in 1984, which prescribes that only newspapers not dominating in the regional market are eligible for additional subsidies.[37] This requirement is applied mainly to party newspapers which received 38 million AS "special press subsidy" in 1989.[38]

Supplementing the federal press subsidy is the subsidy that some Austrian states contribute to newspapers.[39] But in spite of these various press subsidies on the national and state levels, the party newspapers continue to decline. More and more party newspapers have been sold, and it is to be expected that press subsidies will soon be a thing of the past. In 1990 the state of Salzburg, for example, ceased granting its press subsidy which amounted to 5.4 million AS in 1990.

Other Selective Subsidies

In addition to the public subsidies mentioned so far, a number of complementary grants for political parties have been developed in Sweden and Austria. Among these are free electronic media time for political parties in both countries. During election campaigns, Swedish television and radio place free broadcasting time at the parties' disposal. The parties' share of broadcasting time is not based on their size; however, in practice a shift in favour of the larger parties is visible.[40] But no parties are allowed to purchase time for political commercials.

In Austria free media time for political parties is not limited to election campaigns. According to the Austrian Broadcasting Act,[41] political parties are to receive up to 1 percent of the total broadcasting time of each channel. In 1989 a total of 210 minutes of broadcasting time was distributed to the Austrian parties.[42] Moreover, during elections, parties are entitled to additional free broadcasting time according to their respective representation in the Nationalrat. In 1990 the SPÖ got eight, the ÖVP seven, the FPÖ two, and the Green Party one free election advertisements of five minutes each.[43] Parties which are not represented in the Nationalrat are not entitled to any free broadcasting time.

In addition to the forms of selective party financing in Sweden and Austria mentioned above, several other types of specific public funding of political parties are provided in both countries. These include, for example, financial assistance from the state for party youth and other suborganizations and services provided from local governments for the respective local party organizations, such as free copies, subventions for the rent of party offices, free printing of party information in the community newspapers,[44] etc.

In summary, it is clear that in Austria and Sweden a wide range of general and specific direct public subsidies to political parties have been developed at all levels of the respective political systems. Of all types of public funding, the direct general subsidies to party organizations--of which again the vast majority is paid by regional and local government bodies--make up the mass of public subventions. In comparison the total amount of payments per elector made by the governments at all levels of the respective political system in Austria are much higher than in Sweden (See Figure 7.2).

Party Income

The existing data about the income and expenditures of political parties at the national level in Austria and Sweden reveal rather clearly how the introduction of public financing changed the party income and expenditure patterns in both countries at the national level, but they afford no insight into income and expenditure patterns at the regional and local levels. The Annual Reports of the national party headquarters do not include the figures of the regional and local party organizations. Consequently no statements can be made on the parties' total income and expenditure in both countries.

Before we can start with the analysis of the national party income and expenditure patterns, some explanation is in order. With regard to public funding, the political parties in both countries reveal only the total amount of national party organizations. However, the definition of "general public subsidies" differs in each country. In Sweden the Annual Reports, with the general direct public subsidies for the current expenditures of the respective exception of the reports of the Social Democrats, not only subsume all subsidies granted by legislation to cover routine organizational and campaign expenses under the category "public subsidies"; this category also includes public payments for the caucusses. Some parties, Liberals, Greens and Conservatives even include transfer payments from lower party organizations under "public subsidies." In Austria, however, parties subsume only the general payments to party organizations under this category.

The proportion of direct national subsidy of party income in Sweden and Austria shows that in each country the parties are highly dependent on public subsidies. In Austria about 32.4 percent (1989) of the national party organization's income comes from public sources, whereas Swedish national party organizations are even more dependent on public funding. They receive about 69.8 percent (1989) of their total income in the form of direct general public subsidies (Swedish definition).

FIGURE 7.2 Public Subsidies per Elector in Austria and Sweden (1988)

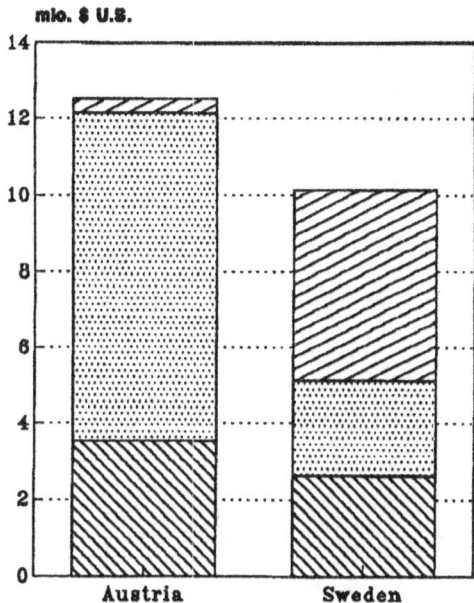

The individual dependency of the respective parties on public funds correlates with its classification as "mass party" or "cadre party."[45] Since the introduction of direct party financing at the national level in Austria in 1975, a typical mass party like the Austrian SPÖ, for example, drew on average 21.6 percent of its income from public sources. The ÖVP, also a mass party, received on average 36.8 percent from public subsidies, and the FPÖ, a typical cadre party, shows the highest proportion of state subsidies with an average of 44.9 percent. The share of public money in the Green Party's income since its first election success in 1987 amounts to an average of 51.8 percent, but this figure has been decreasing continuously since then (See Table 7.5).

In Sweden the parties' reliance on public funding seems to be much higher than in Austria. In the period from 1979 to 1989, the proportion of public subsidies to the total income of all parties taken together amounts to an average of 64 percent. Only the mass party SAP ranks consistently below this average, whereas all other parties normally receive more than 71 percent of their total income from public sources. But when analyzing the figures in the following Table 7.6, one has to keep in mind the fact that with the exception of the SAP all other parties include the subsidies for their caucusses in these figures.

TABLE 7.5 Public Subsidies as Percent of Party Income at the National Level in Austria

Year	SPÖ[a]	ÖVP	FPÖ	GreenParty
1976	32.2	50.6	55.7	
1977	28.0	48.2	45.4	
1978	29.0	43.5	45.5	
1979	16.6	23.8	26.2	
1980	23.6	25.4	42.0	
1981	25.1	38.6	46.7	
1982	20.9	22.0	38.8	
1983	14.9	37.9	31.7	
1984	21.6	36.1	51.0	
1985	24.6	52.2	60.7	
1986	15.5	20.7	48.5	
1987	18.2	45.4	39.3	68.7
1988	18.5	38.8	52.3	49.6
1989	14.3	32.6	45.8	37.2

[a] See Table 7.1 for party names
Source: "Rechenschaftsberichte der österreichischen Bundesparteizentralen 1976-1989" in *Amtsblatt zur Wiener Zeitung*.

The provision of public subsidies to finance political parties seems to be a typical financial strategy in Sweden and Austria. So there are good reasons for the assumption that traditional forms of party funds like donations or membership dues have been declining. An analysis of the Swedish annual reports since 1979 shows that the proportion of membership dues to party income has been relatively stable in varying degrees for each party at the national level. With an average proportion of 12 percent, membership dues are a substantial source of income for the Social Democrats. In contrast membership dues in the Center Party are nearly insignificant at the national level; the average proportion amounts only to 1.7 percent of the party's income. In the Conservative Party, membership dues have a short tradition. They were introduced for the first time in 1965. Since then they have grown continuously and become an important source of income for that party (See Table 7.7).

In Austria membership dues are a reliable source of income, especially for the mass parties, SPÖ and ÖVP. Considering the high membership numbers of the ÖVP and the SPÖ, it is not astonishing that membership dues account for an average of 40.7 percent of the SPÖ's income and for 30.3 percent of the ÖVP's income. The more cadre-orientated party, FPÖ, however, gained only around 4.9 percent of its income from this source until 1988 (since then no

TABLE 7.6 Public Subsidies as Percent of Party Income at the National Level In Sweden

Year	M^a	Fp	C	SAP	Vp	Mp
1979	58.2	82.9	87.8	42.9	77.9	
1980	73.0	82.1	79.2	54.2	77.9	
1981	73.2	84.9	78.0	49.6	69.1	
1982	61.2	87.4	81.6	41.3	74.8	
1983	70.1	84.2	79.8	50.5	72.7	
1984	71.8	78.2	68.1	51.8	65.4	
1985	69.6	62.8	54.9	40.8	68.6	
1986	81.2	56.0	76.5	57.8	69.1	33.8
1987	71.0	76.0	76.4	45.4	59.3	28.0
1988	71.2	76.9	67.6	41.8	58.0	39.0
1989	82.7	85.2	78.0	40.7	48.6	84.0

[a]See Table 7.2 for party names
Source: *Verksamhetsberättelser av de svenska partierna*, 1979-1989.

TABLE 7.7 Membership Dues as Percent of Party Income at the National Level in Sweden

Year	M^a	Fp	C	SAP	Vp	Mp
1979	7.0	4.6	1.9	11.0		
1980	8.0	5.2	2.4	16.5		
1981	7.3	4.9	2.5	14.4	4.7	
1982	8.3	3.5	1.9	9.7	6.0	
1983	9.9	4.9	2.0	14.1	5.1	
1984	10.7	4.3	1.6	11.8	5.1	
1985	8.9	4.9	1.1	12.2	4.0	
1986	11.1	3.4	1.5	15.3	4.0	12.9
1987	11.9	6.2	1.6	10.0	4.3	7.2
1988	10.1	5.3	1.3	8.3	2.1	5.7
1989	10.4	5.0	1.3	9.3	2.5	3.3

[a] See Table 7.2 for party names

Source: *Verksamhetsberättelser av de svenska partierna*, 1979-1989.

TABLE 7.8 Membership Dues as Percent of Party Income at the National Level in Austria, 1986-1989

Year	SPÖ[a]	ÖVP	FPÖ	GreenParty
1986	32.0	31.1	4.4	---
1987	48.8	32.2	4.9	2.0
1988	47.4	29.5	5.4	1.5
1989	34.6	28.4	---	1.5

[a] See Table 7.1 for party names
Source: "Rechenschaftsberichte der österreichischen Bundesparteizentralen," in: *Amtsblatt zur Wiener Zeitung.*

membership dues have been transferred from the lower level to the national party organization). The Green Party, which has only a few registered members, received on average just 1.6 percent of its income from membership dues since 1987 (See Table 7.8).

Despite these differences all Austrian parties have experienced a decline of income from membership dues during the last few years. The SPÖ tried to compensate for this decline by raising membership dues from 30 to 40 AS per month in 1990. This is a solution which is difficult to implement in the ÖVP, because of its decentralised organization. The FPÖ tried in turn to counterbalance the decrease of traditional party income by raising "voluntary" contributions from office holders (party tax). Since 1976 the proportion of party taxes in the FPÖ's total income increased continuously and amounts to 26.5 percent today.

Further traditional sources of income for Swedish parties are lottery and material sales like almanacs, booklets, flags, etc. These types of sources increased in all parties during the last 20 years. Of all Swedish parties the Social Democrats have been the most successful in sponsoring these activities to finance their organization. In 1989 they received nearly 30 percent of their income from lottery and material sales.

Especially during election years a further source of income, voluntary donations from members and contributions from non-members, is important to all Swedish parties. However, large donations from corporations, interest groups and individuals are insignificant in Sweden today. The growing public criticism against any kind of "plutocratic" financing during the 1960-1970s forced especially the Conservatives and Liberals to abstain from soliciting from these sources of income. Today non-socialist parties receive economic support from enterprises only indirectly in the form of advertisements in party newspapers paid for by private companies.[46]

Contrary to Swedish developments, individual and group donations from associations like the Austrian Labor Union or the Federation of Industrialists are still important sources of income for Austrian parties, particularly for the ÖVP and FPÖ. Today the ÖVP receives on average around 11 percent and the FPÖ around 20 percent of its income from private and group donations. For the Greens and the SPÖ, this source of income is less significant. The proportions of all donations in these parties' total income fluctuate around the 5 percent mark. Nevertheless, a clear fluctuation of donation revenue can be seen in all Austrian parties, which can be explained only partly by the "election cycle." It seems clear that for the parties' finances as a whole, donations are unstable income sources (See Table 7.9).

As a result of several scandals (Rabelbauer, etc.) at the beginning of the 1980s,[47] donations to political parties which exceed 100,000 AS (about $8,000) must be listed separately and reported since 1984 in the *Amtsblatt zur Wiener Zeitung*. Two years before, however, a more rigorous regulation was temporarily on the statute book, according to which parties were to name and make public donations of more than 30,000 AS. But as a result of the SPÖ-FPÖ coalition (1983-1986), this provision was eliminated. In the end the limit was fixed so high that one cannot say that the new regulation led to more transparency or openness of party donations in Austria.

Over the years the lack of transparency regarding sources of donations brought about a general distrust in the Austrian public towards all kinds of party donations. This also may be one reason for the decline in the amount of donations, especially for the SPÖ (see Table 7.9). Because of the criticism and distrust of private finance for political parties and as a result of scandals in their own ranks, the SPÖ became wary of all kinds of donations. Today plans are being discussed inside the SPÖ to prohibit donations to political parties.[48] But whether these plans can be carried out against the opposition of the non-socialist parties remains to be seen.

It is clear that in Austria the traditional forms of party financing have changed in the last few years. The proportion of membership dues in the parties' total income is decreasing for all established parties at the national level. Donation revenues are unstable and marginal for the SPÖ. All parties tried to compensate for these declines by various strategies, but all of the measures implemented were not sufficient to balance the decrease of donations and membership dues. Against this background one can assume that the decline of traditional party income sources is one reason for the creation of a new type of public subsidy in Austria, the per elector subsidy in election years. In Sweden, however, the significant amount of public money paid to political parties did not prevent party leaders from financing some of their respective party organizations with the help of traditional income sources.

TABLE 7.9 Donations as Percent of Party Income at the National Level in Austria, 1984-1989

Year	ÖVP[a]	FPÖ	SPÖ	GreenParty
1984	17.8	31.4	0.05	
1985	4.9	22.1	6.9	
1986	14.1	9.8	9.7	
1987	13.9	16.3	7.6	6.2
1988	4.9	15.9	1.4	4.9
1989	12.3	25.7	2.8	5.6

[a]See Table 7.1 for party names
Source: "Rechenschaftsberichte der österreichischen Bundesparteizentralen," in: *Amtsblatt zur Wiener Zeitung*.

Party Expenditure

Annual reports of Swedish national party organizations allow only a limited comparison of various party expenditures. This is due to a very general agreement among the parties according to which every party can still apply different spending categories. In Austria, however, federal legislation introduced a standardization of expenditure categories to make the annual reports of the national party organizations more transparent. In order to be able to make a rough comparison of party spending patterns, three main categories of the Austrian Annual Reports, administration, staff and political activities, have been chosen. The reported Swedish expenditures also have been assigned to these three classifications in the following analysis.

The extent to which the category "political activities" includes campaign expenditures cannot be ascertained by studying the annual reports. In neither country are the costs of election campaigns enumerated separately in these reports. But the Austrian Party Act includes a regulation according to which political parties have to publish the amount of money they intend to spend for the national election campiagn five weeks before election day. Consequently, these specific publications might give some indication of the volume of national campaign expenditures in Austria. According to this information, the Austrian parties spent 80 million AS on their election campaign in 1986 (SPÖ 29,5 million, ÖVP 37,9 million and the FPÖ 13,3 million AS). Because of the fact that these 80 million AS cover just the campaign expenditures of all parties for the last five weeks before election day, one can assume that the real amount of election expenditures is significantly higher.

Both the Austrian and the Swedish parties have their highest expenditures in election years (See Figures 7.3 and 7.4). Because of the fact that in election years party expenditures are normally significantly higher than in non-election years, any comparison over time has to include at least one election year.

During the period 1987-1989, the total expenditure increased for all Swedish parties represented in the Riksdag, whereas the expenditures of Austrian parties fluctuated during the parliamentary term 1986-1990. In 1988 for example, party expenditures were lower than in 1987. Only the Green Party reported a continual increase of its expenditures.

The pattern of expenditures varies in both countries from party to party. During the period 1987-1989, spending for staff made up on average almost 50 percent of the expenditure of the Swedish Conservative and Liberal national party organization. But these two national party organizations also pay for staff expenditures of their respective party organizations on the regional and local levels. If one subtracts these outlays, staff expenditures by the Conservatives and the Liberals met the average (30 percent) of the other Swedish parties. Only the Social Democrats are below average. During the period 1987-1989, they spent only 7.3 percent of their expenditures for staff. In comparison to the expenditures for staff, the costs for administration are much lower for all Swedish parties at the national level. Their proportion of the parties' expenditure is only 3-10 percent.

The share of expenditures for political activities differs enormously in Sweden from party to party. The costs of these activities constituted on average about 69 percent of the Social Democrats' expenditures at the national level during the period 1987-1989 and 55 percent of the Center Party's expenditure, whereas the Conservatives on average spent just 9.3 percent for these items (See Table 7.10).

The differences between the Austrian parties are less apparent. During the election cycle 1986-1990, the proportion of staff expenditures amounted on average to 34.7 for the SPÖ, 28 percent for the ÖVP, 22.4 percent for the FPÖ and 28.7 percent for the Green Party.

Noteworthy is the high share of administration costs of the Green Party. With an average proportion of 19.8 percent during the election period 1986-1989, it is clearly above the average of all the Austrian parties (See Table 7.10). Expenditures for political activities constituted on average nearly 49 percent of the ÖVP's and FPÖ's total costs during the election cycle 1986-1989, whereas the proportion for the Green Party and the SPÖ was on average only 30 percent.

Despite the differences in expenditure patterns described above, one can conclude that with the exception of the SAP the Swedish as well as the Austrian parties did spend the largest share of their respective financial resources on maintaining their administrative machinery.

FIGURE 7.3 Total Expenditure of Austrian Parties at the National Level, 1988-1989

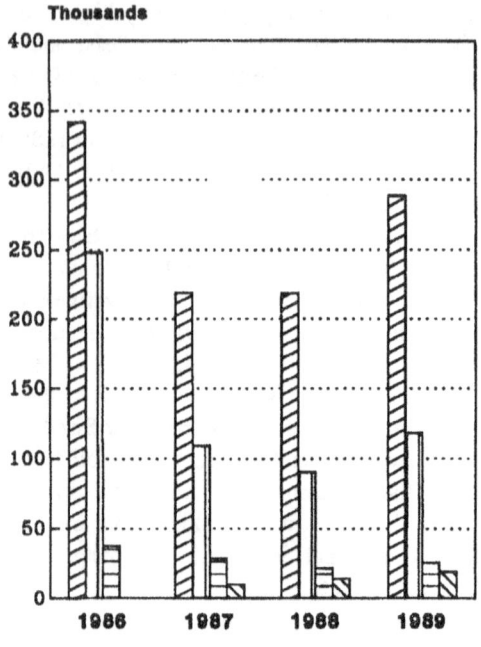

☑SPÒ ⊞öVP ☐FPÓ ◪Green P.

Conclusion

In Austria and Sweden the general direct subsidies paid on all levels of the respective political system are the predominant source of income for all political parties. Whereas in Sweden the lion's share of public payments to political parties is made by local governments, in Austria the highest proportion of public subsidies comes from the state governments. In comparison, the Austrian governments provide more public subsidies per elector for the activities of political parties than the Swedish governments.

The empirical data available for the national level in both countries reveal that public subsidies had different impacts on the parties' financial situation in each country. In Sweden public financing led to an abolition of donations from big business. Furthermore, voluntary involvement of party members (lottery sales and voluntary donations of party members) have increased since public subventions have been introduced. Contrary to developments in Sweden, in Austria traditional sources of income like donations and membership dues have decreased since 1987, and the national party organizations of the mass parties

FIGURE 7.4 Total Expenditure of Swedish Parties at the National Level, 1987-1989

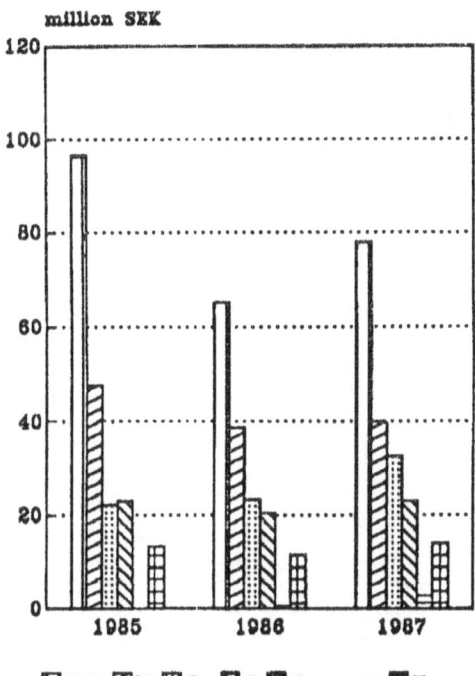

million SEK

☐SAP ☑M ⊞Fp ◩C ☐Green P ☐Vp

SPÖ and ÖVP have not been able to compensate for this financial loss by mobilizing their own members. Consequently, public party subventions had to be increased in Austria in order to finance the routine costs of party activities as well as the administrative machinery at the national level. With regard to plans to abolish donations to political parties in Austria, it is assumed that in the future Austrian political parties will try to create new and additional public financial sources to balance their eroding private sources of income. The election loss by the ÖVP in 1990, which brought about a drastic decrease in public funding for this party, may induce the ÖVP in particular to support additional public funding.

Considering the fact that the lion's share of public subsidies to political parties in Austria and Sweden is spent at the lower levels of the respective political system, a transparency of party income and expenditure at the local and regional levels is absolutely necessary to make any reliable statement about the real significance and effects of public party financing in both countries. But as long as the voluntary agreement in Sweden and the statutory obligation to report party income and expenditure in Austria are limited to the national level, the actual dimensions of party financing remain somewhat obscure.

TABLE 7.10 Patterns of Expenditures in Austria and Sweden (National Level Only)

Austria 1986-1989

Party	Staff				Administration				Political Activities			
	1986 %	1987 %	1988 %	1989 %	1986 %	1987 %	1988 %	1989 %	1986 %	1987 %	1988 %	1989 %
SPÖ	23.8	39.1	42.2	33.9	10.9	14.2	16.8	12.9	54.7	21.8	18.2	27.5
ÖVP	12.6	29.4	37.1	33.1	1.4	3.9	8.6	15.4	78.0	34.2	43.1	40.0
FPÖ	20.0	22.8	23.6	23.2	5.0	6.7	8.3	7.1	62.1	57.8	36.7	31.5
Green Party	----	25.8	30.9	29.5	----	25.7	18.1	15.8	----	28.7	35.6	26.9

Sweden 1987-1989

Party	Staff			Administration			Political Activities		
	1987 %	1988 %	1989 %	1987 %	1988 %	1989 %	1987 %	1988 %	1989 %
Vp	31.6	29.3	28.5	5.0	6.2	3.9	27.6	34.6	14.0
SAP	8.1	5.8	8.2	7.2	5.5	7.9	65.9	74.7	66.1
M	62.2	48.9	66.4	*	2.8	2.7	12.2	6.8	9.0
C	35.6	24.3	39.0	10.9	6.9	10.0	49.9	68.7	46.8
Fp	54.2	46.5	61.4	14.7	5.7	12.4	30.9	42.9	25.2
Mp	*	*	*	*	*	*	28.0	29.0	6.2

Notes

1. Proposition 1965:174, p. 7 and Wolfgang Müller, "Österreichs Regierungssystem" in Hans-Georg Wehling, ed., *Österreich* (Stuttgart: Kohlhammer, 1988),p. 82.

2. Hubert Sickinger and Rainer Nick, *Politisches Geld, Partienfinanzierung in Österreich* (Thaur: Kulturverlag 1990), p. 15.

3. Peter Rabl, "Sündenböcke reichen nicht," in *Profil*, No. 49, 1988, p. 12.

4. *Salzburger Parteienförderungsgesetz*, LGSBl 1981/79.

5. Statens Offentliga Udredningar (SOU) 1951:56, Om Offentlig Redovisning Av Den Politiska Propagandas Finansiering (Lund 1951), p. 59.

6. Nils Andren, "State Support of Political Parties," in *Scandinavian Political Studies*, No. 15, 1968, p. 225.

7. Dick Leonard, "Contrasts In Selected Western Democracies: Germany, Sweden, Britain," in Herbert E. Alexander ed., *Political Finance* (London: Sage Publications, 1979), p. 53.

8. SOU 1972:62, Offentligt stöd till de politiska partierna, 1971 ars partistödutredning (Stockholm 1972), p. 12.

9. Gullan Gidlund, *Partistöd* (Umea 1983), p. 356.

10. Harry Forsell, "Some Aspects of the Communal Party Subsidy in Sweden," Paper delivered at the IXth World Congress of the International Political Science Association, Montreal, Canada, August 19-25, 1973, p. 6.

11. Herbert Dachs, "Öffentliche Parteienfinanzierung in den österreichischen Bundesländern," in *Österreichisches Jahrbuch für Politik* 1985 (Wien 1986), p. 440.

12. Karl-Heinz Nassmacher, "Structure and impact of public subsidies to political parties in Europe: the examples of Austria, Italy, Sweden and West Germany," in Herbert E. Alexander ed., *Comparative Political Finance* in the 1980s (Cambridge: University Press 1989), p. 239.

13. Nationalrat XIII. GP, 150 Sitzung, 02.07.1975, p. 1008.

14. Michael Graf, "Überlegungen zur Parteienfinanzierung aus öffentlichen Mitteln," in *Österreichische Monatsblätter*, No. 1, 1985, p. 19.

15. 1 SEK = $ 0.16 U.S.

16. Leonard, "Contrasts in Selected Western Democracies," p. 56.

17. Lag om statligt stöd till politiska partier, 1972:625.

18. 1 AS = $ 0.08 U.S.

19. *Österreichisches Parteiengesetz*, BGBl 1989/666.

20. Rainer Nick/Hubert Sickinger, "Variations of Political Party Financing in Austria," Paper prepared for a presentation at the conference of the Research Committee on Political Finance, IPSA, Lake Como, 1987, p. 1.

21. *Österreichisches Parteiengesetz*, Art II ^U 2a, BGBl 1989/666.

22. Svenska Kommunförbundet ed., *Kommunalt förtroendevalda och deras arvoden 1989* (Stockholm, 1990), p. 39.

23. Landstings Förbundet ed., Circulär 90:36, *Landstingens medlemskommunernas anslag till partistöd för ar 1990* (Stockholm, 1990), p. 1

24. Hubert Sickinger, *Die politischen Parteien im österreichischen Recht*, PhD Thesis (University of Innsbruck 1990), p. 168.

25. Dachs, "Öffentliche Parteienfinanzierung...," p. 450.

26. Andreas Weber, "Parteienfinanzierung, Nehmerqualitäten," in *Profil*, No. 50, 1988, p. 33.

27. *Bundesrechnungsabschluß für die Republik Österreich 1988* (Wien 1988), p. 19.

28. Interview with the Bundesrat and Party Secretary of the SPÖ Salzburg, 8 March 1991.

29. Gullan Gidlund, *The Cost of Party Performance in Sweden*, IPSA Congress 1988, p. 8.

30. Lag om statlig stöd till politiska partier, in SSF, 1972:625.

31. *Bundesrechnungsabschluß für die Republik Österreich 1989* (Wien 1989), p. 13.

32. Sickinger and Nick, *Politisches Geld*, p. 107.

33. Herbert Dachs, "Über die politischen Akademien in Österreich" in *Österreichische Zeitschrift für Politikwissenschaft*, No 5, 1976, p. 391.

34. *Bundesrechnungsabschluß für die Republik Österreich 1990* (Wien 1990), p. 13.

35. Stig Hadenius/ Lennart Weibull, *Mass Medier* (Stockholm: Bonniers, 1989), p. 86.

36. Peter Musik, *Die Zeitungsmacher* (Wien, 1984), p. 259.

37. *Österreichisches Presseförderungsgesetz*, Abschnitt II, BGBl No. 38/1984.

38. *Bundesrechnungsabschluß 1989*, p. 13.

39. Dachs, "Öffentliche Parteienfinanzierung," p. 450.

40. Gullan Gidlund, "Financing Political Parties--The Swedish Model," ECPR-Paper, Rimini 1988, p. 11.

41. *Österreichisches Rundfunkgesetz* von 1974 (^U 5 (1)).

42. Sickinger and Nick, *Politisches* Geld, p. 98.

43. Ibid., p. 107.

44. Gullan Gidlund, *Det kommunala Partistödet*, Ds C 1985:8, p. 39.

45. Maurice Duverger, *Die Politischen Parteien* (Tübingen 1959).

46. Gullan Gidlund, "Tendenser i svensk partifinansiering," in SOU 1988:47, Kommunalt stöd till de politiska partierna, p. 125.

47. Barbara Wicha, "Parteienfinanzierung in Österreich," in Anton Pelinka/Fritz Plasser ed., *Das österreichische Parteiensystem* (Wien, 1988), p. 500.

48. Interview with the Bundesrat and Party Secretary of the SPÖ Salzburg, 8 April 1991.

8

Campaign and Party Finance in Germany

Hans Herbert von Arnim
Translated by Arthur B. Gunlicks

Introduction

"The parties shall participate in the forming of the political will of the people" (Article 21, paragraph 1, Basic Law; official translation). Given the suppression of democratic parties in the Third Reich, this constitutional provision was an especially progressive feature of the Basic Law (*Grundgesetz*) of 1949, because it recognized the legitimate role of political parties in a democratic system. Now, after more than four decades of "party state" democracy, (the "party state" in Germany refers to a political system in which disciplined political parties, not individual politicians as in the United States, dominate elections and the political process at all levels of government and engage in widespread patronage practices) the kinds of problems associated with parties have changed dramatically.[1] If the challenge after the collapse of the Hitler dictatorship was to establish the parties in a democratic system, today it can truly be said that they are more than well enough established. There is no longer any reason to handle them with velvet gloves or to make them immune from criticism. On the contrary. If it is true that power must be checked if it is not to corrupt, then the parties today are particularly in need of being controlled. In the words of the current German head of state, President Richard von Weizsäcker, they have spread like "fat spots," peering out from behind all state institutions, including those where they do not belong. In short, they have become engaged increasingly in the politics of spoils.[2] Contrary to the intention of the founders of the Basic Law, the parties have emerged as the ruling organizations of the entire sphere of public life. By use of patronage they penetrate the public service, the radio and television networks, the courts, the universities, and other institutions that were conceived by the Basic Law as independent and nonpartisan.

That the role of the political parties has grown beyond measure can be seen above all by their sources of financing. Just as conditions of the community at large have always been mirrored in public finances,[3] so also are the problems of party influences and the danger of abuse of established power reflected clearly in the finances of the parties (including the party groups [caucuses] and party foundations). If one adds together all of the forms of public finance received by the parties, party groups and party foundations during a four-year legislative period. one finds that the sum exceeds far more than four billion DM, on average more than a billion DM per year.

Once public financing of the parties has been established, especially in a parliamentary democracy, there emerges the problem of control. Without effective limits, well meant public financial support of the parties threatens to become a problem. The parliamentary parties fall into the temptation to provide more and more subsidies. Because they control the source of public finance, parliament and the parties represented in it decide alone and in their own interest. Their lack of neutrality calls for controls.

This presents a new set of problems for constitutional theory. According to the conventional understanding, parliament controls the government and the administration. As the representative organ of the citizens and taxpayers, its task originally was to limit state expenditures. In cases where it decides in its own interest, parliament threatens to become the initiator of expenditures and itself needs to be controlled. (The essence of parliamentary democracy, according to which decisions are assumed to be correct, is undermined when decisions are made in the parliament's self interest).

But who is in the position to control the controller? In a democracy, where power derives from the people, who in turn exercise this power above all in elections (Article 20, paragraph 2, Basic Law), attention must be directed first at the voter. But what influence can the citizen exercise with a ballot when the parties are united (or almost united) by means of agreements among the party group leaders, the party treasurers or even the party chairmen to form a kind of grand coalition in questions of party finance, that is, when the voter is rendered powerless by a lack of choice among alternatives? With the aid of such party monopoly, which tends to be justified by those responsible as an example of "unity among democratic parties," the established parties have been able to make themselves largely independent of the people in the area of public party finances (and in the areas of party group and party foundation financing as well as in the compensation of those elected to parliament). The situation is somewhat similar to that in a state in which the voter is confronted by a single party or a united block of parties in so far as he has no opportunity to use his vote as a defense against certain developments and abuses. For the control of the "controlling" parliament, there are--excluding any alternative applications of direct democracy --primarily two institutions of control that remain: constitutional court decisions and public criticism. The Federal Constitutional Court has seen *public criticism* as "the only effective control" over decisions that parliament makes in its own interest.[4] With this statement, however, the Court has attempted to cover up its own active role. In practice developments in party financing are determined to a considerable extent by decisions of the Court. Virtually all of the law concerning party finances was originally judge-made law (which parliament has adopted through regulations or revisions of the party law, tax laws and other laws).

Party Financing

Constitutional Provisions

The Basic Law is silent regarding public political financing. When the Parliamentary Council drafted the Basic Law in 1948-49, the idea of public political financing did not even occur to anyone. Since the parties in the Weimar Republic had been financed exclusively from private sources, the founding fathers (and mothers) of the Basic Law assumed of course that the previous "extraconstitutional" conditions would continue. Public financing was considered to be a constitutionally dubious practice in the early years of the Federal Republic. One of the founding fathers, the Hessian prime minister Georg-August Zinn, reflected later "that the idea of the state supporting the parties financially was completely unimaginable."[5] It was generally assumed-- also by the Federal Constitutional Court--that "the parties are responsible themselves for the financial expenditures associated with their organizations and activities."[6]

Transparency of Party Revenues

The founding fathers saw potential dangers in party financing coming from a completely different direction. They feared the unacceptable political influence of large private contributors and therefore required the parties to account publicly for their income (Article 21, paragraph 1, sentence 4, Basic Law). The voter was supposed to be able to recognize who was standing behind the parties so that he could draw whatever conclusions he wished. Details were to be regulated in a party law to be passed by parliament; however, there was hardly a constitutional mandate left unfulfilled for so long a time as the party law. Especially the parties that received large donations from business sources

(Christian Democratic Union [CDU]/Christian Social Union [CSU], Free Democratic Party [FDP], and the long defunct German Party [DP]) successfully resisted for a long time making such sources public. Finally, the party law was passed in 1967, eighteen years after the Basic Law went into effect.[7]

This demonstrates again the core problem of party financing: the decisions of parliament in matters affecting its own interest create entanglements and temptations which only a God could resist without effective controls. Almost twenty years passed until the Federal Constitutional Court intervened and forced the passage of the party law.

The party law of 1967 contains two major provisions. First, the names of large donors must be made public in the published financial reports of the parties. Until 1988 these included donors who contributed more than 20,000 DM per year; since 1989 the law applies to those that contribute more than 40,000 DM. Secondly, the sources of party funds have to be reported by major categories. Both provisions are inadequate in terms of closing all of the potential loopholes.

The Inadequacy of Public Accounting Provisions. The limit of 40,000 DM for contributions is too high, because donations in this amount can have a massive influence at the regional level. One donor and his or her spouse could each contribute up to 40,000 DM and not be named in the public accounting. There is also no adequate penalty for a failure to publicize the name of a donor. There is hardly any other provision that is ignored so frequently and openly as the publicity requirement. While it is true that since 1983 the tax benefits that party contributions enjoy are dependent on their publication, large donors appear to be more interested in anonymity than in tax deductions. In such cases the incorrect impression is created that the connection between tax benefits and the publicity requirement allows the donor to avoid the latter by not accepting the former. There is an additional possibility of avoiding the publicity requirements: there is no requirement to publicize contributions made directly to parliamentary deputies, although the donor often can achieve at least the same results as with contributions to the party. (The obligation of the federal parliament [Bundestag] deputies to reveal contributions of more than 10,000 DM to the President of the Bundestag in accordance with the so-called "behavior rules" is the opposite of publication, because the declaration is not made public.)

It is a surprising fact that German law provides no penalty directed at bribing deputies, whether the action is initiated by the donor or the recipient, a situation which one criminal law expert has called a "dangerous, disturbing, almost inconceivable loophole."[8] In other countries bribery of parliamentary deputies is almost universally penalized. Since the inquiries made by the courts and parliamentary investigating committees in the Flick Affair (a scandal involving illegal donations to several German parties and politicans by a large business enterprise)[9] and news media accounts of the practices of large donors from the private business sector, we also know that direct contributions to deputies are not insignificant but rather widespread. In the meantime they have assumed an importance that is possibly similar to contributions to the parties, even though public attention is directed exclusively toward party contributions. But the lack of regulation and publicity regarding direct contributions to deputies is of *great practical relevance*.

Publicity Requirements of Income Sources and Loopholes. A further example of a publicity loophole was created in 1984 when the requirement was dropped for a separate listing of certain important sources of party income in the annual party financial reports, including above all the so-called "party taxes" (supposedly voluntary "contributions" or assessments on public salaries paid by elected officials to the party) and bank loans. Both categories are particularly sensitive, which makes a public accounting especially critical. Their exclusion from the annual public financial reports was based on a pretext which reminds one of the most preposterous, distorted formulations commonly found in dictatorial systems: "party taxes" were excluded with the explanation that they were illegal. While this is true, this cannot be the reason for their concealment; rather, it serves at best as a reason for their prohibition. However, they were not prohibited. "Party taxes" are being assessed as before.

Another example of a publicity loophole concerns bank loans, which were excluded from reporting requirements on the grounds that they had to be repaid. This is an argument the speciousness of which can be seen in the proposition that therefore loans in the public budgets in general should no longer be listed separately. In fact, of course, a *separate* category for loans is indispensable.

Publication of Party Expenditures and Party Assets. Since 1984 the Basic Law and Party Law have contained provisions for a public accounting of party expenditures and party assets. The figures appear in the annual public financial reports of the parties and are then incorporated in the annual Party Finance Report of the Bundestag President. While this is the current situation, there was no transparency at all in the 1950s. Instead of following the constitutional mandate of 1949 requiring a public accounting of party income, the parties increased by massive amounts their direct and indirect financing from the public treasury and created a significant tax benefit for donations and membership dues as well as a rapidly expanding system of direct public subsidies.

Tax Benefits for Party Donations and "Equality of Opportunity"

The historical development of party financing is full of complexities and (like the regulation of the party finance system as a whole) can be reconstructed only when one takes into consideration the frequent interventions of the Federal Constitutional Court.

The Tax Benefits of 1954. In 1954 the Bundestag majority consisting of the CDU/CSU, FDP and DP (against the opposition of the Social Democrats [SPD]) passed a law which provided tax benefits for donations and membership dues. Donations and party dues up to ten percent of personal income and two mills of total corporate sales, wages and salaries were made tax deductible. The Federal Constitutional Court declared these provision unconstitutional in 1958, because they gave the recipients of high incomes (and the parties that were most likely to benefit from their generosity) an advantage that violated the principle of "equality of opportunity" (*Chancengleichheit*).[10] Later the Party Law of 1967 provided for a credit of 600 DM (for couples 1200 DM) for donations and party dues. These figures were tripled in 1979.

Avoidance Schemes, Attempts to Gain Amnesty. By the end of the 1970s it was revealed that the parties had encouraged their large contributors to "go around" (*umgehen*) and therefore break the restrictive regulations concerning tax deductions. Thousands of legal cases resulted, some of which have not been completed to this day. The disposition of these cases under the criminal codes was almost made impossible in 1981/82 and again in May 1984 when an attempt was made to introduce a legal amnesty for the many individuals and companies accused of wrongdoing. Both attempts failed, in part because of public protest.

Explosion of Tax Subsidies. The revelations regarding massive tax fraud did not, however, have the effect of securing compliance with the existing rules. Instead the tax deductions were expanded further by new laws. With the help of a special commission, the members of which were named formally by the Bundestag President but actually by the parties, a revision of the relevant laws was pushed through. In accordance with the new provisions, donations and membership dues may be deducted up to five percent of personal income. The obvious incompatibility of this regulation with the Court decision of 1958 was supposed to be overcome by additional public funding. This was to be achieved first by a fifty percent tax deduction for donations and membership dues up to 1200 DM per annum.

The "Equal Opportunity" Rule. The second part of the revised law that was seen to distinguish it from the provisions of 1958 concerned the principle of "equal opportunity" (Party Law, paragraph 22a). The purpose of this very complicated provision which even experts have difficulty understanding is to compensate with public funds parties that receive relatively small total private donations and therefore do not benefit indirectly from the tax deductions received by the donors of the other parties.

The 1986 Party Donation Decision of the Federal Constitutional Court. The Federal Constitutional Court declared the five percent rule unconstitutional in 1986, although to the surprise of virtually all experts and the politicians in Bonn it also approved a tax deduction for donations up to 100,000 DM. This was a maximum limit, and in 1988 the Bundestag provided for tax deductions up to 60,000 DM (for couples up to 120,000 DM).[11] With this revision the maximum tax deduction allowed was increased almost 34 times in comparison with the regulations of 1979 (1,800 DM and 3,600 DM). The Party Donation Decision was met with widespread criticism in the professional literature. It is apparent that the general public can make little use of the provisions which benefit largely the recipients of large incomes. The unexpected change of course in the Court followed the appointment shortly before the decision of Justice Hans Hugo Klein to the decisive Second Senate (the Federal Constitutional Court is divided into two senates).[12] Justice Klein, a former professor of law at the University of Göttingen, had expressed himself in the literature in favor of a thoroughgoing loosening of court barriers to tax deductions for political party [13]

Changes in the Equal Opportunity Provisions. A few years following the introduction of the so-called "equal opportunity" provisions in 1983, it became clear that they contained a "system failure" and benefitted the wrong parties. The SPD, for which the provisions were primarily drafted, did not benefit at all. Instead the chief beneficiaries were the small parties (Greens, FDP and CSU), although these were also relatively successful recipients of donations. A revision of the equal opportunity provisions was carried out in 1988. This occasion was also used to increase substantially the amounts provided. The rules today are even more complicated. Their beneficiaries now are above all the large parties, SPD and CDU.

The revision of the equal opportunity regulations was criticized even during passage in the Bundestag.[14] On the other hand the critics were subjected to strong attacks by the supporters of the new provisions.[15] Now even the parties[16] and sympathetic political scientists[17] concede the serious deficits of the revisions and their probable unconstitutionality, thereby recognizing the legitimacy of the previous criticism.

The So-called "Base Payments" (*Sockelbeträge*). In order to mollify the small parties which lost some of their advantages under the original equal opportunity provisions, an additional source of public funding was introduced: the so-called base payments under Section 18, paragraph 6 of the Party Law (to be described below). This revision took place under severe pressure of time. The party treasurers not only conferred regarding the proposed bill and later changes but also set the timing of the legislative process and persisted in demanding that the new financial regulations go into effect by the beginning of 1989.

The entire course of this legislation confirms the thesis that a parliament deciding in its own interest avoids to the greatest extent possible the passage of restrictive rules and the subsequent disciplining of the parties. Instead, it tends to extract whatever it can from the public treasury.

Discrimination Against Local Nonpartisan Political Groups. In contrast to the above examples, the Bundestag has taken plenty of time (and still continues to do so) in reducing the discrimination in public financing against local nonpartisan political groups. These received no tax benefits whatsoever until 1988. Two decisions of the Federal Constitutional Court in 1985 and 1988 were necessary before parliament finally reacted and the nonpartisan groups were included at least in the tax benefits of the Income Tax Law contributions (50 percent credit for contributions up to 1200 DM). That is hardly comparable to the benefits received by the parties, however. Donors who contribute to nonpartisan groups receive a maximum of 600 DM a year in tax credits (50 percent of 1200 DM), whereas those who contribute to political parties may receive a tax benefit up to 31,800 DM (53 percent [the peak tax rate in Germany] of 60,000 DM). The local nonpartisan groups continue to be disadvantaged, however, especially when one considers that they are excluded from the "equal opportunity" funding and the reimbursement of election campaign costs (including the *Sockelbeträge*) at the *Land* and federal levels. Some of this reimbursement for election costs is used for local election expenditures by the parties. Based on experience up to the present time, changes in the law that would favor the local nonpartisan groups can hardly be expected without strong external pressures. The parties represented in parliament tend to abuse their power to legislate when they can place their extraparliamentary competition at a disadvantage.

Federal Tax Benefits in Germany in the Lead. If one compares the tax benefits for party donations and party membership dues (including the "equal opportunity" funds) in Germany with other countries, it is apparent that with the possible recent exception of France, provisions in other Western democracies do not come anywhere close. The United States even eliminated all tax benefits for party contributions in the Tax Reform Act of 1986. In addition limitations are placed on the amount one may contribute (at the federal level, $5,000 per candidate per election).

Direct Public Financing of the Parties Through the Reimbursement of Election Campaign Costs and the "Base Payments"

At the same time that the Federal Constitutional Court ruled in 1958 against tax benefits for party donations, it suggested that a direct public subsidy would be acceptable. Soon thereafter the 1959 federal budget was provided with funds for the parties in the Bundestag: five million marks in 1959, 38 million by 1965. That was a first in Europe and would have been a first in the world had not Costa Rica in 1954 and Argentina in 1955 introduced public party financing.

The Federal Constitutional Court Pulls the Emergency Brake. Obviously in reaction to the explosive increase of subsidies, the Court placed limits on the current trends when it heard a case in 1966 brought before it by the SPD Government of Hesse and a number of smaller parties. The justices distinguished between the total expenditures of the parties and the costs of election campaigns and declared that only the reimbursement of "necessary costs of a reasonable election campaign" was acceptable; a general party financing (including funds for political education) was not permissible. The Court also declared that public funds were not to exceed one-half of all sources of party income.[18] (Since the Court demanded in addition an Election Campaign Cost Reimbursement Law, the Bundestag had no choice but to pass in 1967 the Party Law that had been mandated by the Basic Law in 1949). The Court put up another barrier in 1968 when it declared that the Bundestag had to take the expenditures for the election campaign of 1965 as a basis and in principle could increase the reimbursements over time only in accordance with the corresponding increases in costs.[19]

Five Marks per Voter. The Party Law of 1967 provided for an election campaign cost reimbursement of 2.50 DM per eligible voter. This amount was increased to 3.50 DM in 1974, applied to the election campaign for the EC's European Parliament in 1979, and increased to 5 DM in 1983.

Therefore the parties now receive a 5 DM reimbursement per eligible voter (not just per actual voter) for federal parliament, *Land* parliament, and European Parliament elections. The focus on eligible votes means, of course, that electoral participation does not affect the total amount of reimbursement. With around 60 million eligible voters in the new united Germany, this means for each of the three categories of election about 300 million DM.

The funds are distributed to the parties and other participating groups based on the proportional results of the elections. The recipients must receive at least 0.5 percent of the vote to qualify. The Rhineland-Palatinate and North-Rhine Westphalia raised the reimbursement in 1990 from 5 DM to 6.25 DM per voter for their respective *Land* elections.

"Base Payments" (Sockelbeträge). In addition to the above funds, the federal government provides the so-called *Sockelbeträge* mentioned above. Every party that receives at least 2 percent of the vote in elections for the federal parliament receives these funds. The base payment amounts to 6 percent of the campaign cost reimbursement for Bundestag elections (about 300 million

DM), or about 18 million DM per party. The amount received is reduced steadily for parties with less than 7.5 percent down to 2 percent of the vote, so that parties with only 2 percent of the vote receive 4.8 million DM. In 1990 North-Rhine Westphalia added a base payment for parties participating in *Land* parliament elections.

Extension of the Public Accounting Requirement to Include Expenditures and Assets. The massive expansion of public party financing made an extension of the public accounting requirement from sources of income to expenditures and assets unavoidable. A public accounting of the uses of public funds is also required. This is an iron principle of budget law and of a democratic state.[20] That is the reason why Article 21 of the Basic Law and the Party Law were amended in 1983. Since then the public financial statements of the parties have shown their expenditures and assets (as well as their debts).

Criticism. Permitting only campaign cost reimbursements while prohibiting a general public financing of the parties, as the Federal Constitutional Court has done, has been criticized frequently over the years. Election campaigns are in fact difficult to distinguish from other activities, because parties by nature are engaged continuously in campaigning. The focus on elections nevertheless makes good sense, because it allows individuals and groups that otherwise have no party status but participate in elections to take advantage of public funding provisions. This helps to prevent the emergence of certain party privileges and keeps the political process somewhat more open.[21]

The constitutional grounds for the limitation of public funding to campaign cost reimbursements, i.e., "freedom of the parties from state control," are not persuasive. Determining the amount of public financing by the benefiting parties themselves in the parliament raises not so much the question of control of the parties by the state as that of the state being manipulated and exploited by the parties for their own purposes. An exaggerated public financing brings about an estrangement between the parties and their members and supporters and promotes their "etatization."[22] Small and new parties and nonparty political forces such as local nonpartisan groups are increasingly strangled financially with the growing amounts of public financing for parties, party groups/caucuses and party foundations. The danger, then, is not so much state control of the parties as a weakening of grass roots party support and a less open political process. The purpose and the irreplaceable function of the Federal Constitutional Court can be found in preventing an uncontrolled self-service by the political parties with all of its negative consequences. The controls over and limits placed on the parties by the Court in public financial cases--in spite of justified criticism regarding details--have been relatively successful. This becomes especially clear when one takes as a comparison those areas over which the Court has not mandated limits, i.e., the public financing of party groups and party foundations.

Public Financing of Party Groups (Caucuses) and Party Foundations

None of the limits drawn by the Federal Constitutional Court since 1966 applies to the party groups. This has resulted in incredible increases in subsidies. The public subsidies for party groups in the federal parliament (*Bundestag*) alone have risen from 3.4 million DM in 1966 to more than 100 million DM in 1991, or an increase of 30 times the original subsidy in 25 years. An increase based on rising costs alone would have amounted to three or four times the original sum. If one adds the subsidies over a four-year legislative period, the payments to party groups are now 400 million DM, that is, they are higher than the campaign cost reimbursements for all-German parliamentary elections which amount to about 300 million DM (not including base payments).

A similar subsidy explosion occurred with respect to the party foundations.[23] The ink was barely dry on the 1966 decision by the Federal Constitutional Court forbidding public financing of political education by the parties when in 1967 public grants amounting to nine million DM for the purpose of promoting activities regarding "social policy and democratic education" by four party foundations were initiated. By 1990 the budget for the Federal Interior Ministry contained an item for this purpose amounting to 165 million DM, whereby these payments were only a part of the total categorical and bloc grants of 545 million DM received that year by the party foundations. In 1966 the total was 14 million DM. (A few years ago a foundation for the "Greens" was created, following their unsuccessful attempt in 1986 to have the foundations declared unconstitutional by the Federal Constitutional Court.)

It is interesting to note that the public financing of the party groups and party foundations has hardly been noticed by public opinion up to now, and it continues to take place almost surreptitiously. In contrast to subsidies for the parties, there is no regular law or justification, even for huge increases, but rather only an obscure budgetary process that provides the financing. In accordance with the 1983 revisions of Article 21 of the Basic Law, the parties have to account for their revenues, expenditures and assets. This does not apply to the party groups and foundations, although one could certainly draw an analogy under Article 21 between them and the parties. Also the material limits that the Court has applied to the parties (e.g., no more than 50 percent of their revenues may come from public financing) do not apply to the party groups and party foundations. This has led to the explosion of public subsidies described above and to a shifting focus, largely unnoticed by the public, from the parties to the party groups and party foundations which now receive much more support from the public treasury than the parties.

Disproportions and Interconnections Between Lack of Controls and Money

In the financing of the party groups and foundations, there is an obvious deficit of transparency and control on the one hand and luxurious financing and explosive growth of public funding on the other hand. The evidence certainly suggests that the inadequacy of publicity and control and the excess of money are mutually dependent. The fantastic growth rates would not have been possible without the consistent shielding from public view of the financial status of the party groups and foundations. When those making the decisions in their own interest are not even required to give a public accounting of the purposes of the expenditures of the public funds received, the assets accumulated, and the debts remaining, then a bottomless barrel exists in which even more public funds disappear.

Therapy

Our diagnosis points to various therapies. At least *three* actions are required:

First, the requirement introduced in 1983 according to which the parties had to account for their expenditures and assets was based on the argument that the parties were being financed to a significant extent from the public treasury. This requirement should be made applicable to the party groups and foundations which receive almost 100 percent of their financing from public sources. It has been shown that this financing is less open to public scrutiny and yet much higher that the subsidies granted the parties.

Second, the party groups and foundations should be required to follow general budgetary accounting procedures and meet their requirements specifically in the relevant budget and accounts. The complete public financing of the party groups has been justified by the Federal Constitutional Court on the grounds that the party groups are "part of the organized state system." For that reason, though, they should be treated like other recipients of public funds and meet the minimum requirements of budgetary rules.

Third, special laws for the party groups and foundations need to be passed. Future increases in public funding should be contained in laws that are published in parliamentary reports and discussed in public debates, with the results published in the legal record. This would permit the media to perform a controlling function and force the parliaments to provide justification open to public scrutiny. The legal regulation of the grants to party groups and foundations is also required by the constitution;[24] however, the Federal Constitutional Court has expressly refused to rule on this question up to now.

Court Cases in Karlsruhe and Münster

On 26 November 1991 the Second Senate of the Federal Constitutional Court heard another in a long series of cases involving public financing of political parties.[25] The Greens and a nonpartisan voter group brought the case before the Court. The Greens asked the Court to rule on the constitutionality of tax benefits for donations and party dues as well as the equal opportunity funds (*Chancenausgleich*). At the same time they declared their opposition to the high publicity threshold that applies to donations of 40,000 DM or more (80,000 DM for married couples). The voter groups assailed the so-called base payments which (as in the case of the tax benefits and the equal opportunity funds) apply only to parties, not to local nonpartisan electoral groups. The decision of the Court is expected in the Spring of 1992.

The constitutional court of the *Land* (state) of North-Rhine Westphalia in Münster is also in the process of deciding a case involving political financing. In the fall of 1990 the *Land* parliament raised the campaign cost reimbursement for *Land* elections from 5 to 6.25 DM per eligible voter, even though the federal party law calls for a reimbursement of 5 DM. It was also the first *Land* to introduce the base payment, even making it retroactive to apply to the last *Land* election held six months earlier.[26] The Greens and an ecology group have brought a complaint before the Court in Münster urging it to rule against these new laws. The decision of this Court, too, is expected sometime in 1992.

Should the Courts decide against the parties, it would hardly be the first time. There is hardly any other area that has been so strongly influenced by judges. The reasons have already been discussed. In the case of public political financing, the parties that control the parliaments decide in their own interests and arrive at monopoly-like agreements that exclude the voters and turn the "control by ballot" argument into a farce. The authority over lawmaking and public budgets can easily tempt the parties to abuse their power and privileges, which leads to an incrustation and obstruction of innovative forces, to putting more distance between the parties and the citizens and to further citizen annoyance with the parties (*Parteienverdrossenheit*). This is where the consequences of the growth of uncontrolled power of the parties (and that of the party-recruited "political classes") and the need to oppose these trends become especially apparent.

Loosening of the Barriers

Especially ripe for elimination are the base payments and the equal opportunity funds. In order to avoid a verdict of unconstitutionality regarding the base payments, the Greens, who along with other smaller parties profit most from such funds, excluded these from their complaint before the Federal Constitutional Court. Instead, they are asking the Court to revise its insistence on reimbursement only of campaign funds for the parties in favor of a public financing of the parties in general. (In the meantime the Federal Constitutional Court has combined the two complaints from the Greens and the voter group, which is of considerable concern to the parties in Bonn). The Greens have received support from the established parties for their argument before the Court, as is demonstrated by a discussion paper prepared by Dr. Uwe Luethje, the general counsel of the Treasurer of the CDU.[27] Assistance has also been provided by a paper written by two political scientists who have ties with the major German parties, CDU and SPD, and who were apparently inspired by Luethje.[28]

This unusual alliance of forces is united in its attempt to eliminate the limitations on subsidies that existed until now for campaign cost reimbursements and to increase the 50 percent limit to 75 percent or more. Such measures would break the dam. Limitations placed on the parties that decide in their own interest have been the most important characteristic of the Federal Constitutional Court's decisions. Whoever calls for a change in such decisions must first explain how the parties are to be controlled in the future. But any other means of control lacks plausibility and therefore effectiveness and would mean even more increases in the future.

The proposal to base decisions regarding party funding on the tasks of the parties and the ensuing financial needs, according to the model of the "Commission to Ascertain the Financing Needs of Radio Stations,"[29] may seem plausible by a superficial observation. But in reality such a commission would be a Trojan Horse that would open the gates to a total public financing of the parties. A similar proposal by Rudolf Wildenmann[30] was correctly rejected by the Federal Constitutional Court in 1966. This method of determining the financing needs of the parties would be wrong, because the needs of competing parties are potentially limitless and therefore controllable only at the sources of funding. Experience suggests that controls would be completely undermined if the parties were successful in appointing their sympathizer to a "Commission to Ascertain the Financing Needs of the Parties."

The Untenable Equality of Opportunity Funds

There is a general consensus that the equality of opportunity funds cannot be sustained in the Court (a point made expressly by Luethje[31]), an assessment which the author was criticized for making before a committee of the federal parliament in September 1988.[32] The error from the beginning was mixing membership dues which do not require equalization funding with donations, on the grounds that the two cannot be separated. The result was that wrong parties were given preference. For that reason the provisions of the law were changed in 1988 and in the process the funding dramatically increased. Membership dues and donations were separated, and a separate equalization fund for each was provided. The result, however, is that the original grounds for the inclusion of the dues, that is, that they cannot be separated from donations, have been abandoned, and the equality of opportunity funds have lost their justification. This has had certain negative consequences for membership dues, which are the least problematic source of party revenues. In the final analysis the equalization funds are additional public subsidies.

If the equalization funds are declared unconstitutional, the tax benefits for large donors who contribute up to 60,000 DM will also become vulnerable. This limit must be reduced sharply, which should not be too difficult because large donors make up only a small fraction of the total revenues of the parties. In compensation the 50 percent credit for donations and dues up to 1200 DM could be increased moderately. This would bring about a connection between public support and private initiative, thus benefiting smaller contributions that do not lead to dependencies for the parties. The argument that a reduction of tax benefits from the current 60,000 DM limit would again create an incentive for bypassing the law is not convincing, because such an incentive already exists at least regarding the limits concerning publicity requirements, for example, the ever increasing direct donations given to influential parliamentary deputies.

Conclusion

The issues raised by public party financing concern more than just money, which in any case is an expression of power and simultaneously a means of expanding power. The question is whether the powerful in the state can use the legislative process to serve their own purpose or whether the rule of law will apply to them as well. It is a question that concerns the relationship of money, power and law in the democratically constituted state.

Appeals to justice are not enough. No party is in a position to regulate itself, because all parties are concerned about their competitive position and of being disadvantaged. So long as there are no constitutional provisions--if necessary made more concrete by the Federal Constitutional Court--that place constraints on all parties, the tendency to expand public financing at the expense of the community will continue. In principle the issue is the appropriate response of the constitution and the Courts to the expansion of the party state.

Postscript

On 9 April 1992 the Federal Constitutional Court rendered its long-expected decision on political finance.[33] Deviating in part expressly from its earlier decisions, the Court declared almost the entire system of public financing to be unconstitutional. This confirms much of the criticism contained in the essay above.

According to the new decision:

- The requirement to publicize only the names of contributors who donate more than DM 40,000 is too generous, especially for donations made at the regional level (see above); the Court set the publicity threshold at a maximum of DM 20,000.

- Direct contributions to parliamentary deputies must be publicized in the future, when they exceed DM 20,000. The publicity requirement includes the President of the *Bundestag*, to whom larger contributions were to be revealed even before the Court's decision (see above).

- The system of equality of opportunity funding is completely unconstitutional (see above).

- The tax benefit for large donations is also unconstitutional (see above).

- The base payments are unconstitutional.

- The Court eliminated the previous limitations on the public financing of election campaign costs. The very real danger that this could lead to excessive public financing was met by the Court's imposition of two restrictions.

First, the Court held to its insistence that no more than 50 percent of the revenue of the parties may come from public funds. Second, the Court established an absolute maximum figure. In the future public funds may not exceed a total amount larger than the average for the years 1989-1992. Increases will be permitted in accordance with the consumer price index.[34] The distribution of the funds has to be on the basis of three criteria: the number of voters, the amount of party dues, and the volume of donations. Details are to be provided by the *Bundestag*.

The Court has obligated the lawmakers to pass new legislation that incorporates all of the above principles by the end of 1993, that is, before the next *Bundestag* and European Parliament elections scheduled in 1994.

The decision affects only the financing of the parties and election campaigns, not the even weightier and more problematic public financing of the parliamentary party groups (*Fraktionen*) and party foundations (see above). It is important that a reform of the public financing of these institutions also be undertaken. Otherwise it appears that a general, overall solution of the problems of German political finance will not be possible.

On 19 May 1992 a decision was also rendered by the constitutional court of North- Rhine Westphalia in Muenster. This *Land* Court rejected the increase in the campaign tax reimbursement from 5 to 6.25 DM per voer and, like the Federal Consitutional Court, overturned the provision of base payments to the parties (See p. 211).

Notes

1. For a general discussion of this point, see Hans Herbert von Arnim, *Die Partei, der Abgeordnete und das Geld* (Mainz: Verlag von Hase und Koehler, 1991).

2. Richard von Weizsäcker, "Krise und Chance unserer Parteien- demokratie," in: *Aus Politik und Zeitgeschichte*, B 42/1982, pp. 3-4; also "Herausforderungen an alte und neue Demokratien," Ansprache vor der Konferenz uber Parlamentarische Demokratie im Europarat in Strassburg am 16.9.1991, *Bulletin der Bundesregierung* 1991, pp. 793-794.

3. The symptomatic as well as original meaning of finances in politics was often emphasized by Joseph A. Schumpeter. See for example, "Die Krise des Steuerstaates," in: Rudolf Goldscheid/Schumpeter (Hg.), *Die Finanzkrise des Steuerstaates*, 1917, and in a later edition by R. Hickel, Frankfurt: Verlag Suhrkamp, 1976, pp. 329, 332.

4. *Amtliche Sammlung der Entscheidungen des Bundesverfassungs- gerichts* Bd. 40, pp. 296, 327. The standard form of citation for decisions of the Federal Constitutional Court = *BVerfGE* 40, 296 (327).

5. See Ulrich Duebber, *Geld und Politik*, (Freudenstadt: Eurobuchverlag, 1970), p. 97.

6. *BVerfGE* 20, 56 (108).

7. For a brief summary in English of German party finance from 1949 to 1967, see Arthur B. Gunlicks, "Campaign and Party Finance in the German 'Party State'," *Review of Politics* 50, No. 1 (Winter 1988), pp. 31-34 and "The Financing of German Political Parties," in Peter H. Merkl, ed., *The Federal Republic of Germany at Forty* (New York: New York University Press, 1989), pp. 229-232.

8. Herbert Tröndle, "Diskussionsbeitrag, " in *Niederschriften über die Sitzungen der Grossen Strafrechtskommission*, Bd 13 (1962), pp. 257-258.

9. For a brief discussion of the Flick Affair, see Gunlicks, "Campaign and Party Finance," p. 39 and "The Financing," pp. 241-243. See also Christine Landfried, *Parteifinanzen und politische Macht*: Baden-Baden: Nomos Verlagsgesellschaft, 1990, pp. 143 ff,; Goettrik Wewer, *Parteienfinanzierung und politischer Wettbewerb*, (Opladen: Westdeutscher Verlag, 1990), pp. 420, 443 ff.

10. *BVerfGE* 8, 51 (64-69).

11. *BVerfGE* 73, 40. Compare the persuasive dissenting opinions of Justices Boeckenfoerde und Mahrenholz (*BVerfGE* 73, 40 U103 ff.

218

12. For a discussion of the organization of the Federal Constitutional Court, see Donald P. Kommers, *The Constitutional Jurisprudence of the Federal Republic of Germany* (Durham: Duke University Press, 1989), pp. 19-21.

13. For a critical review, see Hans Herbert von Arnim, *Parteienfinanzierung. Eine verfassungsrechtliche Untersuchung* (Schriften des Karl-Braeuer-Instituts des Bundes der Steuerzahler Nr. 52), Wiesbaden, 1982, pp. 76 ff.

14. See Hans Herbert von Arnim, "Stellungnahme zur geplanten Aenderung der Parteienfinanzierung im Herbst 1988 vom 17.11. 1988," reported in the documents of the Hearings of the Committee of the Interior of 21 November 1988 (Anhoerung, 190-274); see also *Der Spiegel* Nr. 45 (7 November 1988,) pp. 25-26.

15. See further Hans Herbert von Arnin, *Die neue Parteienfinanzierung* (Schriften des Karl-Braeuer-Instituts des Bundes der Steuerzahler Nr. 67), Wiesbaden, 1989, pp. 130 ff.

16. Uwe Luethje, "Zum Normenkontrollantrag der Gruenen: Anmerkungen, Bewertungen, Schlussfolgerungen," Manuscript dated 12 January 1990; also "Thesen zur Neuordnung des Parteinenfinanzierungsrechts," Manuscript dated 4 July 1991.

17. Werner Kaltefleiter and Karl-Heinz Nassmacher, "Probleme der Parteienfinanzierung in Deutschland," Manuscript 1991, p. 7.

18. *BVerfGE* 20, 56 (113).

19. *BVerfGE* 24, 300 (339).

20. von Arnim, *Parteienfinanzierung*, pp. 102 ff. and pp. 94 ff.

21. Ibid., pp. 94 ff.

22. Landfried, *Parteifinanzen*, p. 14, 275 ff. See also Ibid., p. 95.

23. For a brief discussion of the German party foundations, see Gunlicks, "Campaign and Party Finance," pp. 34-35 and "The Financing," pp. 237-238.

24. Hans Herbert von Arnim, "Zur Wesentlichkeitstheorie des Bundesverfassungsgerichts," *Deutsches Verwaltungsblatt* Heft 24 (December 1987), pp. 1241, 1245 ff.

25. See Hans Herbert von Arnim. "Die Bonner Beutemacher" in: *Die Zeit*, Nr. 48 (22 November 1991, North American edition), p. 5.

26. See Hans Herbert von Arnim, *Wahlkampfkostenerstattung und Grundgesetz, verfassungsrechtliches Gutachten für den Bund der Steuerzahler Nordrhein-Westfalen* (Schriftenreihe des Bundes der Steuerzahler Nordrhein-Westfalen Nr. 18), Düsseldorf, 1991.

27. Uwe Luethje, "Zum Normenkontrollantrag," pp. 17 ff.

28. Kaltefleiter/Nassmacher, "Probleme der Parteienfinanzierung in Deutschland," 1991.

29. Ibid., pp. 25 ff.

30. Rudolf Wildenmann, "Gutachten zur Frage der Subventionierung politischer Parteien aus offentlichen Mitteln," Meisenheim am Glahn. 1968.

31. Luethje, "Zum Normenkontrollantrag" pp. 4 ff.

32. *Protokoll der Bundestagsdebatte vom 9.12.1989*, e.g., pp. 8595, 8598.

33. Aktenzeichen *BvE* 2/89.

34. This was already proposed by von Arnim, *Die Partei, der Abgeordnete und das Geld*, p. 291.

9

Problems of Party and Campaign Financing in Germany and the United States--Some Comparative Reflections

Peter Lösche

Introduction

Political finance is a fascinating subject. It contains the stuff of detective stories. It smells of corruption--individuals or interest groups buying access or favorable legislation, perhaps bribery of a member of parliament or even of a small party. When we talk about campaign and party financing, we focus on "political money."

Why do candidates and parties need money? They fight election campaigns, they maintain interelection organizations, they have to conduct political research. They have to publicize their activities. In other words, candidates and parties need money to gain power or to stay in power.

What do we really know about the impact of "political money"? Does massive spending in election campaigns win votes? (We know that spending too much money can backfire). Can particular bills or administrative acts be influenced by interest group donations? If so, to what extent? What is the effect of political money on the internal structure of a party or--for example in the case of a presidential campaign--of a larger campaign organization? Can contributors try to target different wings or auxiliary organizations within a party in order to promote their particular interest? What is the effect of political money on the relative power of parties within a party system? There are many questions, almost no answers, but a lot of speculation.

When one looks at political financing from a comparative perspective, it is fascinating to observe that in different political systems very similar issues and problems arise and that quite often reform proposals are quite similar. There is, for example, the problem of ever rising campaign costs. Parties as well as candidates are confronted with the potential undue influence of special interest groups. Should there be public funding of campaigns and parties? Should there be free television advertising for candidates and parties? Should there be limits on donations and expenditures? What are the regulations in regard to disclosure? How should the regulations be enforced? Is it even possible to regulate party and campaign finances effectively?

The main problem in campaign and party financing is not corruption, crime, tax evasion, undue influence of fat cats or special interest groups, but the *appearance* of corruption, crime or undue influence. The appearance of wrongdoing and manipulation has brought about increasing public cynicism about politicians, parties, political processes and political institutions. In Germany the catch word *Parteiverdrossenheit*--"annoyance with parties"--reflects the negative feelings people have about parties, especially about the way parties and politicians finance their organizations and campaigns. Any campaign and party finance reform has to focus on exactly this problem, namely, the image of corruption, crime or undue influence. Any campaign and party finance reform has to seek not only to make political financing understandable to a broader public, but also to make plausible that financing candidates, campaigns or parties is part of a normal political process, that political money is not necessarily dirty money.

In the following I will focus on some current issues which are debated vigorously in the United States and Germany. (For example, there are campaign funding reform bills pending in Congress, and the German Federal Constitutional Court has to decide in a case before it on the current Party Law in the Federal Republic [ed. note: see the postscript following the preceeding chapter by Hans Herbert von Arnim.]) These are the problems I want to discuss:

- How should we cope with the alleged undue influence of special interest groups?

- What kind of and how much public funding (including free advertising) should we have?

- What is the impact of campaign and party financing on internal party structures?

- Do the current systems of campaign and party financing promote the "ossification" of our respective political systems?

- Would a limit on campaign expenditures solve most or at least some of the problems that confront us in campaign and party financing?

- How should we enforce campaign and party financing regulations?

Of course, we have to bear in mind that we are dealing with two different political systems, both in terms of institutions and of political processes, two systems which are unique if we look at them closely and analyze them precisely. We find that we are not only comparing different varieties of apples, but different kinds of fruit. To put it more precisely: comparison of our two systems not only stimulates us to reflect on our respective political systems; it also encourages us to engage our political imaginations to the point that we might think about borrowing some features and regulations from each other. While making comparisons, though, we must always keep in mind the more fundamental structural differences between our two political systems:

1) In the American presidential system of government, there is a separation of powers characterized by a permanent competition between the legislative and the executive branches. In a parliamentary system of government the majority in the legislature and the cabinet are politically identical, with the actions of the cabinet supported by strong party discipline in the parliament.

2) The United States has a *candidate*-centered electoral system, in which candidates run, organize and to a considerable extent finance their own campaigns. Political parties are generally weak in organization and discipline. In contrast the Federal Republic of Germany has a *party*-centered electoral system in which parties not only run and finance election campaigns, but also have a virtual monopoly in the political process (party state).

3) In the U.S. the nomination process is much more open than in Germany. The primary system may result in the nomination of candidates that have little or no *party* support. In the Federal Republic candidates are nominated by active party members only; the nomination process is conducted more by one's political peers. While in the U.S. a candidate may have to run an expensive primary campaign, in which he criticizes opponents in his own party, in Germany a candidate generally has to start as an apprentice and move up the career ladder within the party.

4)   While politics in the U.S. at the state as well as at the national level is characterized by an almost permanent campaign, election campaigns in Germany are comparatively brief.

5)   While American elections take place in single-member districts, proportional representation dominates the German electoral system.

Undue Influence of Special Interest Groups?

The alleged undue influence of interest groups used to be and still is one of the most critical problems in campaign and party financing in the United States and the Federal Republic. But it is not so much political reality as the appearance of corruption or crime that is particularly devastating for the political culture in each country. There is no doubt that in both countries corruption and influence buying have been a feature of political reality. But a relatively small number of scandals have blown the problem out of proportion. In general one could argue that the motivation of interest groups in giving donations to parties or candidates is quite legitimate; they want to gain access. Thus, campaign and party donations and lobbying are nothing but complementary means of gaining representation in a pluralist society. While the rules of the game are quite different in the U.S. and Germany, the results of the respective games are not too far apart.

In the Federal Republic there are no limits on contributions whatsoever. The party finance scandals in Germany have been about tax evasion, fraud, and in a very few instances corruption; they were not about illegally high amounts of donations. In terms of party politics German industrial unions are bipartisan (although there is a bias toward the SPD, at least one CDU-member is on each union's federal executive committee). This means that allegations of undue influence via political financing must focus on the role of corporations and employer associations.   These business organizations have institutionalized *staatsbürgerliche Vereinigungen*, de facto auxiliary organizations of the employers associations, which solicit and coordinate campaign contributions from their members and funnel political money to particular parties. Although ideologically employers are closer to the conservative CDU, a kind of incumbency bias can be observed (similar to the U.S.): if and when the Social Democrats are in power, they will receive more and higher donations from *staatsbürgerliche Vereinigungen* and individual corporations (this is true for the federal level as well as for the states (*Länder*). Of course, even very large contributions cannot "buy" one of the two large parties in Germany. Their funding is much too diversified, combining private donations, membership dues, and public funding. However, if a small party cannot operate on membership dues and public funding, it will depend on large private contributions (e.g., the

Free Democrats in the 1960s, 1970s and early 1980s) and an impact can be observed. There is some evidence, but also a lot of speculation, that the Free Democrats left the coalition with the SPD in 1982 to join a cabinet with the Christian Democrats because of large business donations targeted at the right wing of the party. In 1983 one billionaire owner of the department store chain, Horten, gave 6 million DM to the FDP, more than all of the party's membership dues combined in the same year. It is easy to see that the fact that there is no limitation on the amount of donations one can give to a party contributes to the appearance of undue influence by corporate and business interests.

In the U.S. one finds a very different situation. Political action committees (PACs) are regulated comprehensively and in detail. There is a long history of campaign finance regulation, going back to 1907 and 1911.

Corporate as well as union contributions are much more decentralized in the U.S. than in Germany, paralleling the decentralized structure of American interest groups. However, the American Business Industry Political Action Committee, somewhat like the *staatsbürgerliche Vereiningungen* in Germany, tries to coordinate corporate contributions from Washington. But disclosure is handed much more rigorously in the U.S. than in the Federal Republic.

In Germany only contributions over 40,000 DM have to be disclosed, while in the U.S. contributions over 200 dollars are reported. Nevertheless, one also has to deal in the United States with the appearance of undue influence by interest groups and their political action committees. The reason is quite simple: in 1988, 34 percent of the funding for House and Senate general election campaigns came from political action committees. Some 41 percent of House candidates' funds came from political action committees; 47 percent of the funds for the campaigns of House incumbents came from PACs.

In both countries there is considerable suspicion that both candidates and parties depend financially on interest groups. However, the real political problem is the rumor of undue influence or corruption, not necessarily the political reality of undue influence. Nevertheless, there have been enough examples of undue influence in the political process to keep the rumors alive and well. Especially in Germany rumors are encouraged by an authoritarian tradition in our political culture, namely, resentments against parties, political conflict and politics in general.

What can be done? Of course, one could try to educate and enlighten the public. This not only would take a very long time; it might also be in vain. A reform proposal in the U.S., which appears to be radical but is not, might be much more successful. This proposal has been promoted by President Bush and the Republicans. It was introduced in 1989 by the two minority leaders in the House (HR 3425) and Senate (S 727), respectively. Some Democrats have also rallied behind the proposal. It would prohibit contributions from political action committees sponsored by unions, corporations, and other interest groups. The idea behind HR 3425 is very plausible and sensible for both countries: donating money to candidates or parties can be interpreted as an act by a participant in the political decision making process somewhat comparable to casting a vote on election day, and only those who have the right to vote should be allowed to make donations to parties or candidates. Thus, interest groups, corporations, and independent political action committees would be excluded from giving money to campaigns. They would have to focus their effort exclusively on lobbying, which is an adequate and acceptable role for them in the political process.

One can think of ways to get around this kind of prohibition. For example, corporate or union funds could be channeled through selected individuals to candidates or parties. But disclosure and investigative reporting by the media might be a sufficient check on this potential abuse. The main point of this proposal is not to stop forever all illegitimate and illegal contributions to campaigns and parties. This is probably impossible. Instead, the political rationale of the proposal points in another direction: elimination of the appearance of undue interest group influence or even corruption. If and when donations by corporations, trade associations, and unions are outlawed, it might even be possible to tackle the problem of *Parteiverdrossenheit*.

Public Funding

Political scientists have regarded public funding as a means of reducing the dependence of parties or candidates on special interest groups. In Germany public funding has been largely a reaction to increasing campaign costs. Furthermore, public funding is supposed to promote equal opportunity for competing parties and to preserve opportunities for all citizens to participate equally in financing elections.

However, because of public funding a new problem has emerged over the last two decades in the Federal Republic: party dependency on the state, i.e., on public budgets at the federal and *Land* levels. When one adds up the various public funds, parties receive 70-80 percent of their finances from public coffers (not including tax deductions and tax incentives). Thus:

1) According to the proportion of votes cast for them, parties get campaign costs reimbursed for state, federal and European elections (about 6 marks per voter or about 300 million DM for all parties for each election mentioned above).

2) Parties receive about the same amount of money for their political foundations, which legally are independent of the parties; but they provide research, educational and even diplomatic facilities and--to some degree-- patronage for the parties (about a 150 million DM per year go to the foundations).

3)   Free TV time is allocated to parties during election campaigns, based on the share of votes they received at the last elections.

4)   The parliamentary parties, or party groups (*Fraktionen*) also receive substantial public funds which amount to almost 100 million DM per fiscal year in the *Bundestag*.

5)   Finally, according to the most recent amendments of the Party Law, party organizations which gained at least 2 percent of the vote in the most recent federal elections receive "base payment" subsidies from the treasury of the Federal Government (about 6 million DM per year).   This contradicts all decisions of the Federal Constitutional Court in regard to party financing. The Court has ruled that parties cannot be subsidized generally, that only the necessary costs of an appropriate election campaign can be reimbursed. Therefore, the Green Party has challenged the amendment, and a decision of the Court is pending (ed. note: see the postscript following the preceding chapter by Hans Hebert von Arnim).

These examples illustrate the thirst of parties not only for money in general, but for public funds in particular, a condition that has been compared to that of an alcoholic entering a self-service liquor store. What will happen if the supply of alcohol (public money) is shut off? German parties have become addicted to public funds and dependent on the state.

The United States presents a different story. At the federal level there is public funding only for presidential primary and general election campaigns. Twenty-one states have established different public financing schemes for their elections, and about half of these states funnel the money through the parties.

In general neither the parties nor the candidates depend on public funds in the United States.   Rather, public funding--where it exists--promotes the diversification of political money and makes candidates a little more independent of fat cats and special interests.

Free TV time, for example, as a condition for renewing a broadcaster's license, could be granted to American parties, which would determine the allocation of time among different candidates and the party. This would not only cut campaign costs substantially; it could also free candidates and parties--at least to some extent--from the appearance of submitting to undue interest group influence or corruption. Such proposals have been made by political scientists, but they have been vigorously opposed by the Association of American Broadcasters.

There is another dimension to public funding (which one finds also when looking at all types of campaign and party finance resources, but is particularly obvious with public funding), and that is the impact of public funding on the intra-party structure.

Impact of Party and Campaign Financing
on the Internal Party Structure

Today in the Federal Republic, because of the patterns of campaign and party financing, and especially because of public financing, party executive committees on the *Land* and federal levels have become independent of the party membership, that is, independent of membership dues and small donations. For example, party executive committees can do without party members; in regard to campaign and party financing, they do not depend on the grass roots. Rather, campaigns (and to some extent even the party bureaucracy) are financed through the public campaign reimbursement funds, large contributions (from employers associations and/or *staatsbürgerliche Vereinigungen*) and loans that the party executive committee can take out.

This is not a reference to Robert Michels' "iron law of oligarchy" at work in our parties, a "law" that does not fit the intra-party reality today. Rather, party executive committees on the state and federal levels are almost autonomous, rather like independent monarchs not accountable to the membership. Of course, this is a problem of intraparty democracy.

The party leadership in Germany should be made more accountable to the membership in financial matters. Therefore, I would like to borrow from the American example of publicly financed presidential primaries and propose that each mark that a local party committee collects in membership dues and small contributions should be matched with one mark from the public treasury. Thus, the current method of reimbursing parties for their campaign expenditures would be abolished. Public money would not go to the top hierarchy of the *Land* or federal parties; rather, the party hierarchy would depend financially on the grass roots. This proposal would also provide an incentive to organize new members. Furthermore, such a regulation is biased against small parties and favors mass membership parties. In the political reality of Germany such a regulation would mean a challenge for the FDP, a party that not only depends on public finances but even more on large interest group donations.

While party organizations seem to be too powerful and entrenched in Germany, just the opposite is true for the United States. The vast majority of American political scientists as well as many politicians agree that parties should be strengthened for purposes of campaign financing.

A first step in party building could be taken by reducing the importance of political action committees by outlawing all political action committee contributions. A second step could be taken by giving party committees the right to conduct and finance without any limitations organizational activities on behalf of their candidates (such as research, registration and get-out-the-vote drives, mailing, TV and radio commercials). Party committees should be exempt from current limits on donations and campaign spending. Finally, a third step to strengthen parties would be to allocate all public campaign funds (including free TV-time) to parties and not to candidates. With this German approach to campaign financing, parties would have to decide how to use public funds: whether to spend the money and TV-time in marginal districts; whether to allocate a certain share to all candidates or focus on marginal districts; whether to spend some money for promoting the party and its slate of candidates. This proposal may look "un-American" in a candidate-centered system, but today already about a dozen states do channel public funds to parties. There might be some side-effects to this proposal; for example, since parties would gain some power deciding about the allocation of public funds to candidates, it might become attractive again to run for party positions.

"Ossification"?

One criticism made against the current party and campaign financing schemes in the United States and Germany is that of "ossification," i.e., that the current systems favor incumbent parties and candidates; the current party system will be perpetuated forever; and the current parties loose sensitivity toward new issues and challenges.

The argument used in Germany in this context is a simple one. Supposedly there is no equal opportunity for the parties competing for power, because only those parties which received 0.5 percent of the vote in previous elections qualify for public campaign reimbursement. History has proven this charge to be wrong. Public financing was the most important incentive for the highly fractionalized Green groups, movements, and citizen initiatives at the end of the 1970s to stay together as a party in order to be reimbursed for the *Land* election campaigns in Lower Saxony and Bremen. This also was the case in the federal elections of the 1980s. Again, the same is true for the right-wing "Republicans." They are highly fractionalized, but their strong incentive not to dissolve the party is the reimbursement of campaign election costs. Thus, political experience has shown that public party and campaign financing have provided an incentive for small parties to stay together and participate in election campaigns. The differentiation in the German party system came about not the least because of public party financing.

There can be little doubt that the current system of campaign financing in the United States favors incumbents. The situation would change drastically if contributions from political action committees were outlawed and parties strengthened financially in a way that they would have to focus on marginal districts when allocating public funds.

As an outside observer I sometimes wonder about the current debate in the United States on term limitations. In a country for which weak political institutions were designed quite purposefully, political experience should be even more appreciated. Furthermore, I wonder if the de facto seniority system is not the problem when speaking of ossification rather than incumbency. In any case "ossification" in the United States and Germany does not seem to be a result of campaign and party financing.

Limits on Campaign Expenditures?

Many commentators in both countries regard limits on campaign expenditures as a kind of "miracle solution" to all kinds of problems. Expenditure limits are the dividing line between Democrats and Republicans in the Senate right now. All kinds of questions are raised by this proposal:

- Do limits affect free speech (voluntary limits or limits linked to public funding)?

- Can the quality of election campaigns be improved through limits? (In both countries there are negative election campaigns which annoy voters because they avoid political substance; however, if expenditure limits are introduced, campaigns would not necessarily focus on issues. Rather, campaigns could become even slicker and lose all political substance.)

- How should spending limits be enforced?

- Would spending limits have a negative effect on grass-roots participation?

There is one main objection against spending limits: they are easily avoided. In order to enforce spending limits, a complex, highly bureaucratized enforcement agency is required. Therefore, I would argue in favor of a free political market, which, however, should work under certain conditions:

- There should be rigid disclosure to expose anyone who is spending very large sums of money.

- Parties should be strengthened and made more accountable.

- Interest group (PAC) contributions should be outlawed.

In the context of this discussion one issue becomes increasingly important: Even if one deregulates as much as possible, how does one enforce those campaign and party finance regulations which are still in the statute books?

Enforcement

In terms of party financing in Germany there is one structural weakness that stands out: there is almost no enforcement of the Party Law. There are only two provisions that are routinely enforced. First, a professional public accountant (often a party member) has to prepare a party finance report. Second, the parties have to submit this report once a year to the Speaker of the *Bundestag* (the report is then published by the *Bundestag* as an official document). But such reporting requirements did not prevent party finance scandals that were known for decades without any action being taken.

In regard to enforcement, I would like to borrow an item from the Federal Election Campaign Act, namely the Federal Election Commission, an independent regulatory agency (somewhat similar to the German *Bundeskartellamt*, an anti-monopoly agency). Members of a German Federal Election Commission should be elected the same way judges are elected to the Federal Constitutional Court, i.e., by a two-thirds majority in one of the two houses of the legislature. There is no need to explain the proposal in further detail; the parties are strongly and vigorously opposed to a German Federal Election Commission. It would take another party finance scandal to get them to create that kind of agency.

In the United States the Federal Election Commission has been the subject of much criticism and the object of many proposals for the improvement of its enforcement function. Much of the dissatisfaction with the agency is in fact a reflection of the shortcomings of the Federal Election Campaign Act. But the United States at least has an enforcement agency. In Germany institutionalized enforcement is lacking.

Conclusion

Can we learn from each other? I think we can. Since it was possible to transfer American election campaign techniques to West European countries (adapting them to national circumstances), it should be possible to implement in the Federal Republic the kind of enforcement agency found in the United States. The lack of such an agency is one of the most serious problems in regard to party financing in Germany.

The dependency of the German parties on public funds and the need to increase membership participation and the totals of membership dues in order to make the *Land* and federal executive committees accountable to the grass roots is the second major problem in Germany.

The main problem in the United States is the weakness of parties. This forces most candidates for public offices to seek funds from various interest groups and wealthy individuals, therefore opening them to the charge of having been "bought."

This is in fact an important problem that we have in common, namely, the undue influence or the appearance of illegitimate influence of interest groups on parties, candidates, and elected officials. This problem can be solved by pursuing the radical proposal I put forward: outlaw all interest group and corporate contributions to parties or candidates.

Other proposals might be to introduce rigid disclosure requirements and to promote a greater diversification of funds and a better balance among the three major sources of campaign and party financing: membership dues and small contributions; large donations; and public funds.

The goal of political finance reform should be to combat the increasing distrust of parties in the political system, which in the Federal Republic is based on traditional anti-party-sentiments stemming from the political culture of the *Obrigkeitsstaat*. Is there a chance to realize party and campaign financing reforms in the United States and Germany? Amendments of the U.S. Federal Election Campaign Act and the German Party Law have to be brought about by legislators and political parties that profit from the current status quo. Therefore, public pressure is needed.

Since American political institutions are much more sensitive to public opinion, the chances for election campaign reform in Washington are much better than in Bonn. Voluntary expenditure limits are the dividing line between Democrats and Republicans today. But a compromise consisting of the following elements is conceivable:

- public funding of campaigns (supported by Democrats)

- no or very high expenditure limits (supported by Republicans)

- no limits on contributions to party committees (supported by Republicans)

- restrictions on the role of political action committees (supported by Republicans and some Democrats and a majority of political scientists).

In Germany the Federal Constitutional Court has been the most important force in promoting party financing reform. Decisions are pending on the most recent amendments of the law on political parties. Furthermore, with the recent amendments of that law an advisory commission has been installed which is obliged to put forward reform proposals. However, parties will be very cautious in implementing any proposals. Thus, we probably need another serious scandal before fundamental reform steps are undertaken.

PART FOUR

Political Finance
on the Research Agenda
in Comparative Politics

10

Comparing Party and Campaign Finance in Western Democracies

Karl-Heinz Nassmacher

Introduction

A look at any sample of Western (liberal) democracies necessarily leads the political scientist to realize that he or she is dealing with party democracy. Political parties emerge from the analysis as inevitable and indispensable "instruments of democratic government."[1] Accepting this fact brings funding of political competition and party activity into the focus of scholarly evaluation.

Political parties in Western democracies obviously perform functions crucial for the political system. Does this mean that their routine operations as well as their campaign activity are a public service and hence should be supported by public funds? Or can the democratic mass public still rely on private interests (e.g., party supporters or institutional donors) to provide the funds needed to keep parties going? These two strongly interrelated questions have become an issue of public policy in all Western democracies.

Party Government and Political Finance

Money needed to cover the expenses incurred by parties and candidates is provided by citizens who pay one way or another for their specific form of government. At first glance this statement seems to be a truism. Political debate generally emphazises a difference between private contributions and public subsidies as main sources of political funds. Nevertheless, it is always the citizens who finally pay in order to run a democracy, although they may be acting in their capacity as party members, party supporters, members of an interest group, consumers of goods and services, or as taxpayers.

Private sponsorship used to be the normal way of funding political activity in Western democracies. Today, however, public subsidies have become a necessity, for there is no other way to bridge the permanent gap between the amounts provided for political purposes by voluntary giving and the expenditures for the numerous functions of political parties. Experience with political corruption accompanying party fundraising and unequal opportunities for party competition have contributed to the proliferation of public subsidies. Each system of financing has been a specific answer to problems resulting from previous strategies of private political funding. Among the developed industrial democracies, Germany and Britain have chosen almost completely different political paths to deal with the issue.[2] Other nations, like Canada, the United States, Austria or Sweden, which have been the focus of numerous national studies of campaign and party finance,[3] seem to have taken a middle path and share one or the other feature from either end of the policy spectrum.

Parties in Britain (the U.K.) rely almost exclusively on private funds provided by individual supporters and institutional donors, especially the trade union movement and the corporate sector. Party membership has decreased over time. Spending has been adjusted to available funds. Legislation to curtail the flow of institutional donations into the opponent's coffers has been introduced (e.g., the Companies Act of 1967 as well as the Trade Union Act of 1984). Major scandals related to the funding of political parties have not occurred. No tax incentive of any kind for political donations is available to British subjects.[4]

In sharp contrast to the British example, all major parties of (West) Germany have been affected by scandal and revelations of laundered money for party activities, with most cases involving illegal tax exemptions for political donations. A considerable increase in party membership has provided additional funds. An elaborate system of public subsidies to parties and party-related bodies as well as considerable tax benefits for political contributions have provided the funds necessary to build impressive permanent and highly professionalized party organizations and to stage rather expensive election campaigns.[5]

This attempt to compare the different situation of political finance in two countries presents by no means a complete picture. Any comparative study has to focus on funds raised and spent in order to influence the outcome of elections as well as to support the routine operation of political parties. In addition, Khayyam Z. Paltiel has mentioned a third purpose of providing services (for the leadership), especially public opinion polls (surveys), research on public policy issues, training and recruitment of party workers and candidates.[6] All Western democracies must confront questions regarding the financial dimension of party government. Nevertheless, there are many problems of definition and demarcation: Which elections should be considered? Which activity exactly is part of a political party?

Defining Political Party Funding

Establishing the pattern of party financing demands the selection of reporting units. Many sub-units of parties have to be considered separately in order to present a complete picture of party activity; regarding the party as a "holding company" demands data for all potential "subsidiaries." This includes party headquarters at the national level and state (province, *Land*) level, field organizations all over the country, parliamentary caucusses, candidate campaigns, primaries, leadership contests, factions, service organizations and even some Political Action Committees (PACs). Other units that must be included are all party and (serious) independent candidates for all legislative bodies, executive or ceremonial offices elected by popular vote. Elected "heads of state" have to be considered only in Austria, Finland, France and the United States, where the election of a president is an important arena for party competition.[7]

Most data, however, do not include certain aspects of political finance that may be relevant and important, e.g., municipal elections or nomination of constituency candidates. How should spending in the nomination process, e.g., U.S. primaries, or spending on intra-party competition, e.g., Canadian leadership contests or Italian factions (correnti), be handled? Non-partisan elections in most municipalities relieve North American parties of a financial burden faced by their European counterparts. PACs as a specific type of fundraising organization and primaries as a nomination procedure for legislative candidates are unknown outside the United States. Nomination of constituency candidates in Canada is supposed to be more expensive than similar processes in Western Europe, but it is considerably less costly than U.S. primaries. The tradition of rather expensive competition among contenders for the leadership of any provincial or federal party is a special feature of Canadian politics.[8] The costs of nomination and leadership contests or intra-party factions (an important feature of Italian, Japanese and French party politics) can only be estimated by informed observers.

The various elements of a "party structure" consist of the party organization, legislative (parliamentary) party groups (caucusses), and party-directed institutions (e.g., foundations, enterprises). Party structure in most countries conforms to the levels and units of public administration, although there may be specific subdivisions like federal ridings and provincial constituencies in Canada or congressional and state legislative districts in the U.S. Generally supra-national (EC), national/federal, regional (states, provinces, etc.) and local/municipal organizations can be considered as relevant tiers (levels) of party organization.

Due to space and data limitations, this chapter focusses on the national (federal) level. Data for the supra-national, e.g., the European Parliament, or the sub-national levels (states, provinces, *Länder*, etc., where there is a federal system, or local governments) are even more sketchy and incomplete. Research therefore has to begin with those units that provide the most publicity of their activities. Thus even the campaigns run by candidates for mayor of a big city as well as state governors or their parliamentary equivalents will not be within the scope of this study.

Major Problems of Cross-National Comparison

Looking at the current state of research on political finance, a general conclusion reached by Michael Pinto-Duschinsky[9] in 1985 still seems to hold. First, there are too many gaps in our knowledge about financial sources, such as international money, pressure-group activity, secret funds, personal wealth, and changing flow of money due to regulation. Second, there is too little theory based on suitable methodology. Arnold Heidenheimer presented a theory in the 1960s, but we do not have one now. This was also Maurice Duverger's dilemma:[10] Where do we start when theory and data (facts) are equally absent? In addition to this question we must also face the absence of clear and common categories which frustrates most attempts at a cross-national comparison.

Lack of Theory / Conceptualization

Heidenheimer already hinted at the dilemma: "Advances toward the more genuinely comparative study of political finance processes require on the one hand greater amounts of data and information, and on the other unifying concepts which will help relate structures peculiar to various systems in terms of realistically conceived common denominators."[11] Since Heidenheimer and Alexander Heard started cross-national research of political finance,[12] elaborate studies of campaign and party finance (both national and comparative) have focussed their attention on a particular set of countries.[13]

With respect to political finance, there is more information available now in most countries than there was two or three decades ago. Scholarly studies have provided much useful information, and regulations often require periodical reports on political money. We also have hypotheses regarding the impacts of regulation and public funding. Nevertheless the dilemma stated by Duverger in 1951 and re-emphasized by Kenneth Janda[14] in 1980 is still prevalent. Data covering all aspects of party activity are presently not available for any one country, let alone several. Therefore, purists might argue that comparative work on political finance should be postponed until more than one nation has been studied in depth. Like the comparative volumes edited by Herbert Alexander,[15] this study takes a pragmatic approach of looking at the available data without waiting for other relevant, but as yet unavailable, information.

Availability and Quality of Data

Defining the range and focus for comparative studies, a workshop on "Money and Politics"[16] has suggested that a narrow definition of "political money" should be applied which includes money spent by candidates and parties for campaign as well as non-campaign purposes. An attempt to estimate the costs of party democracy can rely on data that have been published in accordance with national regulations in several countries. Any quantitative approach aiming at the costs of democracy is restricted by the individual requirements of specific regulations. In spite of the omissions that are caused by unregulated areas (the financing of leadership contests and intra-party factions being the most important examples), the regulation of election finance has produced considerable information on current expenses, campaign spending and fundraising of political parties in different political systems.

But the data available are still far from complete. Data concerning party and election finance published by public authorities have to be supplemented with additional information gathered by field research. Preparing a comprehensive set of comparable data requires specific computations. Any scholarly interpretation of the data patchwork resulting from different sources of information has to consider the quality of available data as well as the relevance and size of missing data.

The major obstacle to a satifactory comparison of data for political spending in different nations is created by the combined effects of deviating election cycles for individual political systems and creeping inflation. Some effects can be controlled when data given in current money terms are converted into amounts not distorted by the decline of purchasing power for the individual currency. Both economic growth measured by the gross domestic product (GDP) and purchasing power measured by the consumer price index (CPI) qualify as potential deflators. But the data adjusted for inflation still do not resolve the problems created by currency exchange rates that do not represent real purchasing power or the considerable difference in size among individual countries. The latter problem can be resolved by providing amounts per person eligible to vote. If voter registration is the result of outreach activities of the agency in charge (not depending on any effort of the individual citizen), the number of voters listed can be considered reliable data. The reliability of other data sometimes depends on the demarcation selected when defining terms of everyday language for research purposes.

Problems of Demarcation

The term "political finance" carries different connotations. On the one hand political finance is object and result of political processes. The public funding of parties and/or campaigns is determined by policy decisions of politicians. For this reason Gullan Gidlund[17] has chosen political financing as a concept that contrasts with private or plutocratic funding of parties and elections. On the other hand political finance is frequently used as a term that integrates two important aspects of the subject analyzed in this volume, i.e., party as well as campaign finance.

For the campaign and candidate-oriented political cultures of North America, political finance connotes campaign finance in terms of money spent in order to influence the outcome of an election. In Europe the term political finance is frequently used as a synonym for party finance, including both inter-election routine and campaigning. (Considering the effects of the specific electoral system, Japan should be closer to the American, Australia closer to the European, example.) In North America public subsidies were introduced, because electronic media advertising caused skyrocketing expenses regarded as necessary for successful campaigns. Spending limits have been another part of the answer to this problem. None of the European countries (except Britain and France) has introduced anything close to regulations familiar in the U.S. and Canada. Although election campaigns have become more expensive on the European continent, too, parties there face financial burdens unknown to their North American counterparts: a permanent field organization with full-time party agents at the grassroots as well as a party press which is increasingly unable to maintain itself in the newspaper market.

In European countries a substantial segment of newspaper circulation has been controlled traditionally by political parties. In (West) Germany the bourgeois party press did not recover after World War II, and Social Democratic (SPD) papers have been declining steadily from the 1950s to the 1970s. During the 1980s, Italy introduced legislation concerning press subsidies. In Austria and Sweden public subsidies for the press[18] are closely linked to legislative action regarding parties and their funds.

Cabinet government in many democracies has contributed towards the development of disciplined party organizations (the United States and Switzerland are the most notable exceptions). On the other hand some sort of devolution (decentralized government or federalism) has created rival power centers (Britain is the important exception here). The traditional party system in most cases (except the United States and New Zealand) consists of more than two parties, repeatedly under challenge by new party formations.

Besides these aspects, other and older problems of demarcation become relevant. e.g., distinctions between political finance and money in politics (corruption), pressure-group influence, non-party political institutions (especially third party advertising), political money versus the politicians' money, and costs of democracy versus costs of democratic politics. As long as adequately precise criteria for such distinctions are missing, a definition of political expenditure necessarily has to rely on crude estimates for the amount of political money spent.

Although political finance in North America is more closely regulated than party activity in Western Europe, there are unreported monies as well as unregulated areas on both sides of the Atlantic ocean. Among them are issues of demarcation between public administration and party activity, including abuse of legislative privilege (e.g., franking or telephone facilities), diversion of services (or allowances) provided for officeholders (e.g., the administrative assistant of a legislator acting as a party agent) and abuse of government-sponsored advertising during and before "campaign periods."

Subsidies-in-Kind and Indirect Support

In many countries subsidies-in-kind provide infrastructural support for party activities. This kind of support may be provided by the public as well as by the private sector. In Europe and Canada voter registration is the responsibility of public authorities, thus rendering American-style voter registration drives unnecessary. Distribution of ballot papers, mail ballots and advance polls are other cases of public support. Independent advertising (public relations and propaganda) by private groups supporting or opposing current administrations over long periods of time, e.g., Aims of Industry in Britain, also have to be mentioned.

In most Western democracies the electronic media are run by public agencies. No democracy relies entirely on commercial TV; Australia, Japan, Britain, Canada and the United States used a mixture of public and commercial ownership during the late 1970s. Where paid political advertising is not permitted (i.e., in all but four countries, including the U.S.), the parties (in most cases in proportion to their previous voting strength) can use different totals of free radio and TV time for their campaigns. As a general pattern in Western Europe, public broadcasting corporations provide free radio and TV time to all national parties for campaign purposes.[19] The allocation formula favors bigger parties over smaller ones and established parties over newcomers. In any case the provision of free media time is worth a considerable sum of money that European parties do not have to spend during election campaigns.

Free postal services (not just the franking privilege for legislators), reduced rates for direct mail as well as advertising at public expense (e.g., rent for billboards, provision of signs by municipal authorities) and use of assembly halls (for party rallies held in public buildings) may be other examples of subsidies-in-kind that should be mentioned. The net value of such subsidies-in-kind can hardly be estimated. In some countries (e.g., Austria, Sweden and Germany) women's, youth and student organizations (including those associated with political parties) receive public grants for their activities (see Table 10.1).

When West Germany introduced party subsidies by block grant from the federal budget in 1959, the governing parties claimed to perform activities in adult education (i.e., training people to participate in politics). When the Constitutional Court restricted public subsidies to campaign expenses, part of the general subsidy in 1967 was revived in the form of a grant supporting civic education activities of separate institutions closely linked to established parties.[20] Activities of the German "political foundations" range from adult education in residential colleges, training courses at the grassroots, and grants to students or PhD candidates for political research and documentation; the foundations even engage in development projects in third world countries. Financing for these activities is provided by annual block grants from federal and state budgets, supplemented by special grants for specific activities under different programs of public policy.

The Austrian "party academies," copying the German model only partially, are more closely defined as service institutions for the major parties. Their range of activity is limited, and it does not include foreign aid or study grants. The Netherlands support party affiliated but legally separated institutes for policy research (since 1971) as well as political training (since 1978) by matching grants. The public subsidy for any Dutch institute is determined according to the number of parliamentary seats held by the respective party and limited to the amount of income from other sources (party contributions or individual donations) the specific institute has been able to collect.[21] Among Western democracies only Belgium and Norway seem to have similar subsidies and institutions.[22]

Another means of indirect assistance is a tax benefit provided by public law. Tax benefits for political contributions (to parties and/or candidates) by tax deduction or tax credit are familiar to the United States and Canada as well as to Belgium, France, Germany and the Netherlands. The Netherlands started introducing tax deductions for political donations by individuals and corporations in 1951; for income tax purposes parties are treated like charitable organizations collecting donations for causes serving the commonweal/public good. Belgium since 1985 treats individual donations to party institutes in a similar way. France made donations to political candidates tax deductable in 1988 and now applies the same procedure for individual donations to parties, too.

The U.S. (at the federal level and in most states) have eliminated tax benefits for political donations; federal tax credits and tax deductions were terminated in 1987 after only a decade. In Canada federal and provincial tax credits for political donations (up to $1150 for most jurisdictions) and the legal provision for a (non-election time) monopoly of issuing tax receipts have proved

TABLE 10 1 Public Subsidies to Parties and Candidates in Democratic Countries, 1979/1991

Country	Recipient	Interval	Basis	Direct Subsidies	Specific Grants or Services Indirect Subsidies
Australia	Parties	Election	Per vote	Free broadcasting	——
Austria	Parties, parliamentary groups (federal and states)	Annual	Per seat	Billposting, free broadcasting, press subsidies, youth organizations, education for legislators and information (party foundations) patronage positions in nationalized industries	Assessment of salaries
Belgium	Parliamentary groups	Annual	Per seat	Free broadcasting, civic education	Tax deductions
Canada	Federal and provincial parties, candidates	Election	Per vote	Free broadcasting tax credits	Federal and provincial
Denmark	Parliamentary groups	Annual	Per seat	Free broadcasting, press and publications, women's and youth organizations	
Finland	Parties	Annual	Per seat	Billposting, free broadcasting, press and publications, women's and youth organizations	
France	Parties, presidential and parliamentary	Annual election	Per seat per vote candidates	Billposting, free broadcasting, press and publications	Assessment of legislative salaries, tax deductions (continues)

Table 10.1 (continued)

TABLE 10.1 (continued)

Country	Recipient	Interval	Basis	Direct Subsidies	Specific Grants or Services Indirect Subsidies
Germany	Federal and state parties and parliamentary groups	Annual election	Per vote per seat	Free broadcasting, billposting, youth organizations, education and foreign aid (party foundations)	Assessment of legislative salaries, tax credits, tax deductions
Ireland	No direct subsidies	-	-	Free broadcasting	-
Israel	Parties, parliamentary groups	Annual election	Per seat, per vote	Free broadcasting, transportation of voters	-
Italy	Parties, through parliamentary groups	Annual election	Per vote	Free broadcasting, press subsidies, women's and youth organizations	Assessment of legislative salaries
Japan	No direct subsidies	-	-	Billposting, free broadcasting, election advertising for individual candidates	-
Netherlands	Parliamentary groups	Annual	Per seat	Free broadcasting, women's and youth organizations, party foundations (education, research)	Tax deductions
New Zealand	No direct subsidies	-	-	-	-
Norway	Parties, parliamentary groups	Annual	Per seat	'Travel costs of nomination meetings, youth organizations	-

Table 10.1 (continued)

TABLE 10.1 (continued)

Country	Recipient	Interval	Basis	Direct Subsidies	Specific Grants or Services Indirect Subsidies
Sweden	National, regional and local parties, parliamentary groups	Annual	Per seat	Free broadcasting, press subsidies, women's and youth organizations	
Switzerland	Parliamentary groups	Annual	Per seat	Free broadcasting, mailing at reduced charges	Tax deductions (in some cantons)
United Kingdom	Parliamentary opposition	Annual	-	Free broadcasting, free mailing, use of public halls	
United States	Candidates for president and state-wide offices	Election (including primary)	Matching grant in primary, fixed sum in election	Nomination costs (conventions), mailing at reduced charges	Tax check-offs (public funds earmarked by taxpayers)

Comment: "Per seat": amount of subsidy determined on the basis of seats won; "per vote": amount of subsidy determined on the basis either of votes received or of eligible voters.

Source: Originally compiled by Khayyam Z. Paltiel (1981:164-166) from "public documents and secondary sources available in late 1979"; the table has been updated by this author.

to be a very important benefit for federal and most provincial parties. This has especially supported their efforts to solicit rather small donations from individual citizens and small businesses. "Big money in little sums"[23] for the Canadian parties has become a political reality due to an innovative combination of public regulation and organizational effort.

In the early 1950s West Germany introduced a generous tax deduction for political donations which was declared unconstitutional by the Federal Constitutional Court in 1958. A considerable decrease of party income from donations during the late 1970s was one of the major reasons for the 1983 amendment to relevant legislation. When Germany reintroduced the tax deduction for political donations, the limit was finally raised to DM 60,000 (ca. $35,500 in 1991) as the maximum donation to be deducted from taxable income. This amount indicates that tax incentives were intended to foster rather large corporate donations, which nevertheless did not materialize during the 1980s. In addition to substantial tax deductions, Germany has also introduced a tax credit system (following in part the American, in part the Canadian model). Austria, Britain, Italy and Sweden do not provide similar benefits. The net value of tax benefits for political contributions cannot be calculated for different countries; only Revenue Canada has provided the relevant data.[24]

Party and Campaign Expenditures

Expenses for party activity are a subject of comparative research as well as an issue of political debate. Party treasurers regularly argue that their party in particular or all parties of the entire country due to circumstances beyond their control have fallen victim to a cost explosion. Local party workers sometimes believe that their party's headquarters is incurring expenses that are far beyond those necessary. Opposing views like these emphasize the need for a scholarly evaluation of specific items of expenditure, different types of spending and especially the levels of spending for individual countries. Concerning the costs of party activity in national politics, financial reports produced by parties and candidates for the time period between 1974 and 1989 supply sufficient information for a considerable number of countries: Austria, Britain, Canada, Germany, Italy,[25] Netherlands,[26] Sweden, and the United States.

Levels of Spending: The Costs of Democracy

The evaluation of spending by parties and candidates may start with a comparison of the per capita cost of party activity (adjusted for inflation or economic growth). This includes expenses for the party apparatus as well as for election campaigns. Only twice within three decades have political scientists tried to answer the question, "How much money is involved?"

In 1963 Heidenheimer[27] estimated the per capita cost of party activities for "a nine-month election year time span" around 1960 to be 3s9d for Australia, 3s9d for Britain, DM 2.73 for Germany, \$2.53 for the United States, Y 150 for Japan, Lit 1,000 for Italy and I-£ 25.7 for Israel. Heidenheimer's conclusion (repeated in 1970) was summed up by an "Index of Expenditure" using the average hourly wage. The index placed Australia and Britain in the lower stratum, Germany, the U.S. and Japan about twice as high. Italy and Israel were at the high end with ten times the Australian and 32 times the British costs of democracy.

Using information available for the late 1970s, this author calculated in 1986 per voter costs of national politics for a full four-year election cycle for the United Kingdom (DM 5), Canada (DM 7), the U.S. (DM 8), the Netherlands (DM 9), West Germany (DM 21) and Sweden (DM 27).[28] The only reasonable conclusion to be drawn from this data was to label the U.K., Canada, the U.S. and the Netherlands as moderate, Germany, Sweden, (without corresponding figures) Italy and Austria as high expenditure countries. Israel has held its position among the latter group.[29]

A more detailed approach can be applied when using the time series data reported publicly for the national parties in eight Western democracies. Only four of these--unfortunately all of them in the "expensive" category--are at present available for computer processing. A maximum number of 25 parties (national headquarters) from these four countries for a maximum number of 16 years can be counted. Comparing the headquarters totals for all major and minor parties in Austria, Germany, Italy and Sweden during the years 1974 to 1989[30] (Figure 10.1) shows the difference between election and non-election years and the effects of creeping inflation. A marked difference between the two smaller and the two larger democracies under study seems to be quite obvious. Despite the additional expenses caused by campaigning for the European Parliament (in 1979, 1984, 1989), parties in two EC countries have spent less than their counterparts in two non-member nations. Evaluation of additional countries is necessary before further conclusions can be drawn from the data, relating the preliminary findings to economies of scale or a cost push resulting from corporatist structures.

After two decades of reporting (more in West Germany, less in Austria, Sweden and Italy), the question can be asked about how much of the "financial costs of democracy"[31] incurred by political parties is revealed by current reporting procedures. Any answer has to consider those parts of political activity that are not included in the financial reports and compare the figures published to informed estimates of overall spending totals. Reporting procedures in Germany provide for a joint statement of all data concerning income and expenditure of all party organizations at all levels of the political system. During the 1980s the average annual income for a major party amounted to about 200 million DM. For a minor party 40 million DM can be considered a reasonable

FIGURE 10.1   Costs of Party Democracy in Four Countries (Per capita expenses of national party headquarters in US-$ per voter)

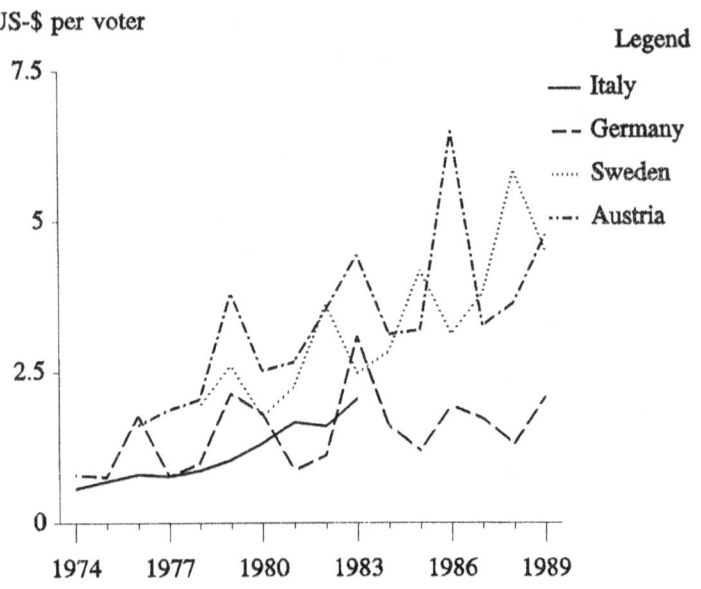

Source: Data published in compliance with national reporting procedure; compiled and processed by International Political Finance Monitoring System, Institute of Comparative Politics, University of Oldenburg.

average. The data, however, do not include parliamentary caucus money and the funds of political foundations or party enterprises. If caucus and foundation[32] financing were included, the average total of the annual costs of party democracy in (West) Germany would add up to approximately one billion DM. Thus two different considerations apply to the German case. First, reported money has to be related to the total amount of political money. Secondly, the national headquarters' share of all political money spent by German parties and their "subsidiaries" must be computed in order to arrive at figures useful for cross-national comparison. The only legitimate claim to be made for (West) Germany (based on the information available) is that about half of all political money is covered by reporting. The national headquarters jointly spend more than 15 but less than 20 percent of all political money available in Germany.

Italian parties provide their reports within three weeks after the end of a fiscal year which is the quickest procedure in Europe. Surprising speed and limitation of reporting to activities of the party headquarters reemphasize Paltiel's warning that Italian reports "must be treated quizzically";[33] from the annual reports published by the parties, not even a guess concerning the total costs of party democracy in Italy seems permissible. The situation in Austria and Sweden, although far from completely transparent, is less obscure. In Sweden the considerable share of public money provided for headquarters' funding, reliable estimates regarding the provincial and local subsidies, and the assumption that the share of public money will not decrease at the lower levels of party organization provide the basis for stating that the financial reports of Sweden's "big five" parties during the 1980s disclosed about one-third of all political money spent in that country. Austrian political funds are less open to public scrutiny. According to scholarly estimates, published balances reported 25 to 30 percent of total income and expenditures; informed party workers assumed that in the early 1980s no more than 12 to 15 percent of all political money was reported to the public.[34]

Types of Spending: Routine and Campaign

With regard to the amount of money that is necessary for party activity, all liberal democracies suggest similar patterns. Election years are characterized by high levels of income as well as of expenditure. The terms "(permanent) organizational spending" and "(extra) election spending" emphasize some aspects not connoted by everyday language. Party headquarters spend considerably more on "routine operations" in election years and, in addition, on special campaign expenses. Any comparison over time therefore has to look either at two election years or at two non-election years. The better approach would be to compare entire election cycles.

Whereas the distinction between "routine" and "campaign" spending is quite familiar to Britain, the equivalent amounts have to be calculated for other countries. The difference between interpolated average (= routine) and actual spending for an election year may be considered to be the amount of campaign spending for that specific year. During the decade from 1974 to 1983, the grand total of expenses by Italian party headquarters increased almost steadily from 37 billion LIT to 139 billion LIT. This may be due exclusively to a trend of creeping inflation. Surprisingly, the expense totals in election years (1976, 1979, 1983) for that country are not significantly different from those in non-election years.

The bulk of the campaign funds in Germany goes into billboards, print media and party rallies. Outdoor advertising is almost completely organized on a "wall-paper" basis. The billboards are decorated with new messages every ten days. This means that during an election campaign the parties put out three different sets of advertising (pasted like wallpaper on the billboards). With respect to the print media, regional daily newspapers and weekly magazines with national circulations account for most of the print media advertising, with the campaigning parties running ads covering one-third to one-half a page. Although

German parties have occasionally attempted to organize something like the Canadian "Leader's Tour" or the "Whistle Stop" of American presidential hopefuls, this has not developed into a specific feature of German election campaigns. The traditional campaign event that involves a considerable amount of expenditure is a party rally convened to listen to and cheer a key speaker who is either a cabinet member or a high ranking member of the parliamentary caucus. These key speakers are "blitzing" the country. Most of the expenditures are for the rent of halls rather than for travel expenses of the speakers.

Although such campaign activities paid for by the party headquarters amount to impressive figures, there is a considerable outlay of fixed costs for permanent party organizations in Austria, Germany and Sweden. On an average, Austrian and Swedish parties spend about half of their annual routine budget for additional campaign expenses in election years.

The central campaign expenses of British parties over time have largely oscillated around the same proportion. Nevertheless the 1987 campaign saw an exceptional increase.[35] In Germany the proportion used to be much higher (about 135 percent of routine expenses for additional campaign spending) for election years 1976 through 1983. Since then German party headquarters seem to have adapted to the "European standard" already mentioned. As private funds become scarce, extra spending on public relations may be on the retreat in Europe.

Items of Spending: Public Relations, Staff and Offices

Ignoring national peculiarities and overly detailed categories, some relevant pieces of information for comparative research can be computed from the standardized reporting forms applied in four countries (at least for the national level). Income from membership dues, private donations, and public subsidies as well as expenses for staff, administration and propaganda can be calculated.

Unfortunately, the data available do not permit us to separate spending on non-party media (TV and radio, print media like newspapers and magazines, billboard advertising) from spending on party media (party-affiliated newspapers, party-produced brochures and leaflets) or spending on meetings, conferences and rallies (aiming at policy development as well as public presentation of party policies and politicians). Most parties report these items under a joint category called "expenses for public relations and campaigns." As can be expected the share of this item as a percentage of total expenses varies in election and non-election years. Different party families[36] have shown similar patterns, in more recent years even including all parties of the left--Greens as well as Communists (cf. Figure 10.2). The most important trend to be discovered from the data is a decrease of propaganda/public relations expenses over time with all party headquarters in Austria, (West)Germany, Italy and Sweden.

The bulk of party funds during the non-election periods is spent on salaries for paid party workers (personnel, staff) and expenses for permanent offices.

FIGURE 10.2 Expenses for Public Relations by Party Family (in percent of total expenses for national party headquarters)

% of total expenses

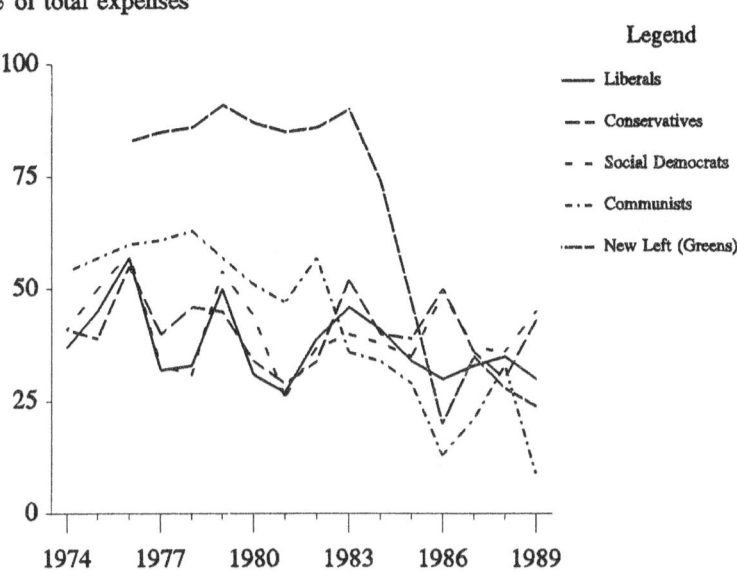

Source: Data published in compliance with national reporting procedure; compiled and processed by International Political Finance Monitoring System, Institute of Comparative Politics, University of Oldenburg.

The latter category includes rent of premises, office equipment and machinery, stationery, telephone charges and postage. Spending on personnel, as a percentage of total expenses for a maximum of 25 reporting units, seems to have increased over time (cf. Figure 10.3). As a general trend, this applies to all types of party organization. The mass parties (defined by a member-to-voter ratio between 12 and 36 percent) indicate an almost linear trend. The pattern for cadre parties (as named by Duverger and defined by a membership of less than 4 percent of their average voting strength) and catch-all parties (term coined by Kirchheimer; member-to-voter ratio between 4 and 12 percent) also depends on election cycles. Nevertheless the general trend seems to be comparable. But this may be due to developments in the realm of funding.

Different Strategies of Fundraising

A more traditional approach towards potential sources of income for political parties would look at membership dues, "voluntary" contributions from

FIGURE 10.3 Expenses for Staff by Type of Party Organization (in percent of total expenses for national party headquarters)

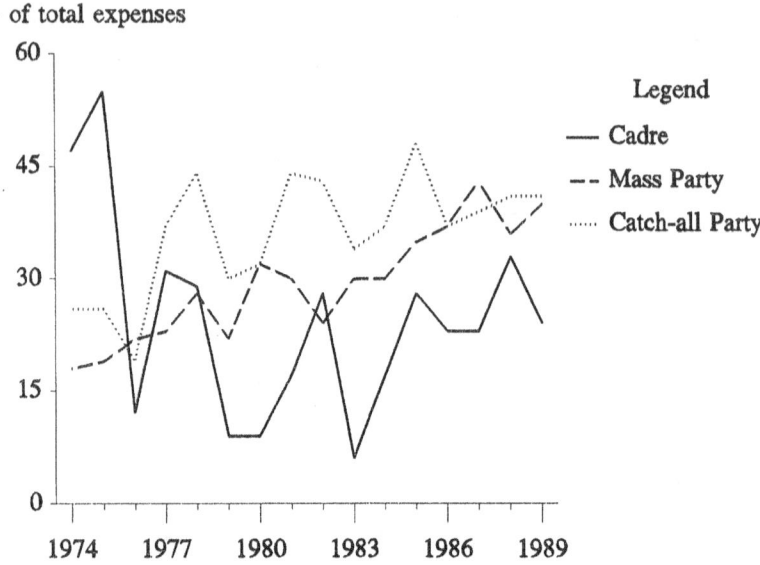

Source: Data published in compliance with national reporting procedure; compiled and processed by International Political Finance Monitoring System, Institute of Comparative Politics, University of Oldenburg.

office-holders, and individual or corporate donations. Rejecting these more traditional distinctions, Gullan Gidlund has proposed to separate "grassroots" from plutocratic financing.[37] The main implication of this alternative is related to democracy as a system of equal political participation by the multitude and plutocracy as a political system dominated by the riches of a wealthy and affluent minority.

Funds from spoils or graft, plutocratic donations and grassroots sources have to be treated separately as different strategies for political financing from private money. In addition to private sources, most Western democracies have developed systems of public financing.[38] Although there is a variety of indirect support for political parties, their activities and their candidates (cf. Table 10.1 above), the term "public funding" is usually applied to direct subsidies only. Subsidies from public funds are given to party candidates, party organizations and parliamentary groups (caucusses).

Income from "Grassroots" Financing

This term is used as a substitute for "membership financing," because it aims at including all money in small sums provided by the rank-and-file of identified party supporters among the general public. It can be divided into (1) membership dues, i.e., the gross amount of income from regular membership subscriptions of party members; (2) voluntary donations from members, i.e., (comparatively small) donations from formal party members in excess of membership dues; (3) contributions from other supporters (loyalists, "faithful"), including those who contribute by means of direct mail, fundraising events, auctions or lotteries.

Income from membership dues is a very traditional and welcome source of party income in Europe. Socialist (workers') parties have card-carrying members who pay various amounts of money (dues) on a monthly or annual basis. Traditional mass parties, such as the Social Democrats in Germany (SPD), apply a rather strict formula for membership dues as a percentage of the individual member's income, whereas other parties like the German Christian Democrats (CDU), which attracted a mass membership only recently (during the early 1970s), obviously did not choose to make dues a major source of party income.

Mass membership parties traditionally maintained their national headquarters from funds collected at the grassroots and funnelled upwards within the party structure. In his sample of 42 parties from Western democracies, Janda[39] found for the 1950s that 17 parties collected more than two-thirds of their total income "from party sources, including membership dues and income from party enterprises."[40] Roughly the same number of parties (19) combined decentralized funding with internal transfers to meet the headquarters' financial needs: "Funds are collected primarily on the local level but large amounts are transmitted upward for distribution by either the regional (state) or national organizations."[41]

More recently the relevance of grassroots funding for the maintenance of party headquarters has decreased. The four-country data (Figure 10.4) indicate that the size of a party influences its ability to raise considerable funds from the grassroots. Size can be measured by voting strength or parliamentary seats. Since all four countries studied here apply a system of proportional representation, no marked difference between these indicators will show. A major party represents more then 30 percent, a medium sized party 15 to 30 percent, a small party 5 to 15 percent and a very small party less than 5 percent of the voters (but still is able to elect some legislators). Only major parties (quite frequently having a mass membership base) collect a significant proportion (about one-fourth) of their central income from party members. For medium sized and small parties, membership dues cover far less than one-tenth of the national budget. These parties obviously rely on other financial sources.

FIGURE 10.4 Income from Membership Dues by Size of Party (in percent of total income from dues for national party headquarters)

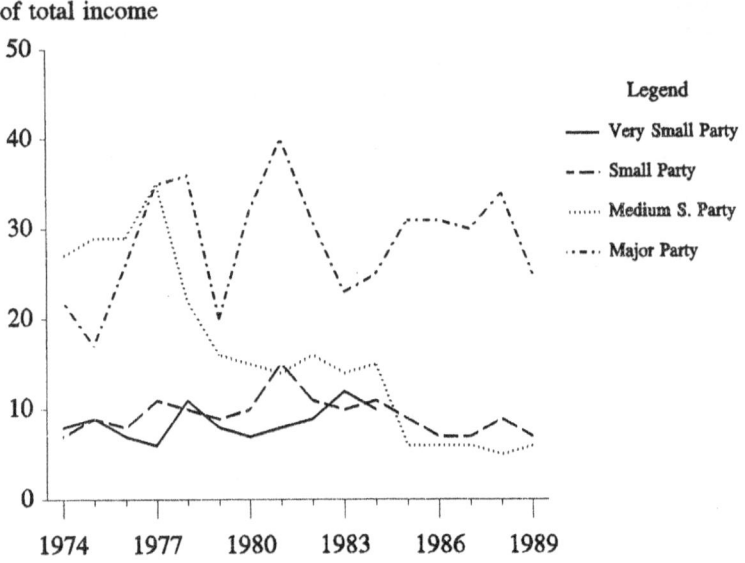

% of total income

Legend
— Very Small Party
– – Small Party
······ Medium S. Party
–··– Major Party

Source: Data published in compliance with national reporting procedure; compiled and processed by International Political Finance Monitoring System, Institute of Comparative Politics, University of Oldenburg.

Income from "Plutocratic" Financing

Donations have always been an important source of income for all right-of-center parties in Europe. Donations-in-kind (such as time, voluntary services, franking vouchers, cars, billboards, pickets, banners, etc.) have to be mentioned, too, although their value can scarcely be estimated adequately. For the "bourgeois" parties, individual contributions from personal income or wealth as well as corporate donors have to be considered the traditional source of funds.

The general term "contribution" applies to different types of donors. One donation may be some small amount given by an individual supporting a party, a PAC or a candidate of her or his personal preference. The second donation may be much larger and given by a corporation, an interest group or an institutional donor wanting to "buy" general access to politicians or influence specific policies. The third "voluntary" donation, finally, may be given in exchange for political favors, such as public contracts, licenses or offices; thus a party in power can profit by exercising public functions. Setting aside sources of income usually regarded as corruption, many donations still reflect specific problems of plutocratic financing.

Certainly a difference has to be made between "small" and "large" donations. Some amount should establish a useful threshold between "participating financially" and "buying access or influence." All individual donations exceeding a certain (but never exactly defined) amount cross the demarcation line towards plutocratic financing. "Large donations" may originate from organizations (e.g., trade unions, interest groups), corporations and individuals. Individual donations by persons entitled to vote (citizens) from their own funds (personal income or wealth) raise the question decided by the U.S. Supreme Court: Is money constitutionally equivalent to speech?[42] Does the unalienable right to speak up on political issues in a public debate automatically include the liberty to spend unlimited amounts of money on behalf of any personal opinion or preferred candidate?

The most difficult problems related to the idea of donating money for political purposes arise with institutional donations by organized interests of society (pressure groups) such as trade associations (including associations of the professions), business enterprises (corporations) and trade unions. Among the more recent examples that require careful scrutiny is the case of corporate PACs. During the 1950s in West Germany a functional equivalent to the American PACs was used to collect corporate funds for the governing right-of-center parties. Similar conveyor organizations (Libertas and Kokumin Kyokai) have been operating in Norway and Japan.[43] The political levy of British trade unions[44] and the collective affiliation of local unions with the Social Democratic parties of Norway and Sweden are other notorious examples of plutocratic financing. Despite these rare cases of institutional donations for the political left, plutocratic financing in general has been applied mostly by right-of-center and other bourgeois parties.

Due to pressures from the left and in response to repeated cases of corruption, different means of regulation have been implemented during the last two decades. A ban on corporate donations by political agreement or national legislation as well as contribution limits for individual donors were meant to put an end to any dependency on plutocratic financing. By introducing a combination of disincentives and incentives, political reformers intended to channel private money of appropriate size and origin into party coffers. Disclosure provisions were designed to discourage corporate and large donors. Tax credits and matching provisions were to induce individual donors to give a rather small amount to political causes, candidates and parties. It is still too early to evaluate the outcomes of different packages of national legislation. While the Canadian example looks very promising, experience in the U.S. appears to be more mixed, and the most recent German approach seems to be a failure.[45]

In the four countries studied in depth here, the dependency of bourgeois party headquarters on income from donations (the only indicator available for plutocratic financing) has declined during the 1980s. In the 1970s the Liberals received an average of 30 percent of their income from this source; the Christian Democrats and Conservatives averaged slightly more than 15 percent. Nowadays these two party families as well as the Social Democrats collect 10 to 15 percent of their central office income

Income from Spoils of Office

When parties want to earn some income from their activities, they may try to turn public offices into "profit centers." Profiteering from administering public offices or by controlling the means of access to them has to be aimed at different target groups. The professional politicians seeking re-election (assessment or party tax) or the public employees wanting to keep their jobs or promote their careers (macing), international or national firms as well as local businessmen needing public permits or licenses (toll-gating) and government contracts (kickbacks) are cases in point. In the past political parties in Western democracies have successfully tapped all four clienteles for donations given more or less voluntarily. The borderline to corruption has always been close and sometimes had to be crossed in order to ensure the flow of party revenue from the spoils of office (graft).

The "macing" of public servants (i.e., the periodic assessment for campaign contributions by the party in power) was common in the U.S. during the period of patronage appointments before the introduction of the merit principle for the civil service.[46] The system continues to flourish where patron-client relations are strong. Puerto Rico in 1940 turned from donations by the sugar interests (a clear example of plutocratic financing) to the macing of public servants, and in 1957 ended up with public subsidies as the dominant source of party income. Between 1940 and 1957 a quota system was established whereby employees of the government were expected to contribute up to 2 percent of their salaries to the governing party.[47]

The so-called party tax on political income (assessment) involves payments by persons directly dependent upon party favor including elected officials as well as managers of publicly owned corporations. Left-wing parties usually demand from their representatives a fixed percentage of legislative salaries. The German SPD requires its deputies in all parliaments (European, federal, state) to contribute almost 20 percent, the Socialist Party in France collects about 30 percent.[48] The Communist parties of France and Italy in their heyday have gone further still, demanding up to 70 percent of the legislative income from their legislators. The bourgeois parties in Austria, France and Germany collect considerably less from their members of parliament.

Paltiel has identified other types of income from spoils: Toll-gating is a system whereby holders of government permits and concessions are required to

FIGURE 10.5 Income from Donations by Party Family (in percent of total income for national party headquarters)

% of total income

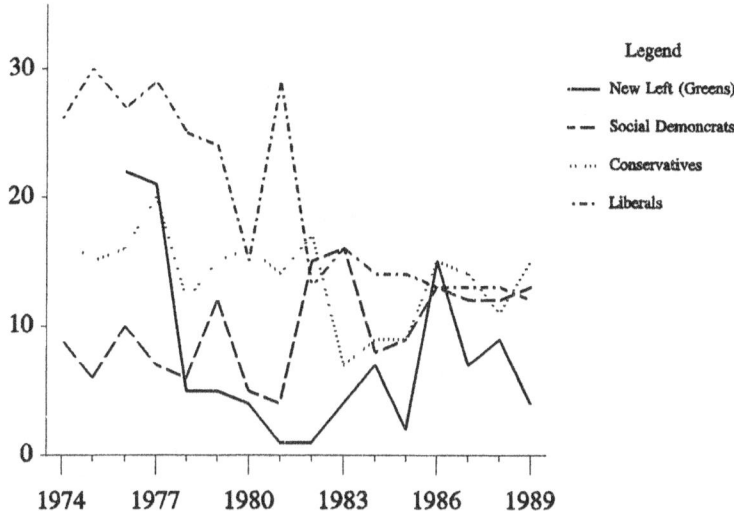

Legend
— New Left (Greens)
– – Social Democrats
· · · Conservatives
·–· Liberals

Source: Data published in compliance with national reporting procedure; compiled and processed by International Political Finance Monitoring System, Institute of Comparative Politics, University of Oldenburg.

make regular contributions--depending on the value of the permit--to the war chests of incumbent parties. Kickbacks (called ristournes in the Canadian Province of Quebec) "are payments consisting of a percentage of the value of all government contracts made to the party in power. Variations of these schemes are probably the most traditional and widespread of the means used by incumbents to reinforce their financial positions."[49] Public inquiries and judicial prosecutions have revealed details of these processes in different jurisdictions. Examples from Austria, France, Italy, Japan and Spain provide major names (especially Lockheed) and scandals derived from this game familiar to democratic politics.

Published financial reports will show only minor amounts of party income from such sources. For obvious reasons there is no category "Income from Spoils" in any model balance sheet provided by public regulation. Only the "party tax" (applied to politicians' income after or instead of federal income tax) shows up in Austrian reports. Germany terminated the category due to constitutional considerations.[50] The reporting scheme applied after 1983 does not include a separate category for the "voluntary" donations or "additional membership fees" from party representatives in legislative bodies. The party tax is still being collected and is now reported jointly with all other income from membership dues.[51] The amount of "voluntary" contributions from legislators and local councillors is different, depending on type of party and type of office. From municipal councillors German parties regulary receive a quarter to a third of the allowance paid; for legislators at the federal or state level, the party tax runs between five to twenty percent of the salary. Assessment of legislators is a common practice of parties in Belgium,[52] but it has never been reported for Italy (except for the Communists, as mentioned above). In Sweden salaries for legislators are considered to be too low for collecting assessments by the party headquarters. On the other hand the largesse of public subsidies in this country obviously has not to be concealed.

Income from Public Subsidies

The information provided so far raises the question of where the bulk of party money comes from. Roughly half of the annual budget for national (federal) party organizations in Austria, Germany, Italy and Sweden is provided by public funds. The share of public subsidies for the individual parties varies between 20 and 90 percent of total net income by year and party. Looking at the average share of party income covered by public subsidies in a country-by-country comparison (Figure 10.6), Austria shows the lowest, but nevertheless a rising level of subsidization. Since 1983 German parties have been receiving the major part of their funds from the public purse. In general, smaller (Italian) parties seem to end up in the upper, larger (left wing) parties in the lower part of the range of public support for the four countries studied in depth.

For Australia,[53] Canada,[54] the United States and the Netherlands,[55] the proportion of public funding is considerably less. Britain and Japan do not provide cash funds but rather subsidies-in-kind. Denmark, Finland, Israel and Norway seem to be more in line with the European nations that have been studied in depth. Because subsidies for parties have been introduced only recently, it is too early to reach any conclusions about France. In all European countries where public subsidies are available, some proportion is distributed to parliamentary groups (caucusses). The entire party subsidy in Italy is formally paid to the parliamentary groups which in turn are legally obliged to transfer at least 90 percent of the total grant to their party headquarters. In Austria parliamentary groups receive the most sophisticated kind of subsidization. Grants to parliamentary groups are computed according to the number of seats held and the salaries of certain public servants (staff with clerical and academic training, respectively). To the amount thus computed a 90 percent bonus is added for publicity activities of the parliamentary groups. Rising costs of political

FIGURE 10.6 Income from Public Subsidies by Country (in percent of total income for national party headquarters)

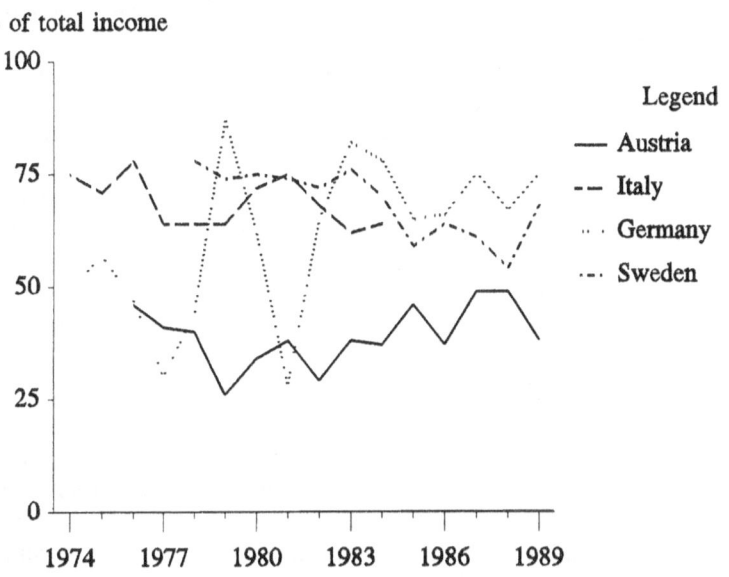

Source: Data published in compliance with national reporting procedure; compiled and processed by International Political Finance Monitoring System, Institute of Comparative Politics, University of Oldenburg.

campaigns have stimulated the introduction of party subsidies. In Canada, Australia and the U.S. public subsidies are closely linked to campaign expenses. While details vary, depending on national peculiarities, the general principle seems to be that a clearly defined proportion of reported and receipted campaign expenses actually incurred by candidates (and parties in Canada or Australia) is reimbursed from public funds.[56] No European country has tied campaign subsidies to actual spending. In Italy parties that compete seriously in elections fought on the national level receive a flat grant as a "reimbursement" of their campaign expenditures after the elections for the national parliament, the European parliament and the regional councils. Austria introduced recently a similar subsidy for the campaign expenses of national parties. In France presidential as well as parliamentary candidates and major parties receive lump sums to cover a substantial part of their campaign expenses.[57]

In Germany the system of party subsidization works the other way round. Due to constitutional considerations, political parties may receive from public funds "an adequate compensation for necessary campaign expenses" only.[58] The party subsidy therefore was built on the fictitious principle that parties are entitled to a reimbursement of campaign expenses based on a fixed amount per voter for elections to the European Parliament, the federal parliament and the state legislatures. Increasing annual installments within legislative periods turn these "reimbursements" into some odd type of flat grants.

Subsidizing the operational costs of national parties is the Austrian, Italian, Swedish and more recently also the French path to public subsidies. The mode of distribution is fixed by law, the total amount by the annual budget. Distribution according to seats in the national legislature applies also in other cases of public subsidization (e.g., Denmark, Finland, Norway). An additional subsidy provided by provincial and local authorities to the regional party organizations is Sweden's innovative contribution to public funding.[59] Such monies are not included in the subsidies paid to national party headquarters. Nevertheless, a portion of the provincial and local subsidies may be transferred to higher levels of the party organization in one way or another.

Comparing the public share of total party income by size of party (Figure 10.7) presents a clue for the politics of public funding. The smallest parties, which serve often as potential coalition partners in the multi-party systems of continental Europe, have been able to claim extremely high proportions of public money to sustain their operations. While the major parties (on an average) receive less than half of their funds from public money, some very small parties in Italy have made public subsidies their major source of funds, permanently drawing about three-quarters of their total income from the national treasury. Public debate of party subsidies obviously has not inhibited this kind of self-service for specific parties. Additional means of control seem necessary when other countries want to check a proliferation of such practices.

Public Controls of Political Finance

With respect to political finance, "the least transparent chapter of party history,"[60] ideas of transparency and control have time and again attracted the curiosity and attention of scholars and reformers. Controlling the flow of political funds can be achieved by administrative regulation or political competition. The general aim of financial accountability (disclosure and reporting) is to enable anyone to raise certain questions of political finance for public debate,[61] or to encourage parties and candidates to raise and spend their funds in ways that do not provoke controversy. The voting citizen is supposed to act as a referee in cases of financial misbehavior.

Disclosure of political donors and reporting on political funds provide the necessary information; news editors and competing parties act as advocates on behalf of the citizens' moral sensitivities. But all of this requires the full disclosure of donations and the reporting of all political money, neither of which

FIGURE 10.7   Income from Public Subsidies by Size of Party (in percent of total income for national party headquarters)

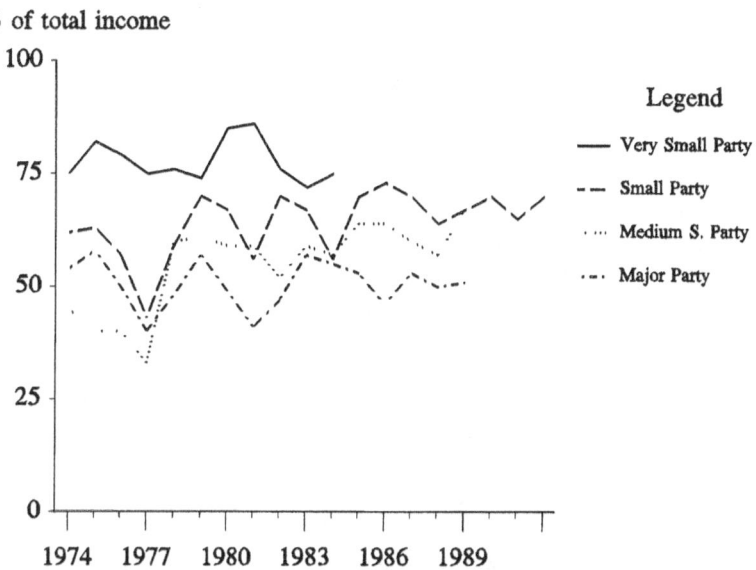

Source: Data published in compliance with national reporting procedure; compiled and processed by International Political Finance Monitoring System, Institute of Comparative Politics, University of Oldenburg.

any European country has yet implemented.[62] Public access to annual reports on income and expenditure and a standard form for these reports (model balance) characterize the European approach to the issue. In North America public regulation of political finance has frequently had the intention of limiting campaign expenses as well as individual contributions. Campaign finance laws regulate the amount a candidate may spend for a campaign or the amount a donor may contribute to a campaign. In addition, Canada and the United States have deliberately established public agencies to enforce specific regulations of political finance.

Disclosure

In North America disclosure of individual donors seems to be at the core of controlling political finance. Disclosure of the donor's identity and the amount of the individual donation is meant to control the flow of private money into campaign coffers. Negative publicity for large donations is expected to discourage donors as well as politicians. The puritan expectation of American lawmakers seems quite simple. If all financial leverage can be made a subject of public debate, politics will be "cleaned up." Public subsidies and tax benefits (in Canada) or matching funds (in the U.S.) provide incentives for candidates and parties to cooperate with such programs of public policy.

Political practice of almost two decades in North American jurisdictions has re-emphasized the general paradox of constitutional reform measures. Implementation of reform legislation breeds the need for more (and more complex) reform legislation. The democratic public and its main agent, the media, take at best an interest in the introduction of reform measures, not in their routine application or in any amending process later on. The elaborate restrictions designed to control the flow of money into the political process have encouraged the professional politicians to engage in a creative search for potential loopholes either in the application of the existing law or when drafting necessary amendments.

European countries have taken a more or less laissez-faire stand towards the control of political finance. They have provided neither spending nor contribution limits,[63] incidental disclosure of large donors only, no independent controlling agencies, and practically no sanctions. Despite some of the principles contained in democratic ideology, Western liberal pluralist democracies maintain a form of "mixed government." Different channels of political action are opened up for groups of citizens; the lower strata can employ their votes, the upper strata their wealth, whether or not their money is subject to disclosure. European emphasis on reporting has not produced results much different from those in North America.

Reporting

Reporting of the major sources of party income and the main items of expenditures was introduced by many European countries[64] in order to achieve some sort of public control over political finance. In Germany reporting includes financial transactions at all levels of the formal party organization. In this respect Germany has always had the strictest regulation in Europe, whereas reporting on expenditure (quite frequently applied by other jurisdictions) was not introduced until 1983. By adding the requirement of reporting expenditures, German legislation only caught up with others. Even after the 1983 amendments, reporting does not apply to the finances of parliamentary groups (caucusses) at the federal, state and local levels of the German political system; nor does it include political foundations and incorporated enterprises (limited liability corporations) run as subsidiaries of political parties.

In Austria, Italy and Sweden, parties report their headquarters' finances only; regional organizations as well as commercial enterprises are not included in the reports. This leaves the reporting of all financial transactions by local and provincial parties to their own discretion and prevents public curiosity from penetrating the finances of party-sponsored publishing enterprises, specific organizations or caucusses (parliamentary groups) at all levels of the political system. There is no publicity whatsoever regarding political funds administered by certain interest groups (Kammern and Bünde) closely tied to specific parties in Austria or by the very powerful (and allegedly well funded) internal factions (correnti) of Italian parties. Only political academies (party foundations) in Austria publish their financial statements separately. Swedish parties even have avoided reporting legislation because of privacy considerations. An agreement in 1980 by the five parties represented in parliament covers only the reporting to one another of income and expenditure and public access to the information thus exchanged.

The 1983 amendments to reporting legislation in West Germany served as an important innovation for all Western democracies. Parties in Germany now have to publish annually a statement of their debts and assets, which is required in no other European country. An annual report of income and expenditure accessible to the public either on request (Sweden) or via mandatory publication in newspapers or parliamentary reports (Austria, France, Italy and Germany) is a common feature of European reporting procedures. Because reporting outside Germany is less comprehensive, transfers between different elements (tiers) of a party organization as well as the setting aside of reserves for election campaigns and debts incurred due to a shortage of funds are not available for any comparative data set.

All regulation based on transparency assumes that public availability of data leads to publicity of political finance in competitive news media. Publicity through print media as well as electronic media is a necessary but not always sufficient precondition for public debate. Public debate which results from some "scandalized" piece of information or revelation can be expected to induce different behavior in a considerable number of voters and by anticipation improves self-control mechanisms built into all parties and campaign organizations by the rules of political competition. This procedure has to run through all the individual steps mentioned and may be completely jeopardized at each stage.[65] Therefore, it seems reasonable not to rely on accidental reporting but rather to insist on systematic enforcement of political finance regulations.

Enforcement

The basic philosophy behind reports of party income and expenditure has been to make party accounts a subject of public debate. None of the European countries mentioned really seems to offer sufficient information for public debate on the issue of party and campaign finance. Most of the debate has been dominated by institutions acting on behalf of the general public, such as parties, pressure groups and mass media. As political money has become an issue of public policy, some political systems (mainly in North America) have created agents for the public interest, e.g., the Federal Election Commission in the U.S. and special divisions with most Chief Electoral Officers in Canada.

European countries have not provided for similar agencies, which Khayyam Z. Paltiel would have argued is a serious failing:

> A system of public financing, full disclosure and an enforcing agency backed by legal sanctions are essential to the success of a reform program for party finance. Disclosure requires systematic reporting, auditing, public access to records and publicity. Enforcement demands a strong authority endowed with sufficient legal powers to supervise, verify, investigate and if necessary institute legal proceedings. Anything less is a formula for failure.[66]

Due to a strong concern for the internal autonomy of political parties, first expressed in a Royal Commission report of 1951 and respected ever since, Sweden has not introduced any statutory control or restriction regarding party funds. Among European democracies, Britain, Denmark and Ireland observe similar principles.

Other European countries exercise different although not very efficient strategies in order to enforce public control of political money.[67] Belgium and the Netherlands demand public auditing of subsidies for party-affiliated bodies. Subsidies to "party academies" in Austria and "political foundations" in Germany are audited in detail by the Federal Audit Offices. In principle the same applies to public funds provided for parliamentary groups. After decades of subsidization, public auditors in Germany only recently started to take their auditing responsibilities very seriously.

The annual reports published by parties in Austria, Germany and Italy (not in Sweden, of course) are audited by certified accountants. This procedure means little more than the fact that a minimum of professional standards is applied when political parties prepare their financial reports. Since no regulation in Western Europe provides for cross-checking of details by an independent enforcing agency, other controlling effects cannot be expected. Any impact specific to the prevalent funding strategy remains unchecked.

Conclusion

Crossing the Atlantic ocean from Europe makes everything look different. The political cultures of North America are campaign and candidate oriented. The term political finance connotes campaign finance, i.e., money spent in order to influence the outcome of an election. In Western Europe the term political finance is frequently used as a synonym for party financing, i.e., the funding of inter-election routine activities as well as campaigns. In Europe campaigns are run predominantly by parties, in America by candidates (and their specific committees).

Major differences between Western Europe and North America result from different approaches towards public funding and publicity regarding political money. In America disclosure of individual donors seems to be at the core of controlling political finance. In Europe the emphasis (if any) is on reporting of the major financial sources and expense items by different parties.

In North America public regulation of political finance puts some emphasis on limiting both campaign expenses and individual contributions. Campaign finance laws limit the amount a candidate may spend for his campaign or the amount a donor may contribute towards the candidate of his choice. Disclosure of the donor's identity and the amount of an individual donation is supposed to help control the flow of private money into campaign coffers. Public subsidies and tax benefits (matching funds) provide incentives for candidates (and parties) to cooperate with such programs of public policy.

In Western Europe public subsidies cover most of the financial needs for operating party headquarters on a permanent basis. Reporting of party income and expenses (occasionally debts and assets, too) was implemented in order to promote public control over political finance. Spending limits are rare, and effective contribution limits are unknown in Europe. Massive tax incentive plans for political donations exist in a few countries only.[68] Any kind of enforcing agency seems to be anathema to European legislators. Swedish parties even avoided any reporting legislation because of privacy considerations.

Of the 19 democracies mentioned in Table 10.1 (above), only 8 have been studied in depth by at least one author. France--for the first time in the comparative study of political finance--has been covered in this volume. The comparative volumes edited by Alexander und Wiberg, respectively, offer at least a general overview of the funding situation in 6 other countries (Australia, Israel, Spain; Denmark, Finland, Norway).[69] For 5 of the 19 countries the information available is still rather patchy and scattered (Belgium, Ireland, Japan, New Zealand and Switzerland).

Further research on campaign and party finance has to focus on the collection of comparable data for more countries. Especially France with its improved data base[70] and some smaller European democracies (such as Belgium, Ireland and Switzerland), New Zealand and Japan as well as the more recent additions to the democratic world in Southern and Eastern Europe are candidates for research. At the same time, researchers should use the data available to test hypotheses on the impact of different funding strategies in various liberal democracies. Such efforts will lead to greater theoretical and empirical progress in the comparative study of political finance.

264

Notes

1. Ferdinand A. Hermens, *The Representative Republic* (Notre Dame, Ind.: University of Notre Dame Press, 1958), p. 162.

2. See Michael Pinto-Duschinsky and Uwe Schleth, "Why Public Subsidies Have Become the Major Source of Party Funds in West Germany, but Not in Great Britain," in Arnold J. Heidenheimer, ed., *Comparative Political Finance* (Lexington, MA: D.C. Heath, 1970), pp. 23-49.

3. Khayyam Z. Paltiel, *Political Party Financing in Canada* (Toronto, Ont.: McGraw-Hill, 1970); Herbert E. Alexander, *Financing Politics* (3rd ed., Washington, DC: CQ Press, 1984); Hubert Sickinger and Rainer Nick, *Politisches Geld--Parteienfinanzierung in Österreich* (Thaur/Tirol: Kulturbuchverlag, 1990); Gullan M. Gidlund, *Partistöd* (Public Subsidies of Swedish Political Parties) (Umea: CWK Gleerup, 1983).

4. Michael Pinto-Duschinsky, *British Political Finance 1830-1980* (Washington, DC: American Enterprise Institute, 1981).

5. Uwe Schleth, *Parteifinanzen* (Meisenheim a.G.: Anton Hain, 1973); Christine Landfried, *Parteifinanzen und politische Macht* (Baden-Baden: Nomos, 1990).

6. Khayyam Z. Paltiel, "Political Finance," in Vernon Bogdanor, ed., *The Blackwell Encyclopedia of Political Institutions* (Oxford, UK: Basil Blackwell, 1987), p. 455 and Khayyam Z. Paltiel, "Party Financing," in *The Canadian Encyclopedia*, Vol. III (2nd ed., Edmonton, Alta.: Hurtig, 1988), p. 1625.

7. This chapter relies heavily on an unpublished paper by Michael Pinto-Duschinsky and Karl-Heinz Nassmacher, "Framework for Comparative Research on Political Finance" (prepared after an ECPR workshop, 1988; see Note 16).

8. The only exception being the New Democratic Party (NDP).

9. Michael Pinto-Duschinsky, "How Can the Influence of Money in Politics Be Assessed?" (Paper presented at the XIIth IPSA World Congress in Paris, 1985), pp. 2, 21-22.

10. Maurice Duverger, *Political Parties* (New York, NY: Wiley, 1954).

11. Arnold J. Heidenheimer, "Comparative Party Finance--Notes on Practices and Towards a Theory," in *Journal of Politics*, Vol. 25, No. 4, 1963, p. 790.

12. Alexander Heard, "Political Financing," in *International Encyclopedia of the Social Sciences*, Vol. 12 (New York, NY: Macmillan, 1968), pp. 235-241; Heidenheimer, *Comparative Political*, passim.

13. See Khayyam Z. Paltiel, "Campaign Finance: Contrasting Practices and Reforms," in David Butler et al., eds., *Democracy at the Polls* (Durham, NC: Duke University Press, 1981), pp. 137-160 and Klaus von Beyme, *Parteien in westlichen Demokratien* (München: Piper, 1982), pp. 241-261.

14. Kenneth Janda, *Political Parties--A Cross-National Survey* (New York and London: Free Press, 1980), pp. xi, 91-92, 111-112.

15. Herbert E. Alexander, ed., *Political Finance* (Beverly Hills, CA: Sage, 1979) and Herbert E. Alexander, ed., *Comparative Political Finance in the 1980s* (Cambridge, UK: Cambridge University Press, 1989).

16. Convened under the auspices of the European Consortium for Political Research (ECPR) by Alec T. Barbrook at Rimini on April 8, 1988.

17. Gidlund, *Partistöd*, pp. 29, 42, 353.

18. For details see Klee, in this volume.

19. Anthony Smith, "Mass Communications," in Butler et al., *Democracy*, pp. 174-175. (In Austria and Belgium political parties are allocated free radio time even during off-campaign periods.)

20. For details see Michael Pinto-Duschinsky, "Party Foundations and Political Finance in Germany," in F. Leslie Seidle, ed., *Comparative Issues in Party and Election Finance* (Toronto, Ont.: Dundurn, 1992), forthcoming. See also von Arnim, in this volume.

21. D. J. Elzinga, "Die Institution der politischen Partei in den Niederlanden," in Dimitris Th. Tsatsos et al., eds., *Parteienrecht im europäischen Vergleich* (Baden-Baden: Nomos, 1990), pp. 560s; Waarborg van Kwaliteit, *Rapport van de Commissie subzidiering politieke partijen* (s'Gravenhage: Ministerie van Binnenlandse Zaken, 1991), p. 35.

22. Ibid., p. 152; Lars Svasand, "State Subventions for Political Parties in Norway," in Matti Wiberg, ed., *The Public Purse and Political Parties* (Jyväskylä: Gummerus, 1991), p. 139.

23. As Alexander Heard, *The Costs of Democracy* (Chapel Hill, NC: University of North Carolina Press, 1960), p. 249, has put it.

24. See Hiltrud Nassmacher and Ina-Maja Lemke, "Steuerliche Anreize für private Zuwendungen," in Karl-Heinz Nassmacher, ed., *Bürger finanzieren Wahlkämpfe* (Oldenburg: BIS, 1992), forthcoming.

25. Giorgio Pacifici, *Il costo della democrazia* (Roma: Cadmo 1983); Gian Franco Ciaurro, "Public financing of parties in Italy," in Alexander, *Comparative*, pp. 153-171.

26. Douwe J. Elzinga, *De politieke partij en het constitutionele recht* (Nijmegen: Art Aequi, 1982), pp. 328-331; Ruud Koole, "The 'modesty' of Dutch party finance," in Alexander, *Comparative*, pp. 200-219.

27. Heidenheimer, *Comparative Party*, pp. 797-798; Arnold Heidenheimer, "Major Modes of Raising, Spending and Controlling Political Funds During and Between Election Campaigns," in Heidenheimer, *Comparative Political*, pp. 11-13.

28. Karl-Heinz Nassmacher, "Die Kosten der Demokratie in Kanada," in William M. Chandler, ed., *Perspektiven kanadischer Politik* (Oldenburg: BIS, 1986), pp. 95-96.

29. Jonathan Mendilow, "Party financing in Israel: experience and experimentation, 1968-85," in Alexander, *Comparative*, p. 143.

30. Effects of floating exchange rates are controlled by the assumption of an average: US $ 1 = DM 2.40 = LIT 1600 = SEK 6.80 = AS 16.90.

31. Heard, *Costs*, p. 8.

32. The figures given here exclude all international activities of political foundations because foreign aid is not an instrument of intra-national party competition.

33. Khayyam Z. Paltiel, "The Impact of Election Expenses Legislation in Canada, Western Europe, and Israel," in Alexander, *Political*, p. 35.

34. This evaluation was also presented in Karl-Heinz Nassmacher, "Structure and impact of public subsidies to political parties in Europe: the examples of Austria, Italy, Sweden and West Germany," in Alexander, *Comparative*, p. 258.

35. Johnston and Pattie, in this volume, figures 1 and 3.

36. Ideological families of political parties as definded by von Beyme, *Parteien*, pp. 43-191.

37. Gidlund, *Partistöd*, p. 42.

38. See Nassmacher, "Structure," pp. 238-247, and Table 10.1 in this chapter.

39. Inter-University Consortium for Political and Social Research, Ann Arbor, MI, Study No. 7534, BV 701 and BV 904.

40. Kenneth Janda, *Comparative Political Parties Data, 1950-1962* (Ann Arbor: ICPSR, 1979), p. 149.

41. Ibid., p. 190.

42. The case was Buckley v. Valeo, 424 U.S. 1 (1976). For some details see Alexander, *Financing*, pp. 40-42.

43. Arnold Heidenheimer and Frank C. Langdon, *Business Associations and the Financing of Political Parties* (The Hague: Martinus Nijhoff: 1968), pp. 169-198; Paul Kevenhörster, *Wirtschaft und Politik in Japan* (Wiesbaden: Otto Harrassowitz, 1973), pp. 89-93.

44. For details see Johnston and Pattie, in this volume.

45. Karl-Heinz Nassmacher, "Citizen Cash," in Nassmacher, *Bürger*, forthcoming.

46. Heard, *Costs*, pp. 145-146.

47. Paltiel, "Campaign," pp. 150-151.

48. Drysch, in this volume.

49. Paltiel, "Campaign," p. 151. For some details see Khayyam Z. Paltiel, "Contrasts among the Several Canadian Political Finance Cultures" in Heidenheimer, *Comparative Political*, p.124.

50. *Bericht zur Neuordnung der Parteienfinanzierung*, Report of a Presidential Commission (Köln: Bundesanzeiger, 1983) p. 188; see von Arnim, in this volume.

51. Hans Herbert von Arnim, *Die Partei, der Abgeordnete und das Geld* (Mainz: von Hase & Koehler, 1991), p. 206.

52. Louis Paul Suetens, "Die Institution der politischen Partei in Belgien," in Tsatsos et al., *Parteienrecht*, pp. 68-69.

53. Ernest A. Chaples, "Public funding of elections in Australia," in Alexander, *Comparative*, pp. 86-88.

54. Karl-Heinz Nassmacher, "The costs of party democracy in Canada: Preliminary findings for a federal system," in *Corruption and Reform*, Vol. 4, 1989, p. 241.

55. Koole, "Modesty," p. 215.

56. Matching campaign contributions for certain U.S. candidates amounts to a public cash advance for campaign spending, thus relieving the recipient of the need to apply for a bank loan during the campaign period.

57. For details see Drysch, in this volume.

58. For an evaluation see Schleth, *Parteifinanzen*, pp. 265-285.

59. Gidlund, *Partistöd*, pp. 240-241, 277-278; see Klee, in this volume.

60. Max Weber, *Wirtschaft und Gesellschaft* (2nd ed., Tübingen: J.C.B. Mohr, 1925), p. 169 (translation by author).

61. *Bericht zur Neuordnung*, p. 181.

62. Details of national regulation are summarized in Paltiel, "Campaign," pp. 154-159 (=Table 7-1).

63. Except for France, which has placed limits on both donations and expenditures, and Britain, which has limited the spending of constituency candidates.

64. Britain is again the most important exception; see Johnston and Pattie, in this volume.

65. Empirical evidence--from case studies or longitudinal analyses--on any successful process of control is not yet available.

66. Khayyam Z. Paltiel, "Candidate and Election Finance," Study No. 22, Royal Commission on Corporate Concentration (Ottawa, Ont.: Queen's Printer, 1976), pp. 108-109.

67. Dian Schefold et al., "Rechtsvergleichende Ausblicke," in Tsatsos et al., *Parteienrecht*, pp. 843-845.

68. See Table 1 above.

69. Alexander, *Comparative*, and Wiberg, *Public Purse*.

70. See Drysch, in this volume.

About the Contributors

Hans Herbert von Arnim is professor of public law at the Post-Graduate School of Administrative Sciences in Speyer, Germany. He is the author of numerous books and articles on German campaign and party finance, and he has received considerable public attention for his revelations and criticisms of a number of party finance practices and pensions schemes for *Land* (state) legislators.

Thomas Drysch is a doctoral candidate and research assistant for Professor von Arnim at the Research Institute for Public Administration at the Post-Graduate School of Administrative Sciences in Speyer, Germany.

Arthur B. Gunlicks is professor of political science at the University of Richmond, Virginia. He is the author of *Local Government in the German Federal System* (Duke, 1986) and the contributing editor of books on German federalism and local government reform and reorganization in the United States and Europe. He has published numerous articles and book chapters on political parties, local government, federalism, and party and campaign finance in Germany.

Paul S. Herrnson is an associate professor of government and politics at the University of Maryland at College Park. He is the author of *Party Campaigning in the 1980s* (Harvard, 1988), and he has published several articles and book chapters on American politics.

Ruth S. Jones is professor of political science at Arizona State University. She has written and consulted extensively on state-level campaign finance and public campaign funding. She has published several articles in professional journals and chapters in edited works. She currently is working on a manuscript on state-level public campaign funding in the United States.

R. J. Johnston is Vice-Chancellor of the University of Essex. Prior to assuming that position, he was professor of geography at the University of Sheffield. His main research interest is electoral geography, and he is the author or co-author of several books on electoral geography in Great Britain, including *A Nation Dividing? The Electoral Map of Great Britain, 1979-1987*, co-authored with Charles Pattie.

Gudrun Klee is assistant professor of political science at the Institute of Comparative Politics at the University of Oldenburg in Germany. She studied political science at the Universities of Munich, Hamburg, and Linköping (Sweden). Her current research interests focus on party financing in West European democracies and Scandinavian politics.

Peter Lösche is professor of political science at the University of Göttingen, Germany. He has been a visiting professor at the University of California, Santa Barbara, and he is the author of numerous books and articles on German and American political parties, political finance, labor unions, and general politics. His most recent book is *Amerika in Perspektive*, 1989.

Karl-Heinz Nassmacher is professor of political science at the Institute of Comparative Politics at the University of Oldenburg in Germany. He has published books on Austria, the EC, German local government, and political parties, and he has authored numerous articles on local government and campaign and party finance in Germany and abroad.

C. J. Pattie is lecturer in geography at the University of Nottingham. Until 1989 he was a research fellow in geography at the University of Sheffield. He is the co-author with Ron Johnston of *A Nation Dividing? The Electoral Map of Great Britain, 1979-1987*, and he is currently conducting research on British electoral behavior in the 1990s.

William T. Stanbury is UPS Foundation Professor of Regulation and Competition Policy in the Faculty of Commerce and Business Administration, University of British Columbia, Vancouver, Canada. He is the author of over 200 publications dealing with various aspects of government activity, privatization, interest group behavior, and political finance. His study for The Royal Commission in Electoral Reform and Party Financing is *Money in Politics:Financing Federal Parties and Candidates in Canada* (Toronto: Dundurn Press, 1991).

Index

274